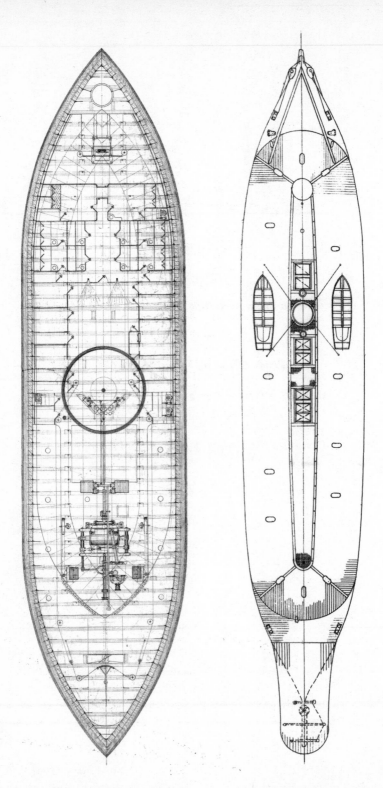

The *Monitor* and the *Merrimack*. The ironclads are not drawn to relative scale:
the Union ship was 179 feet long with a 41½-foot beam; the Confederate, 275 feet by 51 feet.

IRON DAWN

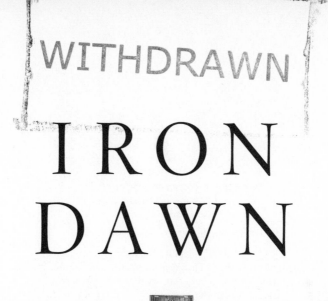

THE *MONITOR*, THE *MERRIMACK*,

and the

CIVIL WAR SEA BATTLE THAT

CHANGED HISTORY

RICHARD SNOW

SCRIBNER

New York   London   Toronto   Sydney   New Delhi

SCRIBNER

An Imprint of Simon & Schuster, Inc.
1230 Avenue of the Americas
New York, NY 10020

First Scribner hardcover edition November 2016

SCRIBNER and design are registered trademarks of The Gale Group, Inc.,
used under license by Simon & Schuster, Inc., the publisher of this work.

For information about special discounts for bulk purchases,
please contact Simon & Schuster Special Sales at 1-866-506-1949
or business@simonandschuster.com.

The Simon & Schuster Speakers Bureau can bring authors to your
live event. For more information or to book an event,
contact the Simon & Schuster Speakers Bureau at 1-866-248-3049
or visit our website at www.simonspeakers.com.

Interior design by Kyle Kabel

Manufactured in the United States of America

1   3   5   7   9   10   8   6   4   2

Library of Congress Cataloging-in-Publication Data

Names: Snow, Richard, 1947–author.
Title: Iron dawn : the *Monitor*, the *Merrimack*, and the Civil War
sea battle that changed history / Richard Snow.
Description: First Scribner hardcover edition. | New York : Scribner, 2016.
Identifiers: LCCN 2016006965
Subjects: LCSH: Hampton Roads, Battle of, Va., 1862.
Monitor (Ironclad) | *Virginia* (Ironclad)
Classification: LCC E473.2 .S67 2016 | DDC 973.7/31—dc23
LC record available at http://lccn.loc.gov/2016006965

ISBN 978-1-4767-9418-1
ISBN 978-1-4767-9420-4 (ebook)

Interior and insert illustration credits: pages 85, 175, and 183: Collections of the Mariners'
Museum; page 329: Prints & Photographs Division, Library of Congress. The portrait
of Lincoln in the insert is from the Mellon Collection. Other images are in the author's
collection; many of the engravings appeared in two highly popular publications of the
era, *Frank Leslie's Illustrated Newspaper* and *Harper's Weekly*.

To the memory of my father and mother:
Richard B. Snow, who served in the Atlantic aboard
a latter-day ironclad during another war;
and Emma Folger Snow, who endured those years of
separation with the same lonely tenacity that he did

The sinking of all the world's old sea-bitten names,
Temeraire, *Victory*, and *Constellation*,
Serapis, *Bon Homme Richard*, *Golden Hind*,
Galleys of Antony, galleys of Carthage,
Galleons with gilded Virgins, galleasses,
Viking long-serpents, siren-haunted galliots,
Argos and argosies and the Achaean pride,
Moving to sea in one long wooden wall
Behind the huge ghost-flagship of the Ark
In such a swelling cloud of phantom sail
They whitened Ocean—going down by the head,
Green water seeping through the battened ports,
Spreading along the scrubbed and famous decks,
Going down—going down—going down—to
    mermaid-pools,
To Fiddler's Green—to the dim barnacle-thrones,
Where Davy Jones drinks everlasting rum
With the sea-horses of his sunken dreams.

—Stephen Vincent Benét
John Brown's Body

Contents

IRON
DAWN

CHAPTER I

Terrible Havoc: March 1862

One of a galaxy of patriotic tokens and medals struck
in honor of the Union ironclad.

Her creator had come up with the name—*Monitor*—and he meant it to have the broadest implications. Not only was his ship to cast her stern gaze on all Southern deviltry, but "there are other leaders who will also be startled and admonished by the booming of the guns from the impregnable iron turret." These leaders, he said, dwelt in Downing Street, London.

But neither the rebellious South nor the Lords of the Admiralty would have felt much admonished had they seen the USS *Monitor* on her maiden voyage.

It wasn't a long trip, just from Brooklyn down to the Chesapeake Bay, but during the journey she had nearly sunk twice in twenty-four hours. She had no business being out on the open sea in early March when the Atlantic is full of brutal caprice; she should still have been making cautious trial river voyages near the yard in Greenpoint where she'd been built. Workmen had been hammering away at her iron skin right up to the time she raised anchor and steamed down through the Narrows of New York Harbor and out into the ocean.

The first few days of her life were encouraging. She hadn't sunk like an anvil, as many had predicted, and after some adjustments she went in the direction the helmsman wanted. The few inches of freeboard stayed above water, and the deck remained dry once she got to sea. Soon enough, though, a gale was kicking her around, and nothing about her was dry, inside or out, and most of her crew, with no sails to set or ropes to haul, could only brace themselves against sweating metal bulkheads in a drizzling darkness falteringly lit by oil lamps and engine fires. They could all feel the sea, but none of them could see it because they were sealed in below the waterline—in a submarine, really, although the word did not yet exist to describe a kind of boat. They were sailors, they knew the ocean and its ways, but this duty was new to them. They'd never sailed in a ship like this one. Nobody had.

The captain got seasick—no shame in that; Lord Nelson always had at the start of his voyages—and then many of the men did too. They were helped topside to lie, sketchily shielded from the spray by canvas sheets, on the only part of their ship that was above water now: the turret (although this was so new a development that many of them called it the "tower"). Below inside it were the guns—only two of them, and all but untried. They were good cannon, big seven-ton Dahlgrens, but their inventor, Major John Dahlgren, wished they'd never left port. There hadn't been time to test them properly, and it seemed likely there wouldn't be until they were fired in battle.

The prospect of that battle was what had brought the *Monitor* and its men, half-trained and ill prepared, out into the March Atlantic. Some four hundred miles to the south, in Norfolk, Virginia, the Rebels were building—had built—a vessel sheathed in iron. Unlike the *Monitor*, its upperworks rested on a wooden hull; it wasn't all iron. But what showed above the waterline was, and the vessels guarding the immense natural harbor of Hampton Roads, and thus Chesapeake Bay, the finest ships in the Union fleet, were all made of wood.

If the Rebel ship could blast its way past them, she might very well steam up the Potomac and bombard Washington, or into New York Harbor and knock apart the financial resources of the Union. This was a machine that could end the war. Or so they thought in Washington and New York, and who was to say they were wrong?

So the *Monitor*, hurried from the laying of her keel to her launching, hurried now, while the seas grew taller and the wretched men shivering on the top of the turret watched the frill of sparks on her stacks and prayed nothing would douse the fires that kept sending them up into the Atlantic night.

The fires stayed lit, barely, but at one point the ventilators failed and the ship filled with poisonous gases, and the insensible men pulled from the fumes out onto the turret were at first thought to have died.

But by luck and improvisation and feats of considerable bravery, they made it at last to better weather and the sight of Capes Henry and Charles, the doorposts of Chesapeake Bay. Late on the afternoon of March 8 the sailors began to hear gunfire, distant and steady, and William Keeler, the *Monitor*'s paymaster, saw "little black spots . . . suddenly springing into the air, remaining stationary for a moment or two & then gradually expanding into a large white cloud—these were shells & tended to increase the excitement."

When the *Monitor* was close enough to take a pilot aboard, he said the Southern ironclad had come out that very morning and made "terrible havock among the shipping." It most certainly had. As darkness settled, the sky to the west remained bright with the burning wrecks of Northern warships. The *Monitor* was steaming toward the worst disaster the US Navy had ever suffered, one that would not be surpassed until a December Sunday eighty years in the future. "Oh, how we longed to be there," wrote Keeler, "but our iron hull crept slowly on & the monotonous clank, clank of

the engine betokened no increase of its speed." Everyone above
decks stared at the distant fire playing on the undersides of smoke
clouds and wondered if, after the months of frantic work on their
ship, and the nightmare little voyage they'd just taken aboard her,
they had arrived a few hours too late.

WE TEND TO SEE THE Civil War largely as a contest waged
on land. Say "Civil War" and your listeners may think of Pickett's
Charge on the third day of Gettysburg, or the shredded cornfields
at Antietam, or the mortal roads that led to Appomattox. It is
unlikely they will envision the agglomeration of extemporized
hardware that Lincoln called "Uncle Sam's web-feet" even though,
as the President said, "at all the watery margins they have been
present. Not only on the deep sea, the broad bay, the rapid river,
but also up the muddy bayou, and wherever the ground was a little
damp, they have been, and made their tracks."

In the war's last year, a Union captain named Charles Steedman
said of Rear Admiral David Glasgow Farragut, "That little man"—
Farragut was just under middle height—"has done more to put
down the rebellion than any general except Grant and Sherman."
Steedman's thinking he had to make the remark suggests that even
then people needed reminding that the naval war was as crucial
to Union victory as the land operations. Yet the Civil War navies
have always been in relative eclipse.

The reason is clear: the numbers of those who served on land
and on sea are violently disproportionate. The Navy absorbed only
5 percent of the Union's manpower. It was a fighting outfit, but its
losses for the entire war were outstripped by any number of single
days of combat ashore.

Stonewall Jackson, William Tecumseh Sherman, Grant, Lee,
we all know, and, yes, probably Farragut (yet who can name his
flagship?); and on the Confederate side, what naval figure comes
to mind?

One place where the Civil War Navy does get equal billing with the Army is on the south side of the triumphal arch in Grand Army Plaza in Brooklyn. There, two bronze groups from the turn of the last century by the sculptor Frederick MacMonnies are named in honor of *The Spirit of the Army* and *The Spirit of the Navy*. They're pretty terrific, and well worth a visit (Manhattan itself is oddly stingy with Civil War monuments). On the left as you face the monument is the Army, officers and men forever charging up Flatbush Avenue beneath the frozen tumult of a winged horse; on the right, the Navy. These sailors seem closer to our time, perhaps because they are less formally uniformed, and perhaps because at the front of the plinth is a black man. He's kneeling, but not, as in so many allegorical statements of the era, in gratitude for having had the shackles knocked from his wrists. Instead he's holding a big Navy Colt revolver, clearly ready, even eager, to use it. He looks tough as hell.

The naval group seems the more interesting, the more modern, of the two.

And if a sense of modernity is there, it is absolutely fitting. The Civil War was full of grim modernity, from twentieth-century firepower to an industrial state supporting a vast citizen army. But nowhere is that modernity more striking than in what is often considered the most traditional and hidebound of services.

If it is difficult to summon from memory the conflict's naval leaders, almost everyone can name its two most significant warships. Of course the alliteration helps, but there's more to it than that. Many naval battles—Trafalgar, Midway—have bent the course of history in hours or even minutes. But none has fomented in a short day's work a whole new kind of warfare, has in one noisy morning made an ancient tradition obsolete.

Although some aspects of the meeting of these two ships carry a tang of the miraculous, their battle wasn't in itself a miracle. The fight, or something like it, had been bound to happen, given the trajectory that military technology was taking when it occurred. Still, how likely is it that this first encounter of a brand-new kind of machinery, and an equally new idea, would also have immediate results? It is a little as if a week after the Wright brothers first flew at Kitty Hawk, they had taken their airplane out to sea and won a signal victory for their nation.

Whose victory it truly was is still argued today. What has long been beyond dispute is the courage of the two crews—one six times the size of the other—who took to sea to fight in untried vessels that were at least as dangerous to themselves as to their enemies. Their foray into the unknown has left us with the only two Civil War vessels we can automatically name: the *Monitor* and the *Merrimack*.

CHAPTER 2

Augury

The Charleston floating battery seen from the side,
with its hospital behind.

With the possible exception of President James Buchanan in the waning days of his administration, Major Robert Anderson held, in the early spring of 1861, the least enviable job in the newly disunited states.

Anderson, who had a distinguished record of service against Chief Black Hawk and in the Mexican War, was in charge of the US garrison in Charleston, South Carolina, and thus responsible for the military installations that guarded the harbor there. Under normal circumstances he would have been perfectly comfortable in this post: born in Kentucky in 1805, he saw himself as a Southerner, had owned slaves, and felt at home in the prosperous world their labor made possible.

The circumstances, however, were far from normal. Abraham Lincoln had been elected president half a year earlier, and six weeks later South Carolina had seceded from the Union, viewing itself, before other states joined it, as an independent nation.

Anderson and his command became the object of increasing suspicion and hostility. The major found little guidance in the paltering semi-orders that sporadically came in from Washington: *Give up Nothing!* and at the same time *Do Nothing to annoy the South Carolinians!* As a martial mood settled on the tiny new republic, he realized that this growing social isolation could easily become an honest-to-God siege.

If that happened, it would be over quickly. Among the works Anderson was responsible for was Fort Moultrie on Sullivan's Island, a finger of land that hooks out into Charleston Harbor. He had his men busy strengthening it, but if the danger came from the quarter he now expected, his defenses would be worthless. The fort had been designed to withstand an attack from the sea by some foreign power, not from behind by its owners.

The question of ownership was urgent. Representatives of the infant government were up in Washington punctiliously offering to buy South Carolina's defenses, saying they hoped this real estate transfer would ensure them a peaceful departure from the Union.

Anderson wanted peace with all his heart; and if there was to be a war, he most keenly wished not to start it. A devout man, he prayed daily that the crisis could be resolved without bloodshed. But he knew Charleston's military properties were not for sale. He couldn't defend Fort Moultrie, or any of the shore batteries. Out in the middle of the harbor, though, stood Fort Sumter on its man-made island. Under construction for thirty years, it still wasn't finished. Nevertheless, the fort was formidable, with brick walls forty feet high and up to twelve feet thick. Once there, Anderson could make a stand if he had to.

Such was the atmosphere in the city that the major made his move as if under enemy guns: by stealth and at night, on December 26. That he was wise to do so is confirmed by the rage that greeted his occupation of Sumter, encapsulated in the *Charleston Courier*'s account of the maneuver, which began, "Maj. Robert Anderson, U.S.A., has achieved the unenviable distinction of opening civil war between American citizens by an act of gross breach of faith."

If not quite war yet, it felt enough like one to the garrison in Fort Sumter: monotonous days, drab rations—little was coming over from the shore—and a constant mutter of speculation about whether supplies and reinforcements were on the way.

In the meantime, South Carolinians had occupied all the vacated federal positions and were surrounding Sumter with a necklace of batteries on the harbor islands.

Early in the charged New Year of 1861, they began a project that greatly interested Anderson. In Marsh's Shipyard on the Charleston waterfront, well in view of the fort, carpenters were hammering together a peculiar structure. They worked under the direction of Lieutenant James Randolph Hamilton—the descendant of a South Carolina governor—who had resigned his commission in the US Navy to take command of the ambitiously named Navy of South Carolina. With no fleet at his disposal, Hamilton set about building a movable waterborne gun platform. Looking something like a cross between a barn and a covered bridge, the floating battery was a hundred feet long by about twenty-five feet wide, built of heavy pinewood logs hewn a foot square. Its broad face was pierced by four openings easily recognizable as gunports. Around them grew a shell of boiler plating that, once laid down, got crosshatched with vertical strips of railroad iron. Eventually a pair of 32-pounders and two 42-pounders—cannon that threw balls of those weights—would be trundled aboard. These were big guns, and Hamilton counterbalanced their weight with a six-foot-deep wall of sandbags along the back of his battery. Beneath the sandbags lay the magazines that held the vessel's gunpowder; the shot it would propel was under the deck just behind the cannon. If this maritime creature were not odd enough, it was joined by a floating hospital containing several beds and two operating tables, riding on a separate raft that would tag along behind the battery sheltered by its iron façade.

Some members of Company D of the South Carolina Artillery Battalion, who would be working the battery's guns, were sufficiently skeptical about its armor to name it "the slaughter pen."

Others thought it would capsize before the iron sheathing could be tested.

Their doubts were echoed happily by one of Anderson's engineering officers. Captain John G. Foster wrote a report saying, "I do not think this floating battery will prove very formidable" as "it can be destroyed by our fire before it has time to do much damage."

His commander wasn't so sure. Major Anderson had been an artillery instructor at West Point, and his gunner's eye didn't like what it saw taking shape on the Charleston shore. He was worried enough to write Washington: "I should like to be instructed on a question which may present itself in reference to the floating battery, viz: What course would it be proper to take if, without a declaration of war . . . I should see them approaching my fort with that battery? They may attempt placing it within good distance before a declaration of hostile intentions."

The question evidently demanded a cabinet meeting, at which, in a flash of spirit, Buchanan said that Anderson should "crack away at them." But that boldness quickly evaporated. The President wanted to slow the momentum of the gathering conflict until he could hand off this colossal can of sharp-fanged worms to his successor.

So what Anderson got in response was a spate of nothing disguising itself as a directive:

"If . . . you are convinced by sufficient evidence that the raft of which you speak is advancing for the purpose of making an assault upon the fort, then you would be justified on the principle of self-defense in not awaiting its actual arrival there, but in repelling force by force on its approach. If, on the other hand, you have reason to believe that it is approaching merely to take up a position at a good distance should the pending question not be amicably settled, then, unless your safety is so clearly endangered as to render resistance an act of necessary self-defense and protection, you will act with that forbearance that has distinguished you heretofore."

In late February a Charleston-based *New York Times* reporter, clearly of strong Union leanings and generations away from any pretense of journalistic objectivity, watched the battery being launched. "Arrived at the Palmetto Wharf, I saw a small crowd gathering, which each moment increased, as the news spread through the town. By 8 ¼ o'clock at least 5,000 people were present, and the unknown quantity, called by many the 'slaughter pen,' rolled heavily and clumsily into her new element. They haven't christened her, and when they do, it is my private opinion that it will be done in the blood of all who embark in her. I hope the Richardson Guards [a recently formed South Carolina volunteer regiment] will say their prayers, even if they never did it before, and make their wills in some sort of earnestness, for they never will see Charleston again. . . . God help those who do go, if the tide should turn her round and present her unprotected side to Major ANDERSON'S death-dealers, at only six hundred yards. Only the gun-side is plated, and the roof of that part looks very like an old-fashioned rope-walk. . . . Lieutenant HAMILTON . . . is a brave man, even unto rashness; he can give no better proof of it than his intention to herd the boys who are ambitious of seeking a bloody grave."

The battery stayed put for a while, an object of fascination not only to Charleston citizens, who visited it daily, but up North as well. The *New York Herald* put on display for its readers a log identical (said the *Herald*) to those used in the battery. Another log was offered to P. T. Barnum for display in his Broadway "museum." Barnum was interested until he heard the price: his unsurpassed entrepreneurial instinct told him that $150 was too steep.

ABRAHAM LINCOLN WAS INAUGURATED ON March 4. In his address that day he made clear that Fort Sumter would remain a federal possession: "The power confided to me will be used to hold, occupy, and possess the property and places belonging to the Government." In closing, he spoke directly to the citizens of South Carolina and of the six other states that had joined her in secession: "In *your* hands, my dissatisfied fellow-countrymen, and not in *mine*, is the momentous issue of Civil War."

In early April the momentous issue was most immediately in the hands of Brigadier General Pierre Gustave Toutant-Beauregard, who had studied artillery tactics under Anderson at West Point. He had left the US Army to take command of the ten thousand Rebel troops now gathered in Charleston.

On the first day of April Beauregard telegraphed the Confederate capital in Montgomery, Alabama, "Batteries ready to open Wednesday or Thursday. What instructions?" There was no waffling from *this* government. The word came back: issue an ultimatum. Evacuate the fort, Beauregard ordered, or he would, in the military euphemism of the day, "reduce" it. Anderson determined to hold on as long as he could with his command of 127 men, which included 8 musicians and 43 noncombatant workers who were willing to stick it out with him.

On the night of the eleventh, steam tugs towed the floating battery across the harbor to the tip of Sullivan's Island, and it anchored there a mile from the fort. The balky, inconvenient vessel was at least capable of staying on top of the water. Nor did what the *Times* reporter called "the novel coercive weapon" gratify him by pivoting its naked backside to face Anderson's guns.

At four thirty in the morning of the twelfth, Beauregard gave the order, and a mortar crew on James Island sent a shell arcing upward. The dawn was still distant enough for the gunners to follow the sparking trail of the fuse through its reflection in the harbor waters. It exploded directly above Sumter's parade ground.

Forty-six other guns immediately joined in. The *Charleston Mercury* exuberantly reported, "Upon that signal, the circle of batteries with which the grim fortress of Fort Sumter is beleaguered opened fire. The outline of this great volcanic crater was illuminated with a line of twinkling lights; the clustering shells illuminated the sky above it; the balls clattered thick as hail upon its sides."

Anderson waited until full daylight before ordering Captain Abner Doubleday, his second-in-command, to open fire. Sumter fought throughout that day. With all he had to occupy him, Anderson took time to note that the floating battery had justified his apprehensions about it. The hospital protected in its lee got one client, when a cannonball punched against the plating to wound a soldier. But that was all: as the clanging hours passed, shot after shot struck Lieutenant Hamilton's battery; some caromed upward off the pitch of its roof; some knocked themselves into the water against the inward-sloping lower face; none pierced it.

A Union artillery captain in the fort wrote that the guns playing on the craft "were 32 and 42-pounders, and some curiosity was felt as to the effect of such shot on the iron-clad battery. The gunners made excellent practice, but the shot were seen to bounce off its side like peas."

Meanwhile Hamilton's guns kept up a steady fire, shattering masonry and raising clouds of brick dust. The *Mercury* said, "The celebrated Floating Battery" has "fully vindicated the correctness of [its] conception." It was "quite hidden from our view by the smoke from its own guns, but it was not difficult to see the effective execution of its 42 pounders upon the north parapet of Fort Sumter."

By the next day most of the wooden buildings inside Sumter's walls were burning, and Anderson's ammunition was all but gone. On the afternoon of the thirteenth, he surrendered.

The thirty-four-hour bombardment had sent some 4,000 shells into the fort, 490 of them from the floating battery. By a miracle (one all too rarely repeated in the red years to follow), none of the defenders had been killed, nor had any of their adversaries.

In the aftermath, Anderson was able to surrender with full military honors: the war was a jolly new adventure to the victors (the *Mercury*'s headline called the bombardment a "Splendid Pyrotechnic Exhibition"), and their success had left them magnanimous. Anderson's men were allowed to keep their arms, and he the flag. Waiting steamers carried them to New York City, where good food and drink and general adulation did much to blunt the memory of the hard months of isolation in Charleston Harbor.

Anderson went on to Washington, where in his reports he stressed the floating battery. He had seen its iron carapace shed the best he could fire at it. If someone conceived the idea—and it wouldn't require much imagination on the part of these new enemies—of mounting a steam engine inside the battery, the result could be dire for the wooden warships that made up the entirety of the US Navy.

Captain Doubleday said he too came back North believing "that South Carolina not only intended to build iron-clad batteries, but was thinking of iron-clad ships, to sink our wooden navy, and at some future time capture our Northern harbors." He wrote of the threat to "members of Congress; but no one at the North seemed to give the matter a second thought, or imagine there was any danger to be apprehended in the future."

CHAPTER 3

Disgrace

The *Merrimack* when she was still the pride of the United States Navy,
but soon to become its most fearsome opponent.

If Fort Sumter's spirited defense at the eleventh—the twelfth—
hour helped salve the Union's bruised martial amour propre,
what went on four hundred miles to the north at the Gosport
Navy Yard was an unmitigated, all-but-inexplicable disaster.

Gosport was a year away from being rechristened with its cur-
rent name, the Norfolk Naval Shipyard, although it is actually in
Portsmouth, Virginia, across from Norfolk on the west bank of
the Elizabeth River. Ten miles downstream the Elizabeth joins the
Nansemond and James Rivers to form Hampton Roads, the vast
natural harbor—one of the largest in the world—that opens onto
Chesapeake Bay.

Gosport was the best-equipped Navy yard in America. Only
Boston came close. Both had granite dry docks, but such was the
scale of Gosport's that, more than 180 years after taking in its first

ship for repair, the dock is still in daily service. Around this prodigy spread a smoky industrial metropolis of foundries and machine shops, ship houses capable of building the most advanced war vessels, smithies, gunners' lofts, rigging lofts, forges, sawmills, timber sheds—all the fixtures necessary to run a complex naval world of wood and iron and cordage.

While Beauregard busied himself training his guns on Sumter, Gosport was host to a dozen warships. Some were relics, albeit imposing ones: the quarter-century-old, 140-gun *Pennsylvania* was the largest sail-driven warship ever built in America. She was a ship of the line, since the seventeenth century the biggest and most heavily armed class of all fighting vessels, but having lived her expensive life between the War of 1812 and this brewing contest, she had never fired her broadside in battle.

The most advanced ship there was the steam frigate *Merrimack*, 4,236 tons, forty guns (the least of them many times more powerful than anything the *Pennsylvania* had ever mounted). All her guns, however, were ashore. The *Merrimack* was only five years old, but in this transitional epoch between wind power and steam power the newcomer could be unreliable. Every steam warship carried a full complement of masts and sails, which would be used on long voyages to conserve fuel, and in case just such a misfortune might visit their engines as had beset the *Merrimack*'s. Her still-young power plant had worked itself into uselessness; its components lay scattered about the yard in various stages of abandonment or repair.

Commodore Charles S. McCauley had charge of Gosport. He'd first gone to sea as a boy midshipman aboard the frigate *Constellation*, had fought on Lake Erie in the War of 1812, had commanded ships in the Atlantic and Pacific and in the Mediterranean, had been the guest of honor at a celebratory White House dinner in 1856. But he was sixty-eight now, and the years had made him cautious.

McCauley found no more help in his Washington orders than Anderson had. He too was told to defend his small territory while doing nothing to irritate his increasingly belligerent neighbors. A Pennsylvania man and a firm Unionist, McCauley—despite his years of hard service—was frightened of the twenty-two officers who reported to him. Almost all were Southerners; he both doubted their loyalty and feared driving them into the widening arms of the secession movement. Seven states were gone, but the Upper South, which included supremely important Virginia, might still be cajoled into loyalty. McCauley was all for cajoling. He was said to be a drinker; if so, his liquor irrigated no Dutch courage, which, in the end, is better than no courage at all.

Robert Danby, the yard's chief engineer, was a Unionist and eager to get the *Merrimack* out of Gosport before the storm gathering at Sumter broke over Norfolk too. McCauley told Danby it would take at least a month to resurrect the ship's steam plant. Danby found this preposterous and said so in a letter to Benjamin Franklin Isherwood, the Navy's newly made engineer in chief.

Still in his thirties, the powerfully built Isherwood—his broad chest made him seem shorter than his five feet ten inches—had the reputation of being the "handsomest man in Washington," which probably didn't sweeten the opinion of those who also found him the most abrasive one. His supporters liked to speak of his frankness, but this quality manifested itself in a straightforward rudeness that needlessly brought him many enemies.

In part, his character had been formed by the difficult service to which he'd devoted most of his life. Being a naval engineer in the years before the Civil War meant that you were responsible for the fuming, dimly understood, deeply resented machinery that had begun to show up in warships only a generation earlier.

Seniority counted very much in the Navy, and its high officers saw themselves as the inheritors of a tradition that stretched back through all the centuries during which their predecessors had worked beneath what was invariably described as "towering clouds of sail." Any of Sir Francis Drake's captains set down on the quarterdeck of the *Pennsylvania* would instantly have understood her; and any of them seeing the greasy, clanking new netherworld inhabited by the marine steam engine would have been disgusted. So were most of the Navy men Isherwood met on his way up.

That climb had started surprisingly early, even in an era when children routinely went to work not so long after they'd learned to dress themselves. Isherwood was born in 1822, the son of a New York City doctor who died soon afterward. He was raised by a stern, strong-willed mother, who, when he was nine, enrolled him in the Albany Academy, a school that subjected its students to what would today be considered a rigorous college education and was apparently run like a penal colony.

One Albany graduate looking back upon his time there imagined adopting a coat of arms that bore "the crimson shield, signifying gore, upon which is emblazoned the figure of a boy rampant, with the hand of one unseen holding him in position, while above, as a crest, are two rattans [whips] crossed." The harsh routine didn't suit one boy a year ahead of Benjamin, Herman Melville, and eventually it drove away Benjamin himself. Although he had won several prizes at the school, he got expelled for "serious misconduct." He was fourteen years old.

Albany Academy had educated its malefactor soundly enough to land him a job as a draftsman in the locomotive shops of the Utica and Schenectady Railroad, where he qualified as a "practical steam engineer" at the age of sixteen.

In 1842 Congress permitted the Navy to found an engineering corps, and the men who had been tending to the workings of the new steam warships were brought into the service. The infant bureau looked good to Isherwood; in the spring of 1844 he joined the US Navy as a first assistant engineer.

Two years later he was sent to Veracruz and the Mexican War aboard the USS *Princeton*, the most advanced ship in the American Navy, or any other. Rather than being driven by elaborate external side-wheels that offered a big, fragile target, she was the first warship to have a propeller—or *screw*, as naval parlance then and now puts it. The screw was turned by machinery that lay below the waterline, hard for enemy gunfire to reach. But this made the

Princeton's deep engine room an inhospitable place during summer blockade duty in the Gulf of Mexico. The temperature stood at 115 degrees for days on end, and the stench from the simmering filth in the bilge was enough to make seasoned sailors pass out during their watch. But his comfortless post got Isherwood familiar with the most sophisticated naval technology of the day.

He left Mexican waters to wade into the controversies that eddy about any new enterprise. Charles Haswell, the Navy's first engineer in chief, who appointed Isherwood, had spent hectic, grinding months designing new ships for the rapidly growing steam navy, and the last of them, the *San Jacinto*, was a total failure. Asked to comment on its properties, Isherwood showed his combative temperament by writing that the engines were "a disgrace to the service and the corps" and "a standing monument of Mr. Haswell's incompetence and folly."

Haswell was so demoralized by this—and doubtless too by the demands of his unprecedented job—that he simply walked away from the *San Jacinto* and the Navy. Isherwood joined in the acrimonious faction battles that were shaping his corps, all the while designing engine after engine. Some of them failed, but one gained so wide a popularity that it became a standard in the fleet and would be known as the "Isherwood engine" during the war that lay just over the horizon.

When steam plants first appeared in naval vessels, nobody knew what status should be accorded the men who tended them. Deck officers believed engineers weren't sailors at all, just hired mechanics, no more deserving of rank than a blacksmith. The engineers' dubious position was reflected in an 1849 act of Congress establishing pay scales: a frigate captain got $5,000 a year, a chief engineer $1,500. Even so, the same act did attempt to raise the engineer's standing, allowing him to dine with the other officers in the wardroom.

Isherwood became the most controversial engineer in the new fraternity with his insistence on a theory that defied the shaky orthodoxies of the day.

The debate boiled down to the important point of how much steam was needed to push a piston. Common practice held that the steam should be cut off shortly after entering a cylinder; its expansive qualities would do the necessary work. This argument sat well with naval frugality: the less steam needed, the less fuel burned.

Isherwood's experience told him that no matter how energetically the steam might expand, the technology of the time could not seal a cylinder tightly enough to take advantage of it. He called for more steam to drive each stroke.

The engineers did not explore this difference in an atmosphere of comradely collaboration. Rather, as the great historian of technology Elting Morison put it, "The discourse was stabilized at a level of most sordid dialectic." In the spirit of Isherwood's calling his boss Haswell a disgrace to the service, his opponents decried him as an "ignorant child," a "merchant of pure nonsense" trying to sell the "manifestly absurd." When in 1859 Isherwood published his findings in a fat two-volume work called *Engineering Precedents for Steam Machinery*, one of his critics responded with astounded indignation that Isherwood had had the effrontery to offer "*mere hypotheses* of his own that he has printed in a *book.*"

Despite this base tactic, Isherwood had gained admirers in Washington. The engineer in chief who had replaced Haswell found the job no more congenial than had his predecessor and, like him, abruptly quit. In March the new President, Abraham Lincoln, wrote his new secretary of the navy, "Sir: I understand there is a vacancy in the office of Engineer-in-Chief of the Navy, which I shall have to fill by appointment. Will you please avail yourself of all the means in your power for determin[ing] and present me with the name of [the] best man for the service." Gideon Welles chose Benjamin Isherwood.

WHEN THE YOUNG ENGINEER IN chief received Robert Danby's contemptuous letter about the *Merrimack*'s inability to be ready for sea inside of a month, he had held his new post for less than a month and barely knew his boss. Still, he did not hesitate to run the letter right in to Welles, whom he urged to get the *Merrimack* out of Gosport. Welles agreed and sent orders to McCauley: "SIR: In view of the peculiar condition of the country, and of events that have already transpired, it becomes necessary that great vigilance should be exercised in guarding and protecting the public interests and property committed to your charge. It is therefore deemed important that the steamer *Merrimac* should be in condition to proceed to Philadelphia . . . in case of danger from unlawful attempts to take possession of her, that she may be placed beyond their reach."

Welles should have stopped right there; instead, he added, "It is desirable there should be no steps taken to give needless alarm." So when McCauley had the *Merrimack* towed to the ordnance wharf to take on her guns, and some Norfolk secessionists began complaining, he ordered the work stopped.

All this happened between April 10 and the twelfth. The bombardment of Sumter spurred Welles to send a stiff directive to McCauley: "Sir: The Department desires to have the *Merrimack* removed from the Norfolk to the Philadelphia Navy-yard with the utmost dispatch. The Engineer-in-Chief, Mr. B.F. Isherwood, has been ordered to report to you for the purpose of expediting the duty, and you will have his suggestions for that end carried promptly into effect." Although once again this too was to be done "without creating a sensation but in a quiet manner." Along with Isherwood, Welles sent Commander James Alden, who was quietly to take over the *Merrimack* once she was ready to sail. Isherwood could get the ship's engines in order, but he couldn't command her at sea.

Meanwhile, Welles cast about for a crew. The *Merrimack*'s full complement was six hundred seamen; Welles found he could lay his hands on sixty-three.

Isherwood and Alden arrived in Norfolk on the fourteenth, the day after Anderson surrendered Sumter. They at once discovered it was too late to carry out their mission unobtrusively. "To my surprise, all Norfolk seemed to be full of it," Alden wrote. He and Isherwood made their way through knots of scowling citizens and across the river to Gosport, where McCauley greeted them with the news that the workers—there were fourteen hundred—had walked off their jobs.

Isherwood examined the *Merrimack* and was dismayed by what he saw: "The engines were in a wretched state. All the braces were out of the boilers, having been removed with a view to the substitution of other and larger ones, and the entire machinery was in a disabled condition." He and Alden went together through the quiet yard, trying to find the far-flung pieces of the ship's steam plant. Despite the dispiriting tour, Isherwood drastically revised McCauley's estimate of how long it would take to make the *Merrimack* operational. He and Danby were able to recruit some mechanics and laborers with the promise of exorbitant wages, and they set to work. There followed a hell of effort that showed the chief engineer at his most galling: hour after hour of angry impatience. But he also possessed a raucous, optimistic energy that heartened his workers even as he berated them. He might be infuriating, but he worked every bit as hard as any other hand, and he obviously knew exactly what he was doing.

On April 17, Virginia took the step the entire North had feared. Once the state seceded, most of McCauley's officers left the Union with her. Despite the upheaval, Isherwood and Danby, badly worn but greatly pleased, appeared in McCauley's office at four that afternoon to report "the machinery ready for steam." Isherwood had repaired the *Merrimack* in just three days. He told McCauley "that fifty-four firemen and coal heavers had been engaged and were ready to go on board, and asked him if I should fire up at once." McCauley seemed "startled," Isherwood said, and "replied not that afternoon, adding that if I had steam on the next morning it would be time enough. Accordingly, a regular engine-room watch was kept during the night and the fires were started at daybreak."

Thursday the eighteenth dawned clear after a night of rain, and the *Merrimack*'s stack was feeding volumes of coal smoke into the cloudless spring sky. Isherwood had swapped the chains that had held the ship to the pier for ropes, so that the axmen he'd posted could free her in an instant.

"At about 9:00 AM I called on the Commodore and reported the engineer department ready for leaving; that Chief Engineer Danby, the assistant engineers, the firemen, and the coal heavers were all on board, with steam up and the engines working at the wharf. The only thing wanting was his order to cast loose and go. He then, to my great surprise and dissatisfaction, informed me that he had not yet decided to send the vessel, but would let me know further in the course of a few hours."

While McCauley waffled, "I called his attention to the fact that the instructions of the Department were peremptory." It was too late to fret about ruffled Virginian feelings, Isherwood insisted, and although the *Merrimack*'s sparse crew made Philadelphia an impossibility, she could still get across the harbor and shelter under the guns of Fortress Monroe, whose garrison's loyalties were not in doubt.

McCauley remained adamant. Exhausted and seeing his considerable accomplishment in hurrying the *Merrimack* back into life being squandered, Isherwood wrote that the commodore "sat in his office immovable, not knowing what to do. He was weak, vacillating, hesitating, and overwhelmed by the responsibilities of his position. . . . He behaved as though he were stupefied."

Alden, in the meantime, was offering $1,000 to any civilian pilot who would guide the *Merrimack* to safety across Hampton Roads: two years' pay for two hours of work. But whether Alden found a pilot or not made no difference because when, at two o'clock, Isherwood returned to McCauley to again seek permission to cast off, "he informed me that he had decided to retain the vessel, and directed me to draw the fires." That is, to shut the *Merrimack* down and leave her dead in the water.

Isherwood walked back to the ship and passed along McCauley's orders to the equally frustrated Danby. "As I witnessed the gradual dying out of the *Merrimack*'s engines, I was greatly tempted to cut the ropes that held her, and bring her out on my own responsibility." But this was the Navy, and orders were orders, and anyway engineers could not hold deck command. Isherwood wrote, "With great sorrow, I dismissed my men, waited until the engines made their last revolution [and] left the yard."

He didn't leave quite so easily as that suggests. The nascent secessionist authorities in Norfolk had learned of his attempts to snatch the *Merrimack* away from them, and now they wanted to seize him as a prisoner of war. A friend of Isherwood's got wind of this and told the engineer to stay put in his room at the Atlantic Hotel while the friend booked a cabin on the Chesapeake Bay steamer under his own name. He returned to the hotel, smuggled Isherwood into his carriage, and got him aboard the steamer and locked in his cabin without anyone's taking notice. The angry crowd that formed before the Atlantic Hotel found its quarry fled.

The Old Bay Line steamer deposited Isherwood in Washington on the morning of the nineteenth. He and Alden went immediately to Welles, who was furious. More at Alden, though, than at Isherwood: the one had, after all, got the *Merrimack* ready to sail; the other had refused to sail her. Both men, however, were justified in their final failure to take action. Events were moving swiftly, but not fast enough to show how things would stand with the yard in just a few hours, let alone what would become of the *Merrimack*. To have taken the ship out in defiance of McCauley's orders would have been an act of mutiny unprecedented in American naval annals.

For his part, Welles at once relieved McCauley and tried to "rush reinforcements," as the phrase goes, to Norfolk. There were few to rush, and however quickly those on hand might have got there, it was too late. On Saturday the sloop *Pawnee*, mounting eight nine-inch guns and carrying 349 men of the Third Massachusetts Infantry, entered Hampton Roads. Also aboard was Commodore Hiram Paulding, the most senior line officer in the Navy Department. He discovered that in a final exercise of his authority, McCauley had ordered all his ships scuttled to keep them from falling into the hands of a still largely illusory opposition. Their sea cocks had been opened to let water flow into the holds, and although not all were yet on the bottom, nothing could be done to save any of them. Paulding relieved McCauley of his command.

The new arrivals might have been able to hold the yard against the scattering of Virginia militia on its outskirts, but panic was spreading, fueled by all those silent forges and abandoned machine shops and listing ships, and the phantom secessionist host threatening to storm Gosport. Commodore Paulding ordered the yard destroyed.

A squalid carnival began, with barrels of turpentine sloshed along the decks of already foundering ships and two thousand pounds of powder laid to blow up the superb dry dock. Hundreds of cannon had to be attended to: men wielding eighteen-pound hammers tried to strike off their trunnions, the twin fat iron pegs that sprouted a third of the way down their barrels and rested on the carriages that supported the guns. With these gone, the cannon would be useless forever. But not surprisingly the trunnions were strong. Paulding reported to Welles, "100 men worked an hour with sledge hammers, and such was the tenacity of the iron that they did not succeed in breaking a single trunnion." In the end the would-be destroyers had to settle for driving spikes into the guns' touchholes (removable, with some effort) and then rolling them into the water (retrievable with almost no effort in a dockyard).

Sailors put matches to long powder trains and got clear. The *Merrimack* burned, the fire running along her masts and shrouds so that for a little while she was an incandescent diagram of the rigging plan of a mid-nineteenth-century man-of-war, and, although none of the men who had put her to the torch could know it then, a fiery epitaph for half a millennium of naval warfare. But—and this would have the largest ramifications—the flames did not reach her engines.

Poor McCauley offered one last difficulty. Having sunk his actual ships, he now declared his intention to go down with a metaphorical one and refused to leave his office, waiting there for the fire to take him. Harried officers from the *Pawnee* had to go and fetch him from his would-be pyre.

The ton of gunpowder meant to destroy the dry dock never exploded. Some Southern patriots claimed credit for dousing the fuse, but nobody knows what happened, save that the crucial facility went intact to its new owners.

The cannon, hundreds and hundreds of them, were rescued to see service throughout the Confederacy. Decades later, the Union admiral David Dixon Porter was still indignant about those guns: "A number of them were quickly mounted at Sewell's Point to keep our ships from approaching Norfolk; others were sent to Hatteras Inlet, Oracoke, Roanoke Island, and other points in the Sounds of North Carolina. Fifty-three of them were mounted at Port Royal, others at Fernandina and at the defences of New Orleans. They were met with at Fort Henry, Fort Donelson, Island No. 10, Memphis, Vicksburg, Grand Gulf, and Port Hudson. We found them up the Red River as far as the gunboats penetrated, and took possession of some of them on the [railroad flat] cars at Duvall's Bluff, on White River, bound for Little Rock. They gave us a three hours' hard fight at Arkansas Post. . . ." But, Porter concluded, "In the end they all returned to their rightful owners."

The real Union catastrophe at Gosport came from the least expected quarter. Isherwood, turning over and over in his mind his mutinous impulse to seize the *Merrimack* himself, wrote that had he done so, "the disasters which followed her detention, and which are my justification for the desire to take the matter into my own hands, would not have happened."

CHAPTER 4

The First Necessity

Stephen Mallory, the effective and imaginative
secretary of the Confederate Navy.

In the euphoria of secession, anything seemed possible to the
Confederate States of America. The newborn nation could
count on the inherent valor of its sons, untainted by the mercantile
grubbing of the mongrel drones in the industrial North; and it had
cotton. In those early days, the talk was all of cotton. King Cotton,
if withheld, would cripple the North and beggar the mills of Great
Britain. Cotton was more than just a valuable commodity: it was
the mainspring that drove Western civilization. Here is Senator
James H. Hammond of South Carolina speaking two years before
Sumter: "Would any nation make war on cotton? Without firing
a gun, without drawing a sword, should they make war on us, we

could bring the whole world to our feet. . . . What would happen if no cotton were furnished for three years? . . . England would topple headlong, and carry the whole civilized world with her, save the South. No; you dare not make war on cotton."

And couldn't it be used even more effectively? Alexander Stephens, the Confederacy's freshly minted vice president, thought so. He proposed taking 4 million bales from the 1860 and 1861 crops while at the same time buying fifty ironclad steamships. The cotton, loaded aboard the ironclads, could run past whatever interference the North might devise and be warehoused in Europe. Once the price rose to fifty cents a pound, the stock would be sold, at a stroke feeding $800 million into the Confederate treasury.

Surely word of the vice president's plan reached Stephen Russell Mallory, and it must have given him a brief, bleak gleam of amusement. Fifty ironclads! The secretary of the Confederate Navy was doing his best, his vigorous and highly competent best, to scratch up just one.

Mallory knew a lot about ships and the sea. Born in 1813, he had grown up in Key West, Florida, a town on a low, three-mile-long island that drew its sustenance from the sea. But not by fishing. The string of islands that makes up the Florida Keys curls out to the west for 140 miles, paralleled to the seaward by a coral reef whose peaks and hollows brew vicious currents that have been the despair of mariners since the earliest days of colonization. Key West, in contrast, fronts a deep, sheltered harbor, and from there men set out to save the lives of shipwrecked sailors and salvage the vessels on which they had come to grief. This fortuitous trade had, by the 1830s, made Key West the richest town in Florida.

Admiralty law held that the first person aboard a wrecked and abandoned ship was, in effect, her owner until the vessel could be delivered over to the courts. The salvage rules that governed the ship from its striking the reef to the apportionment of its cargo and remains were many and complex. Mallory early started to master them. In 1828 Congress gave a court at Key West jurisdiction over shipwrecks throughout all south Florida; three years later, Mallory, still in his teens, was appointed inspector of customs, a post that brought him into close contact with the merchant marine.

A quick student, he made his way with increasing confidence through the maze of maritime law. He had a tenacious fixity of purpose that revealed itself in his courtship of Angela Moreno, a Spanish girl he first saw when she was fifteen and he a couple of years older.

She got under his skin and stayed there. After four years of trying, Mallory managed to get her alone and, he said, "began very nervously and formally the story of my love." In response she glared at him and picked up a candlestick; she "looked as if about to hurl the candlestick at my head." But he held his ground, stammering out that he wanted to marry her, and that he was willing to wait two years before his next proposal. "You need never renew your offer," she said, "for I will never listen to it again."

Two years later he wrote saying the offer stood, and that if she turned him down, he would join an expedition against the Seminoles. She told him to go fight the Indians.

So Mallory spent the winter of 1837 splashing around in the Everglades. The commander of the expedition, Lieutenant Lewis Powell, met the Seminoles and was routed by them. Mallory never came under fire, but "I had a very pleasant & somewhat independent position assigned to me, with the command of a fine body of seamen & my own superb long, center board, schooner rigged, whale boat. . . . I enjoyed capital health, good spirits, and reaped much useful experience, self reliance & benefit generally from my service."

His eight-year campaign ended far better than had Lieutenant Powell's six-month one. Back in Pensacola in April 1838, Mallory again found his now twenty-three-year-old quarry. "What in the world has brought you here?" Angela Moreno asked, surely rhetorically.

"You have. I came to see you alone—Refuse me & I go back at once; but not to give you up, for I am determined to marry you."

And Angela said, "I had determined to accept your offer if you ever renewed it."

They were married in Pensacola that July.

A FEW YEARS EARLIER MALLORY had entered political life as the Key West marshal. His work began at nine thirty in the evening, when the town bell let the citizenry know it was time "for the cessation of business and pleasures." Thereafter Mallory was to put the arm on "any Negroes, bond or free, appearing on the street without authority," and to deal with "merrymaking by fiddle, drum, or any other kind of noise."

From this modest beginning, Mallory grew in stature as a public figure, and in time the young lawyer began to be seen as congressional material. In 1851 he went to Washington as a senator, and two years later became chairman of the Senate Naval Affairs Committee. As the nation moved toward war, Mallory, though not eager for secession, vigorously defended the institution of slavery. When the decades of compromises that had prevented a sectional rift finally failed with Lincoln's election, Mallory made his last speech to the US Senate, a mixture of not entirely persuasive remorse and wholly convincing defiance: "I cannot feel . . . but profound regret that existing causes imperatively impel us to this separation. . . . Throughout her long and patient endurance of insult and wrong, the South has clung to the Union with unfaltering fidelity . . ." Now, though, "be our difficulties what they may, we stand forth a united people to grapple with and to conquer them. Our willingness to shed our blood in this cause is the highest proof we can offer of the sincerity of our connections."

The Confederate Congress, meeting in Montgomery, Alabama, to invent a nation, chose Jefferson Davis as its first president on February 9, 1861. Two weeks later it established the Confederate Navy, and Davis, who had worked amicably with Mallory for years in the Senate, asked him to be its secretary. Mallory was something of an anomaly in Davis's cabinet, a Roman Catholic in a conclave of Protestants—with the quite extraordinary exception of Judah P. Benjamin, the Confederate secretary of war, then of state, who was Jewish. The two men were close friends.

Some thought Mallory too soft for his post. One reporter wrote that he was a "stumpy, 'roly-poly' little fellow . . . for all the world like one of the squat 'gentleman farmers' you find in the south of England." He had a plump, boyish countenance that suggested self-indulgence. Later, a Confederate War Department secretary said he had seen a note from Mallory inviting a colleague "to his house at 5 PM to partake of 'pea soup.' . . . His 'pea soup' will be oysters and champagne, and every other delicacy relished by epicures. Mr. Mallory's red face, and his plethoric body, indicate the highest living." Worse, many thought him timorous and questioned his loyalty. But his entire career as Navy secretary ratifies his energy, determination, and wholehearted fidelity to the Confederacy. He was one of only two members of Jefferson Davis's cabinet to hold their posts throughout the war.

With the consolidation of the disaffected states, the government moved to Richmond, and Mallory set up his offices there. A hastily compiled guide suggests the improvisatory nature of his new quarters. The seat of power was in the Mechanics Institute—on Ninth Street, between Main and Franklin—with the Navy Department to be found on the "2nd story, right hand side."

Behind the door that bore his name, Mallory took up the strands of his responsibilities while an unseasonably warm spring added to his discomforts (although one Confederate Army officer saw a tactical advantage in it, writing his wife, "We are having terribly hot weather here, and it does us good to think how it must toast the Yankees").

In his steaming rooms, Mallory sorted through the tools he had to work with. Burdened with too many shortages, he found himself with one troublesome surplus. Of 677 Southern-born US Navy officers, 321 had resigned their commissions to serve the Confederacy. Mallory had six ships to put them on. Of course shore batteries would need manning in the South's many harbors, and he would attend to that. But he saw his nation's role in the sea campaigns to come as far more than a defensive one. He knew the North would try to establish a blockade along the Southern coastline, and he wanted something to counter it.

Some of his actions in the Senate hinted that Mallory might take a conservative, even reactionary approach to his duties. He had campaigned vigorously if unsuccessfully for the reinstatement of flogging in the US Navy, even suggested that the service couldn't exist without it. But now, facing a naval war with a nonexistent fleet, he looked forward.

Just a week after Gosport Navy Yard burned, Mallory wrote the Confederate House Committee on Naval Affairs, "I regard the possession of an iron-armored ship as a matter of the first necessity. . . . Inequality of numbers may be compensated by invulnerability. Not only does economy, but naval success, dictate the wisdom and expediency of fighting with iron against wood, without regard to first cost." He would write his wife, "Knowing that the enemy could build one hundred ships to one of our own, my policy has been to make such ships so strong and invulnerable as would compensate for the inequality in numbers."

A Southern joke, possibly from the time, has a reporter questioning an official of the fledgling service.

Q: "Sir, is your navy iron-plated?"

A: "Sir, our navy is barely even contem-plated."

Mallory knew it would take decades to build a wooden fleet even remotely commensurate with what the Federals already had in hand. A new kind of warship, an iron warship, could redress the balance.

The thought had not originated with Mallory. Athenaeus, a second-century Greek grammarian and writer, says that in the third century BC, Hieron, king of Syracuse, built a ship whose hull was sheathed with lead plates fastened with copper bolts. If Athenaeus is to be believed, it was quite a vessel, a sort of proto–cruise ship with such luxuries as a marble bathroom, four-berth cabins, a library, and an aquarium. It also had a nice celebrity connection, in that the windlass used to launch it was designed by Archimedes.

In 1592 a Korean fleet under Admiral Yi Sun-sin used hundred-foot-long vessels protected with half-inch iron plating—called *kobukson*, "turtle ships"—to repel a Japanese invasion.

The idea wasn't taken up in the West for another 250 years until, during the Crimean War in 1855 at the Battle of Kinburn, the French reduced Russian forts on the Black Sea with three iron-plated floating batteries.

Mallory may not have known about the *kobukson*, but he'd received full reports on the Kinburn action from American observers.

Earlier and closer to home, two inventive New Jersey brothers named Robert and Augustus Stevens had talked Congress out of a quarter million dollars to build what was probably the first iron-clad warship ordered by any navy. Work on the "Stevens Battery" went forward slowly, but not cheaply, and a decade into its halting growth, in 1852, the Senate faced the question of whether to provide the money necessary to finish the job.

With little to show after ten years of riveting, the Stevens brothers were up against a largely hostile Senate. Mallory argued to save the battery. He won more funding, although not enough to finish the ship (it would be sold for scrap thirty years later), but he never lost faith in the project.

Now he was in a position to act on his conviction. Mallory figured that he didn't need a lot of ironclads, but he had to have *some.* If they were to carry the war to the enemy, they—unlike the Charleston floating battery—must be self-propelled.

Mallory first looked overseas to Europe, where the two great naval powers of the day were hard at work building large iron warships. France already had the thirty-six-gun *Gloire*, and England had responded with the just-launched forty-gun HMS *Warrior.* The former had iron plates sheathing a wooden hull; the latter was all iron. (Miraculously, it still survives, magnificently preserved, a mid-Victorian marvel that would be well worth a visit to Portsmouth even if Lord Nelson's flagship, *Victory*, were not there.) The idea of ironclads had taken such firm hold across the Atlantic that when Mallory was planning his invincible weapon, a hundred armored ships were either building or afloat in Europe. The British, who had already heard more than they wanted to about "Yankee ingenuity," dispensed a good deal of Olympian amusement about how far the Yankees were behind in this seagoing revolution.

Still, not one of these new creations had come close to meeting another in the ultimate test of combat.

Mallory's navy in the war's first year received a precise $14,605,777.86 out of government expenditures of $347 million; only the Confederate "Executive Mansion" was more meagerly funded. Still, Mallory hoped to buy his iron warship ready-made, and he sent envoys to Britain and France to try. One of them, James Bulloch, succeeded in commissioning raiders that played havoc with Union merchant shipping; the other, James North, contented himself with stealing a sum worth £30,000 from the Confederate treasury. Neither man was able to persuade any government to part with an ironclad.

Mallory would have to build his own. The same determination that had won Angela Moreno served him well here. Out on the western rivers, they were already hanging metal siding on steamboats, but Mallory had something more ambitious in mind than nailing stove iron to matchwood upperworks. He demanded a warship so ambitious that it is not too fanciful to view its building as the Confederacy's Manhattan Project.

It began with a message, dated May 30, slapped out over the telegraph wires from Gosport, that could not have made too great an impression on Mallory, besieged as he was by fragments of information pelting in from everywhere south of Washington. But the terse announcement was one of the most consequential communications in all naval history: "We have the *Merrimack* up and are just pulling her into dry dock."

CHAPTER 5

Old Father Neptune

An engraving of Gideon Welles as secretary of the Navy.

Save for a few haunting portraits of adolescent recruits, all the subjects of photographs from the Civil War era look at least a decade older than they are. It is surprising to remember that at the time of his inauguration, the immemorial face of Abraham Lincoln belonged to someone who had just turned fifty-two. Even so, Gideon Welles, who was in his late fifties when he joined Lincoln's cabinet, looks as old as Neptune. And that is the fond, mildly teasing nickname Lincoln gave his Navy secretary: Old Father Neptune.

Welles, like every politician, had enemies, and many of them made fun of his appearance. That wasn't hard to do. Years earlier, when his hair was still brown, he had ordered a curious wig, a high, wedge-shaped burst of fibers that had of course failed to turn white when his copious beard did. If this toupee was a reflection of the man's vanity, he was cavalier about it. He would put on the hairpiece in the morning, then pay it no further attention. When he became agitated, it would twitch about on his large head like a cat trying to get comfortable.

Massachusetts governor John Andrew once came to call on Welles asking, "Where can I find that old Mormon deacon, the secretary of the navy?"

The supple New York politico Thurlow Weed, who had first supported Welles's appointment and then, when his keen nose sniffed a change in the wind, opposed it, told Lincoln that if the President would "stop long enough in New York, Philadelphia or Baltimore to select an attractive figurehead, to be adorned with an elaborate wig and luxuriant whiskers, and transfer it from the prow of a ship to the entrance of the Navy Department, it would, in my opinion, be quite as serviceable as his Secretary, and less expensive."

With his shrewd combination of toughness and affable deflection, Lincoln replied, "Oh, wooden midshipmen answer very well in novels, but we must have a live Secretary of the Navy."

A *New York Tribune* reporter saw what Lincoln did. He wrote that Welles was "a curious-looking man: he wore a wig which was parted in the middle, the hair falling down on each side; and it was from his peculiar appearance, I have always thought, the idea that he was an old fogy originated. . . . In spite of his peculiarities, I think Mr. Welles was a very wise, strong man. There was nothing decorative about him; there was no noise in the street when he went along; but he understood his duty, and did it efficiently, continually, and unvaryingly. There was a good deal of opposition to him, for we had no navy when the war began, and he had to create one without much deliberation; but he was patient, laborious, and intelligent in his task."

Welles did not come to the task nearly so well equipped as his

Southern counterpart Mallory had. Just after he got to Washington, Lincoln told him, "I know but little about ships."

Welles knew less.

AN ACCIDENT OF GEOGRAPHY PUT Gideon Welles in charge of the US Navy. He thought he would be getting that eternal plum of the spoils system, a postmastership—in this case, *the* postmastership. But Montgomery Blair was made postmaster general. He was from Maryland; Simon Cameron, the secretary of war, from Pennsylvania; Secretary of the Treasury Salmon Chase, from Ohio. Lincoln needed a New Englander to balance things.

Gideon Welles was born in 1802 in Glastonbury, Connecticut, a few miles downriver from Hartford. His father, Samuel, owned a shipyard, a store, and a farm; the neighbors called him the Squire.

Gideon's boyhood was shadowed by death. His invalid mother died when he was fourteen, and two years later, his older brother Sam drowned while swimming near his father's docks. Gideon brooded and hung about the local cemetery, where his grandfather's tombstone offered the flinty solace "The wise in God will put their trust, / The young may die, the aged must."

After a while, his father brusquely told the melancholy boy that he was getting stupid and sent him away to the Protestant Episcopal Academy in Cheshire. Gideon was a lackadaisical student, his appreciation of Latin such that he told his classmate and lifelong friend Andrew Foote—who would one day be a rear admiral in the Navy Gideon oversaw—that he wished Rome had suffered the same fate as Carthage.

Shortly before Gideon's twenty-first birthday, his father wrote him, "You will soon be your own man now, remember that you are made for other purposes than merely to amuse yourself with the curiosities of this world—God blessed you with Talents—which you ought not to lie rol'd in a napkin."

Welles was already nurturing a vocation, although not one that would have pleased the Squire. He wrote in the notebook he had taken to carrying, "When vexed by the petty ills of life . . . [I] seize my pen and forget the cause of my uneasiness in writing something that might imitate verse to mix with the . . . pieces of prose which I may have idly and almost thoughtlessly composed."

He wanted to be a writer. He is not remembered as one, but writing would be a great comfort to him during the war, when he kept the diary that not only relieved the endless aggravations of his office, but—although a private exercise—survives as the greatest day-by-day account of one who held high office during those burning years.

By writing, he mounted the first rungs of his career. In the summer of 1823 he sent a sentimental sketch to a weekly called the *New York Mirror* and was thrilled to read in the September 13 issue that "The Deserted Orphan," a "beautiful little story . . . will appear next week." He sold the *Mirror* four more stories. They gained him entry into a Glastonbury group that liked to call itself The Literate.

His tiny triumph helped him become tax collector for Glastonbury, in 1823, and thereafter he was involved in politics for the rest of his life. When the new Democratic Party began to coalesce around Andrew Jackson, he joined it and, having landed a job on the *Hartford Times and Advertiser*, wrote vigorous (his opponents said strident and "illiberal") editorials for the candidate in the 1828 campaign. Jackson lost Connecticut, but he won the presidency and made Welles the state's Democratic Party manager. In the state assembly he echoed Jackson's feelings about hereditary privilege by complaining that Connecticut's problems came with "a political spice from Old Yale College. . . . I am ashamed . . . to say of the civil and political complexion of my state [that] a degraded, bigoted, hide-bound, aristocratic, proud, arrogant and contemptible policy governs her, through designing hypocrites, and artful and unprincipled knaves."

When he went to Washington to meet Jackson ("His person is very tall and spare, his phiz remarkably long, his eye quick, roving and penetrating"), he discovered that the office of Hartford post-master had already been awarded to Benjamin Norton, a man he didn't like. Welles had already become a skilled enough politician to unseat Norton with such sure-handed efficiency that for years afterward the total demolition of a rival was known in Connecti-cut legislative circles as "Nortonizing."

Welles himself got the Hartford postmastership at the begin-ning of Jackson's second term. By that time he had married. On a trip west to Harrisburg, Pennsylvania, to view the Democratic Party's first convention, the twenty-four-year-old Welles had vis-ited his uncle, Elias Hale, and met his daughter Mary Jane, a grave, brown-eyed ten-year-old. Six years later he gallantly offered to act as Mary Jane's guardian during her stay at Brace's Seminary for Young Ladies in Hartford. He met her at the steamboat landing on the Connecticut River and just days later wrote her much older brother Reuben, "Were I not so old and so foolish, I should believe myself more than half in love with my fair cousin."

Soon he was pursuing a difficult courtship. Mary Jane's mother was against the marriage; she had another suitor in mind for her daughter. After months of "sickening, deadening suspence," Welles prevailed, and he and Mary Jane Hale were married on her eigh-teenth birthday in July 1835. It proved a remarkably happy match, although one often darkened. Of their nine children, only three lived to become adults. But the couple drew strength from one another through good times and bad for the rest of their lives.

IN 1844 THE NEWLY ELECTED James Polk rewarded his loyal Connecticut supporter by putting Welles in charge of the Navy Department's Bureau of Provisions and Clothing.

The recipient's enthusiasm for this bounty shows in one curt, joyless diary entry: "Business causes induced me to accept this place."

Welles had been a good postmaster, and he was a good head of Navy supplies. The job was demanding. America was fighting

Mexico, and although Welles had nothing to do with the operation of warships, he had to make sure the men working them were
properly fed and clothed off Mexican shores in climates much
warmer than they'd prepared for. He did well, and although his
service taught him nothing about gunnery or the obstreperous
new marine steam engines, it proved invaluable when he had to
cope with broader naval duties.

Administrations changed, and Welles was out of office in 1849.
The "business causes" that he'd gloomily invoked when offered his
post were in far better shape. His investments in western lands
had turned out well, but now he was unhappy about the course
his party was taking.

He was not an abolitionist. He had no fondness for slavery, but
he believed it had been recognized by the Constitution and so was
part of the legal fabric. Now he was convinced that the Southern
Democrats were trying to spread slavery into the territories in
hopes of making the institution a national one. To him, this was
an assault on the states' rights that were so much a part of his Jef-
fersonian convictions.

He left the Democratic Party after thirty years, transferring
his faith to the new Republican Party and becoming a member
of its National Committee. Abraham Lincoln came to speak in
Hartford on March 6, 1860. Welles would never have dreamed
of presenting his ideas about slavery in the homely terms that
Lincoln did, but the candidate's ideas perfectly expressed Welles's
beliefs:

> "If I find a venomous snake lying on the open prairie, I seize the
> first stick and kill him at once. But if that snake is in bed with my
> children, I must be more cautious — I shall, in striking the snake,
> also strike the children or arouse the reptile to bite the children.
> Slavery is the venomous snake in bed with the children. But if
> the question is whether to kill it on the prairie" — slavery in the
> territories — "or put it in bed with other children I think we'd
> kill it."

When Welles came away the morning after the Hartford speech from his first meeting with the candidate, he was on Lincoln's side. "This orator and lawyer . . . was made where the material for strong men is plenty, and his huge, tall frame is loosely thrown together. He is every way large, brain included, but his countenance shows intellect, generosity, great good nature, and keen discrimination. . . . He is an effective speaker, because he is earnest, strong, honest, simple in style, and clear as crystal in his logic."

At the Republican National Convention in Chicago, Welles steered the Connecticut delegation into his candidate's camp. In November Lincoln carried Connecticut, as he did all New England. Welles was "very jolly" over the outcome, but saw ahead "dissolution of the Union, and other terrible calamities."

ON MARCH 1, THREE DAYS before Lincoln was to be inaugurated, Welles received a telegram from Hannibal Hamlin, the vice president–elect, summoning him to Washington. He left that same day, confident he'd be offered a cabinet position, and believing— and wanting—it to be that of postmaster general. He wasn't able to get in to see Lincoln until the morning of the inauguration, when he discovered that "the President & Vice President prefer, I think, that I should take the Navy portfolio. The President stated that this was his arrangement."

Welles went to his office, passing under the same portraits of the heroes of the War of 1812 that he had last seen when he was fired from his naval supplies job. As soon as he got behind his desk, chaos engulfed him. The last time Welles had been there, he'd been worrying about what kind of butter to purchase for the Navy; now he had to whistle up a fleet.

He had some ninety ships to work with, half of them out of commission, only twenty-four steam-powered, and few anywhere nearby. The *Hartford*, from whose deck Farragut would damn the torpedoes in Mobile Bay three years hence, was showing the flag off the Chinese coast. Some of the best were lying on the silt at the bottom of the Elizabeth River.

He began summoning home the ones still afloat and started building, he said, "a class of vessels different in some respects from any that were in service, to act as sentinels on the coast." These were wooden, shallow-draft steamers that could carry their eleven-inch bow gun across bayous and up skinny rivers. The name they acquired, 90-Day Gunboats, said how quickly they got built. But even three months was too long, and Welles began buying civilian ships indiscriminately. Anything with a working steam plant would do: towboats, excursion steamers, harbor tugs, right down to the ferries that plied Manhattan's East River (these tough city kids would give a surprisingly good account of themselves in the years ahead). The motley assemblage gained a less dignified nickname than the gunboats: the Soapbox Navy.

The secretary chose as his main hiring agent George D. Morgan. Welles trusted him, and with reason. In six months Morgan bought eighty-nine ships for $3.5 million, which was close to a million under the initial asking prices. But he was also Welles's brother-in-law, and he made $70,000 in commissions, a huge amount of money for half a year's work. That did not sit well with the press. Nothing Welles did seemed to.

The war went badly for the North from the start. In the first big battle, Confederate soldiers routed the Union army thirty miles west of Washington at Bull Run on July 21. Less than a month later, Northern forces met Southern ones at Wilson's Creek in Missouri, the result codified in the name that immediately attached itself to the engagement: Bull Run of the West.

Two days after the earlier reverse, Lincoln had drafted a nine-point memorandum on what his forces should do now. Item 1 was "Let the plan for making the Blockade effective be pushed forward with all possible despatch." But the gathering of blockaders went largely unnoticed by the press, which felt things were being handled as ineptly at sea as they were on land.

That was all Welles's fault, wasn't it? He became the object of

angry glee in the Northern press: that wig, his whole appearance—
a lot of reporters mysteriously decided that he bore a physical resemblance to Marie Antoinette—came under steady written and
drawn assault. The popular *Frank Leslie's Illustrated Newspaper* published a quatrain about him:

> Retire, O Gideon, to an onion farm,
> Ply any trade that's innocent and slow.
> Do anything, where you can do no harm.
> Go anywhere you fancy—only go.

He didn't go. But his job was intolerable. Lincoln had asked for
a blockade not just of Southern ports, but of the entire coastline.
Welles initially opposed the strategy. Blockades were deployed by
nations at war with one another, and he feared that imposing one
on the rebellious states would amount to recognizing the Confederacy as a legitimate entity. Better, he said, to close Southern
harbors, as any nation would do had they been seized by pirates.

Lincoln, however, looked overseas. Great Britain, having used
blockades as a strategy, would respect one: the practice had been
codified by international law. But Britain would not tolerate the arbitrary cordoning of various cities, especially by the United States,
this bumptious newcomer that had already proved such an irritant
during its young life. That would be seen as trifling with England's
maritime rights, which her famous fleet could assert.

So Lincoln ordered a blockade, and Welles found himself responsible for policing thirty-five hundred miles of coast from Cape
Henry to the Rio Grande, the same length of rivers, and two thousand miles of the Gulf; in all, just over nine thousand hostile miles
of notched, broken, rocky, fort-studded, swampy, and forested
shoreline. No navy had ever attempted so immense a job.

Welles ignored as best he could the ridicule and, scaling what he
called a "mountain of letters," assembled his converted ferryboats
and summoned-from-afar men-of-war. After a grueling half year he
could take some satisfaction in having one hundred ships on station.

He had also assembled a cadre of officers he could trust. In the beginning he was as unsure as poor McCauley had been about the loyalty of his captains. Many of the Southern-born ones resigned their commissions at once; others asked for foreign duty so they would not have to fight their countrymen. The latter group angered Welles just as much as those who immediately went South. To all who did not support the Union, he was implacable, never forgiving "the host of pampered officers who deserted their flag . . . when their loyalty should have upheld it."

But the winnowing was over. The blockade had been established and would stand and grow stronger. The secretary of the navy was well along with his blockade by August when he almost certainly read a newspaper item from the South (where reporters weren't nearly as merciless to him as his countrymen were). Attempts at military secrecy in the war's early years were all but nonexistent. On August 11, 1861, the *Mobile Register* published, "It would seem that the hull of the *Merrimack* is being converted into an iron-cased battery. If so, she will be a floating fortress that will be able to defeat the whole Navy of the United States and bombard its cities. Her great size, strength, and powerful engines and speed, combined with the invulnerability secured by the iron casing, will make the dispersal or the destruction of the blockading fleet an easy task for her. Her immense tonnage will enable her to carry an armor proof against any projectile and she could entertain herself by throwing bombs into Fortress Monroe, even without risk. We hope soon to hear that she is ready to commence her avenging career on the seas."

CHAPTER 6

The Once and Future *Merrimack*

A 1907 postcard advertising a Coney Island spectacular that
re-created the Hampton Roads battle offers a fairly accurate view of the
Merrimack in dry dock. There are no known photographs of her.

The article may have disturbed Gideon Welles; it infuriated
Lieutenant John Mercer Brooke, who wrote in his diary, "The
Mobile Register contains information in relation to the Merrimack
of much value to the enemy. Editors are doing infinite harm in that
way. I shall begin to think that even the South can not tolerate a
free press."

Brooke was one of the officers whose resignation so angered
Welles, and likely more than that of most of them, for Brooke was
an uncommonly able man.

Born into a Virginia military family, he grew up on army posts,
but not for long: his mother died when he was twelve, and his
father got him an appointment in the Navy. In 1841, at the age of
fourteen, he reported for duty as a midshipman aboard the USS
Delaware, a ship of the line commanded by Charles McCauley, who

twenty years later would inadvertently furnish him with his most important professional challenge.

During his relatively brief schooling Brooke had been strongly drawn to mathematics, and he was fascinated by technology. The *Delaware* paid a great deal of attention to gunnery, and he learned it under the sure tutelage of a rising lieutenant named David Farragut. Brooke proved himself sufficiently adept a student to be admitted, in 1846, to the two-year-old insitution that would become Annapolis.

Having graduated, he went back to sea, first aboard the *Delaware*, and then the highly advanced *Princeton*, whose workings would have intrigued him. During these years he embarked on a difficult courtship that in some ways mirrored those of both Stephen Mallory and Gideon Welles. Like Welles, he fell in love with a cousin, Lizzie Garnett, and like Mallory, he had a hard time proposing. When the day came, Lizzie remembered, he "had everything so jumbled up together and spoke so fast that I could hardly collect my thoughts." Lizzie got the drift, though, and told him she had "never liked anyone else." They married in 1849.

By then Brooke was on the revenue cutter USS *Washington* making surveys of the Atlantic coast. From its birth, the US Navy had relied on British charts, but now wanted to outgrow its dependence. Brooke's grasp of science served him well in this duty and he enjoyed it. He asked to be assigned to the Naval Observatory, which oversaw the charts he had helped create.

The request granted, Brooke quickly distinguished himself by inventing a simple, ingenious sounding device that, lowered over the side of a ship, could accurately register the depth of the ocean floor below. The Navy adopted it and sent Brooke off around the world. He conducted the first survey of the east coast of Japan; he charted the shores of Alaska and Siberia; he plumbed the seabed three miles down.

Home at the end of the decade, he got a pleasant surprise. Having paltered about it for years, Congress—goaded by Stephen Mallory—finally awarded him $5,000 for his sounding device. He picked up his payment from the Treasury Department in the early spring of 1861, and immediately invested it in Confederate bonds.

Years later he wrote, "When the State of Virginia seceded, in accordance with my convictions, I laid down my pencil on the chart of 'French Frigate Shoals' which I was drawing, went to the Navy Department and handed in my resignation." Gideon Welles refused to accept it. On May 14 he wrote Brooke coldly, "Your letter of the 20th ultimo tendering your resignation as a Lieutenant in the U.S. Navy has been received. By direction of the President your name has been stricken from the rolls of the Navy from that date." In effect, a dishonorable discharge.

Brooke had spent much of his peripatetic boyhood in the North, and many of the following years overseas. But once he'd cast his lot with the Confederacy, he did so wholeheartedly, telling his wife, "Politically speaking it will be best for the South to have war for some time to break up all the old connecting ties. I despise the North." At about the same time, he wrote, "We at last have a homogeneous country. I never wish to have anything to do with the late US or rather the Northern people."

Brooke was commissioned a lieutenant in the Virginia Navy on April 23 and ordered to report to the commander of the state's forces, Robert E. Lee, who had resigned his commission the same day Brooke had. He wrote Lizzie that "Genl Lee is a Second Washington if ever there was one." For his part, Lee knew what he had in Brooke and put him to overseeing the acquisition of every type of weapon from sidearm to field gun. Although reluctant to leave Lee—"He is a true man in every sense of the word"—Brooke wanted to stay with his old calling and wrote Mallory asking for "a commission in the permanent Navy of the Southern Confederacy when such a navy shall be organized."

He got his appointment on May 2. Four days later he sent Mallory a letter that echoed the secretary's thinking on the sea war ahead: "The strict blockade which the U.S. Government proposes will render the importation of arms very difficult, and the process of manufacture is too slow to provide a sufficient number even if we had the best machinery. It has occurred to me that if the French Emperor is favorable to the Confederate States, an iron plated ship might be purchased in France loaded with arms and brought into port in spite of the wooden blockade."

The two met for the first time a month later. On June 4, "a hot oppressive drizzly day," Brooke wrote Lizzie from Richmond, "Mallory arrived here from Montgomery last night. I had some conversation with him but it was quite late and he was very tired." A week later he wrote Lizzie again: "Mallory wants me to make some calculations in regard to floating batteries which I shall do today."

Brooke was far more discreet than the *Mobile Register.* He didn't divulge even to his wife the radical form the floating battery was to take.

Perhaps Mallory suspected from the start that he was being naïve to think France or Britain would part with their new iron warships, for when he met Brooke, he was already planning to launch a home-built one. A few days earlier he had telegraphed a Confederate officer in New Orleans, telling him to find iron plate "of any given thickness from two and one-half to five inches." Nothing doing: no shop in Louisiana could make it. The same news came in from Georgia, Kentucky, and Tennessee. But the Tredegar Iron Works in Richmond had said it could roll out plate two inches thick, and Mallory asked Brooke to make a fighting ship out of that. The secretary said, "He entered upon the duty at once."

Brooke was almost finished with his preliminary designs by June 19 when he wrote his wife that he'd spent the day refining them. He envisioned a metal shed—or casemate—"inclined at the least angle that would permit working the guns." He called for ten cannon, and the sloping sides mandated a vessel of considerable length, as there would not be room to have the two rows of broadside guns mounted back to back as they were on conventional warships. Rather, they'd have to be staggered, allowing room for their crews to stand side by side when the recoil kicked the cannon backward. The ship's shield would be laminated—three one-inch-thick plates laid on top of one another—and backed with two feet of timber. Brooke wasn't happy about the laminating; he wanted single three-inch plates, but that was beyond Tredegar's capabilities.

This metal canopy would rest on a submerged hull. The idea of tilted sides to deflect shot was not new: it had been used on the ships that fought the Kinburn batteries in the Crimean War and had just proved its worth on this side of the Atlantic with the floating battery in Charleston Harbor.

Brooke's conception of the hull, however, was revolutionary. Later, when Mallory reported on the ship's progress to the Confederate House of Representatives, he said, "The novel plan of submerging the ends of the ship and the eaves of the casemate . . . is the peculiar and distinctive feature. . . . It was never before adapted." Brooke lit on the idea of a submerged hull because the iron carapace would be so heavy. "It was apparent that to support such a shield," the bow and stern of the vessel would have to be so broad and blunt "as to prevent the attainment of speed. . . . It occurred to me that fineness of line, protection of hull, and buoyancy with light draft could be attained by extending the ends of the vessel under water beyond the shield." He received a patent for the idea.

Brooke made sketches of his vessel and on June 23 brought them to Mallory. They looked good to the secretary, but Brooke was not a naval architect, or "ship constructor" as the discipline was then known. So John Luke Porter was also at the meeting.

PORTER, WHO WAS BORN IN Norfolk in 1813, had spent his life near warships. His father owned a shipyard; it had to be sold when he died, but by then John, though only seventeen, already had become a ship carpenter capable enough to bring in a salary that could support his mother and, when he was twenty, allow him to marry. In time he advanced from carpentry to being a ship constructor. He wanted to become a US Navy constructor, a civilian position that nevertheless meant the builder worked only for the service and followed its dictates. Porter passed the exam in 1857 and, made the Pensacola Navy Yard's constructor, moved to Florida with his family.

On January 10, 1861, the state seceded. Washington ordered Porter up to Norfolk, where he found "everything in the Yard was disorder and confusion. The workmen were standing around in groups. No one was working." He looked the place over, made a perfunctory appearance before the fuddled and frightened McCauley, and then went to join his wife, who had preceded him North to set up a home.

He later said McCauley should have been court-martialed for his performance during those days. This seems harsh coming from Porter, who evidently offered his commander no help whatever. Virginia seceded, the yard burned, and, although Porter said, "I did not think from the beginning of the War that the Confederacy could succeed," on April 20, "I then resigned my appointment as Constructor in the U.S. service and reported for duty to Commandant Forrest. The Commandant had assumed command of the Yard for the State of Virginia."

Commandant Forrest was Flag Officer French Forrest, who had been serving under his previous flag for half a century. He'd joined the Navy the year the War of 1812 began, fought on Lake Erie, and helped get the Army ashore at Veracruz during the war with Mexico. Now in his midsixties, and looking like an allegorical portrait of a magnificent old warrior—cascades of white hair framing a fierce, wise, weary, hawkish face—he had thrown over his commission and come South along with a number of older officers who, the sour-natured Raphael Semmes, commander of the famous commerce raider *Alabama* during the war, said offered "nothing but their patriotism and their grey hairs."

Gray hairs notwithstanding, Forrest took over the task of organizing Gosport with skill and vigor.

He ordered Porter to help repair the yard. There was a lot to work with, and the news was all good. Along with the spectacular haul of cannon, the flames had spared a quarter million pounds of gunpowder and, scrupulously assessed, clothing worth $56,269 and $38,763 worth of food, lots of chain and shot, and the superb dry dock.

Porter's initial efforts had nothing to do with ships, but that soon changed. As early as 1846, his son wrote years later, "Mr. Porter conceived the idea of an ironclad vessel which would be able to go to sea and still be shot proof." He'd sent his plans to the Navy Department and never received a reply. When he met with Mallory and Brooke, he brought with him a model of his shotproof ship. In many ways it chimed with Brooke's ideas, as it too featured an iron casemate with sloping sides, although this shield rose sheer from the water, presenting the problems that Brooke hoped to avoid with his submerged hull. "I was afraid," wrote Brooke, that Porter "would, having an idea of his own make objection to my plan but he did not[,] regarding it as an improvement."

Nonetheless, Brooke's premonition of friction between the two men turned out to be accurate. For years after the war the two would querulously argue about which was the guiding spirit in the ship's genesis. The dispute continues to this day, but what is beyond argument is that a formidable partnership was born in Mallory's office. Even looking back from the promontory of a century and a half, it is difficult to imagine how, given the tools they had, the two could have created a more devastatingly effective engine of war.

MALLORY TOLD PORTER TO DRAFT finished plans for the ship. For its power plant the secretary turned to Brooke and a third member of the meeting, William P. Williamson, the chief engineer of the Confederate Navy. Like Porter, Williamson had years earlier conceived and drawn up an ironclad warship, and he and Brooke were already friends; Brooke called him Willie.

Brooke and Williamson visited the Tredegar works. The factory built locomotives, after all, so it should have been capable of increasing the scale a bit to make ships' engines.

Joseph Reid Anderson, who owned Tredegar, was an ex–Army officer still in his forties who had in twenty years built his ironworks from a small, dying, debt-ridden failure into the industrial behemoth of the South. He knew what he was talking about when he said the job would take months, if indeed it could be done at all.

The two men went away discouraged, but after a while Williamson thought of the *Merrimack*. French Forrest had been told to refloat her. Although he'd groused about what he thought was a waste of money that could better be spent on almost anything else, he'd paid a civilian firm $6,000 to raise the hulk and pump it out. Now, charred down to the copper that sheathed the hull and slick with river slime, it was resting in the Gosport dry dock.

Brooke and Williamson went to Norfolk to see what might be salvaged, and Porter almost certainly joined them there. The three men walked around the rim of the dock, looking down at the blackened, reeking hull. The engines glinted dully, spavined and despised—but possessing the inestimable virtue of actually existing. Moreover, the hull looked sound. Why not save months of work and tens of thousands of dollars by building the ironclad on top of the *Merrimack*'s timbers?

Brooke thought this made sense; so did Porter; and so too, when they presented the idea to him, did Stephen Mallory.

BACK IN APRIL 1854, WHEN America contained only one Congress, it had authorized the construction of "six first-class steam frigates to be provided with screw propellers." Half of the fourteen steam-powered ships in the US Navy at the time were driven by paddle wheels; these new vessels would have their source of propulsion safely beneath the water. The six ships were meant to be the most advanced in the world, both an advertisement and a warning that US maritime strength had caught up with that of the European powers.

They were named for American rivers—*Niagara*, *Roanoke*, *Minnesota*, *Wabash*, *Merrimack*, and *Colorado*. The *Merrimack* was the first built. The advantage for her was that she would get the most careful planning and the best materials; the drawbacks were those that beset any prototype: it reveals every mistake that must be spared its successors.

The *Merrimack* was laid down in the Charlestown Navy Yard, across the Charles River from Boston. Two hundred and seventy-five feet long and displacing four thousand tons—and with a deep draft (the vertical distance between the waterline and the bottom of the hull) of twenty-seven feet—she was made of well-seasoned live oak. But for all the hopes of her advancing American sea power, she was a conventional sailing ship. A handsome one, to be sure, but her hull was uncomfortably narrow for the machinery it had to contain. In the morning time of steam at sea, the new arrival was still used as an auxiliary to help in storms and maneuvering in battle.

This is not to say that the machinery was an afterthought. The *Merrimack*'s engines, built at the West Point Foundry in Cold Spring, New York, were twelve feet high, fifteen long, and nearly thirty wide, fed by massive boilers that were the only part of the plant that didn't make trouble.

Twenty thousand spectators came to see the *Merrimack* launched on June 14, 1855. In deference to the American Temperance Society, founded in Boston thirty years earlier, she was christened not with wine but with a flask of Merrimack River water broken across her bows, a pallid baptism for a ship that would have a career unique in naval history.

The components of the engines began to arrive from Cold Spring a month later and started to cause difficulties as soon as they were installed. The machinery added 129 tons to the ship's weight, but despite its imposing dimensions—the two cylinders were six feet in diameter—consumed much of the energy that should have been turning the propeller shaft simply keeping its own innards in motion. Designed to push the *Merrimack* at a cruising speed of

ten knots, it could barely make more than six, and that at the exorbitant cost of forty-five tons of coal for every twenty-four hours'
steaming. When Benjamin Isherwood examined the ship's engines,
he wrote, "The enormous cylinder capacity caused the steam to
have a low average pressure on the pistons . . . and the vacuum,
owing to air leaks, was very poor. The arrangement and proportion
of the air-pumps were faulty and productive of the same results."
Beyond being weak and costly, the plant was in constant conflict
with the ship, thrashing at wooden bracings not sturdy enough to
support it properly, and chewing up its bearings.

These failings were invisible when the *Merrimack* was gusting
along under her full spread of fifty thousand square feet of new
canvas, and when she visited Britain in the fall of 1856, she was
hailed by one Royal Navy observer as the "finest vessel of her class
that has ever been christened." That enthusiast must have come
up when wind alone drove ships; British engineers shared Isherwood's dark view of the power plant.

The engines continued to make trouble. After the British visit,
the *Merrimack* returned to her birthplace for a complete mechanical overhaul. Whatever good it might have done did not last long;
on November 14, 1859, the ship ended its last cruise under the
Stars and Stripes at Gosport. Two weeks later she was taken out of
commission and pieces of the delinquent engines scattered around
the yard, not to be reunited until Isherwood's vain attempt to save
the frigate for the Union.

ON JULY 11, MALLORY WROTE Forrest, "You will proceed with
all practicable dispatch to make the changes in the *Merrimack*, and
build, equip, and fit her in all respects according to the designs
and plans of the Constructor and Engineer, Messrs. Porter and
Williamson." He added, "Time is of the first importance in the
matter."

Time certainly was. Mallory knew he was in a race. The Union
might as yet have no thought of building a vessel that could counter

his projected ship, but surely the North's industrial muscle and mechanical ingenuity would bring on a swift response once the US Navy found out what the Confederate Navy was up to.

Porter set to work drafting meticulous plans for the conversion on a prodigious scroll of paper twenty-seven feet long. His designs immediately drew the criticism of almost everyone who was privy to them, including French Forrest, who, having thought the vessel not worth raising in the first place, now was certain that building a metal fortress on top of a waterlogged wooden carcass would give the *Merrimack* the distinction of being the only warship to sink twice within a year.

"I received but little encouragement from anyone," Porter wrote. "... Hundreds, I may say thousands, asserted she would not float. Some said she would turn bottom side up; others said the crew would suffocate; the most wise said the concussion and report of the guns would deafen the men. Some said she would not steer; and public opinion generally about here said she would never come out of the dock. You have no idea what I have suffered in mind since I commenced her, but I knew what I was about, and I persevered."

While he was persevering, Brooke was back amid the flare and din of the Tredegar works seeing to the plates. Tredegar did as much as Lee and Stonewall Jackson's military prowess to keep the Southern cause alive. The first mortar that fired on Sumter had been born there, as had the shell it sent into the fort; and the foundry would still be casting Confederate cannon four years later when Richmond fell. Tredegar was the fourth-largest ironworks in America, surpassed only by three in coal-rich Pennsylvania, and without it Mallory's ship would never have existed. When Brooke arrived there, he found a thousand men at work making everything from light brass field pieces to huge guns for coast fortifications, while forty forges burned in the blacksmith shop night and day.

Brooke's business was with the rolling mills. The owner, Anderson, contracted in July to supply the iron for the vessel at six and a half cents a pound. On August 24 the Confederate Congress moved "that there be appropriated ... for repairing and fitting the steamer Merrimac as an ironclad ship, the sum of one hundred and seventy-two thousand five hundred and twenty-three dollars." By September, the task was consuming Tredegar. Much of the iron came from the Baltimore & Ohio Railroad's tracks in northern Virginia, which Jackson had his troops ripping up from their captured roadbeds for the purpose.

The inch-thick plates Brooke had initially called for to make his three-layer metal sandwich were fairly easily worked. But with the job under way, Brooke received an order from Mallory: "You will without delay proceed to test the iron plates now being prepared in the Tredegar Works, in the best manner to determine what their powers of resistance to shot and shell will be when placed on the Merrimac according to the plans accepted."

Brooke must have felt some relief to be able to try out his shield before lives depended on his calculations of its strength, but the order added burdens to what was a bad time for him. The insidious spiritual erosions of wartime separation were already at work when he wrote Lizzie—who had not come to the hectic new capital city and was in Lexington, Kentucky—saying he was "very miserable" because of the "cruel charges" she had made against him. She seems to have taken his prolonged absence as neglect. "My love is strong," he protested, "and for you thus deliberately to charge me with want of affection and to say that I wean you from love of life, I who would lay down my life for you, whose only consolation is to be loved by you is too hard."

Brooding, he left Richmond to test his ship's sheathing beyond the reach of newspaper reporters. He went to Jamestown Island, where in 1607 the first permanent English settlement in America had put down the roots of the republic he was now working to dismantle. Jamestown, fifty miles southeast of Richmond, was private enough for his purposes. The town had been abandoned for nearby Williamsburg by the late 1600s, and all that was left of its desperate, heroic life was the mellow rose brick of the tower of the ruined church, then more than two centuries old, that stands there today.

He brought with him sixteen carpenters who set up a target "from a plan proposed for the *Merrimack*'s shield" that was twelve feet square with three layers of inch-thick iron backed by twenty-seven inches of wood, its face sloping upward with a tilt of thirty-six degrees. Spurred along by what seemed to be distant cannon fire (but turned out to be thunder), the workmen had the substantial structure finished by August 30. "The target was completed this morning," Brooke wrote in his diary, "and I am now only waiting for a boat to take the carpenters away. It is desirable that they should not witness the experiments as they live in Richmond and would probably report to their friends, leading to the publication of the whole affair in our indiscreet newspapers."

On the last of day of August, with the potentially too-chatty carpenters on their way back to Richmond, the crew remaining on the island charged an eight-inch gun with a solid iron ball and ten pounds of powder, trained it, and fired. "At a distance of 300 yards," the shot "perforated the iron and entered 5 inches into the wood." The three-inch layer of plates wouldn't do.

"It was then thought proper," wrote Brooke, "to increase the thickness to 4 inches. A new target was constructed, of which the plates were two inches thick, forming two layers. Eight-inch shot, with ten pound charges . . . were fired against the target. The outer plates were shattered, the inner were cracked, but the wood was not visible through the cracks in the plating."

Brooke returned to Richmond to announce the change of plans to Tredegar. The new two-inch plate came accompanied by new problems. The ironworks had no equipment able to punch bolt holes through it and had to resort to time-consuming drilling instead. As the ironclad took shape, plans shifted, and some of the plates had to be reworked three and four times before they were ready for installation.

Gosport was able to offer Tredegar some help with the work. On the eve of the war, the US government had installed a new iron punch that turned out to be strong enough to bang through the two-inch plate, and French Forrest set it to work on the *Merrimack*'s armor. (That punch was a wonder: eighty years later it was being kept busy by the demands of World War II, and it wasn't scrapped until well along in the unsentimental 1950s.)

By the fall the ironclad had become Tredegar's largest single project. The cost of materials went up, and in September the works had to raise its price for iron to seven and a half cents per pound. One of the Tredegar partners wrote, "We are now pressed almost beyond endurance for the heavy iron work to complete one of the war vessels *now ready for operations.* It is a most fortunate thing that we could render this assistance to our little Navy—It could not have been done anywhere else in the Confederacy."

Brooke was feeling pressed beyond endurance himself and probably was not much helped by Mallory's visits to Tredegar to "encourage the work." Brooke wrote, "I find that hard work particularly at night is hurting my eyesight again. I do have enough to do. Cant attend to all of it. Feel exhausted every day and only weigh about 133 pounds." He glumly reported spending his twelfth wedding anniversary at the ironworks; but he saw to it that the plates got made. When the final shipment went off to Norfolk on February 12, 1862, Tredegar had rolled 733 tons of iron for the *Merrimack.*

But getting the iron forged was only part of the problem. In early November a Tredegar official complained to Gosport, "We have iron for the Navy Yard that has been lying on the bank for 4 weeks—several sizes are ready to go down, the Rail Road has been unable to transport it."

In its voracious birth throes, Mallory's ironclad would—directly and indirectly—hobble the railway system of half the South.

Richmond is only ninety miles from Norfolk, a short run over the Richmond & Petersburg Line, and at the outset of the war five railroads fed into the city—but none of them very far. In the infancy of railroads, drayage companies—the truckers of that horse-drawn age—pressured the Virginia legislature to make it illegal for any two rail lines to connect. So on every journey, freight had to be transferred by hand—slave hands—from train to wagon to train.

When the first shipment of finished iron was ready, a Tredegar agent wrote to Thomas Wynne, the superintendent of the Richmond & Petersburg, "The Navy Department is pressing us to send forward the heavy iron for the steamer Merrimac. We have some 70 to 100 tons of iron already to ship. . . . You will please state if you have a sufficient No. of flats to forward the iron promptly."

Flats were flatcars, and Wynne replied that he didn't. The fighting fronts were not so far away, and the Army Department constantly requisitioned rolling stock to move infantry and field guns.

Forrest ordered his agent, William Webb, to find routes between Richmond and Norfolk. Shuffling through an infinity of railroad schedules and the hastily sent orders that overrode them, Webb, a most capable man, patched together paths that skirted all the rival demands. At one point he was getting his iron to Norfolk by sending it over the Petersburg line to Weldon, North Carolina, where the Seaboard & Roanoke took over.

Once the plates had made their circuitous way to Gosport, they needed to be fastened to the *Merrimack*'s hull. Porter had to work out how to set all that iron on a wooden frame.

The craft of building wooden ships had developed over centuries to a point where well-handled vessels could stay afloat under the worst that nature could fling against them. But no shipwright had ever before had to figure out how to balance eight hundred tons of metal—for that was what the *Merrimack* finally had to carry—on a submerged hull.

The task Porter oversaw had more to do with bridge building than with house framing, and his heavy wooden skeleton was complex and demanding. "Many of the inboard arrangements," he wrote, "are of the most intricate character and caused me many sleepless nights."

Porter's trusswork was 150 feet long and 24 wide and, once sealed with pitch to make it watertight, got covered with a four-inch-deep sheath of white oak. Two layers were beneath that: foot-thick pine and five-inch-thick pine, with a salting of locust throughout. All this before the iron went on, and all of it held together with bolts. These were metal dowels, rust-proof brass and copper in places exposed to the water, and iron, which gripped more tenaciously, above decks.

So when it came time to attach the plates, the workers drilling the final holes had to grope their way through invisible geometries of bolts already in place. It was maddening work. The "hole borer" would pick a spot and turn his auger, hoping not to hit a bolt. If he did, his bit would break, and the useless hole would get plugged with a wooden cylinder (these enjoyed the vivid name *treenails*, turned in pronunciation into the inscrutable word *trunnel*). Then, with a fresh bit, the borer would try another spot. This blindman's buff explains the constant requests to Tredegar for plates with revised bolt-hole positions.

The sole comfort for the builders was that they had no shortage of good wood. As with so much matériel at Gosport, those stores had escaped the torch, and plenty of seasoned timber was on hand.

Every other need of the ship, however, was becoming increasingly difficult to meet. Urgent demands—and every demand was urgent—came into Gosport from all over the South, and Mallory found himself at odds with the Army as he competed for supplies. The *Merrimack*'s engines needed oil to function, and Forrest was able to acquire hundreds of gallons of it from a captured Union ship. Coal proved more elusive, but Forrest realized he had valuable bargaining chips in the hundreds of cannon that had fallen into his hands. He established a barter system: you can have so many guns, but I won't release them until I get some coal. He was able to acquire seventy-three tons, and, through shrewd trading, the pig iron necessary to produce ammunition for the ship's guns.

CHAPTER 7

Guns

John Dahlgren, the "father of American naval ordnance,"
with one of his cannon aboard the sloop of war *Pawnee*.

T hose guns were as important to the success of this untried machine as was its armor. Indeed, armor would have caused little
fuss at all had not artillery undergone, over the past few decades,
developments as sweeping as those that were putting steam engines
in ships. Like so many changes in that accelerated century, this one
came quickly. Just as Drake's seamen would have found themselves
at home in the rigging of Nelson's *Victory* two hundred years later, so
would one of his gunners have understood the far larger but basically
unchanged pieces that decided Trafalgar. Both fired solid-iron shot.

A generation later, by the 1840s, the venerable order had been
changed by a revolution in weaponry that was largely the work of
one of Napoléon's ablest artillery officers, Henri-Joseph Paixhans.

61

All Europe stood in fear of French gunnery on land. At sea, it was a different story. French ships and French cannon were often superior to their British counterparts, but the French navy almost always got beaten in fleet actions. Paixhans wanted his navy to match the fighting qualities of Britain's and saw cannon as the instrument to do that. Around 1820 he wrote that French warships should "use guns which shall drive the heaviest shells horizontally, like a cannon shot, and with equal force and accuracy."

The all-important word in this sentence is "horizontally"; there was nothing new about shells themselves.

A shell was an iron globe, filled with gunpowder and topped with a fuse that made it burst when it reached its target. On land they had been used for centuries, but the squat guns—mortars— that fired them were heavy and required a stationary platform, both disadvantages at sea. Moreover, shells had to be lobbed in a high arc. This was satisfactory if the target was an immobile fort, but nearly useless in a naval engagement.

During the last war the French had again and again tried to use shells at sea, with results far more detrimental to them than to their enemies. Napoléon lost six frigates and possibly five ships of the line to premature explosions. The shells' savage volatility was exacerbated by the difficulty of firing them. For all their ferocity, they were delicate in comparison with solid cannonballs. The charge needed to propel a solid shot with authority would crush a shell to fragments in the breech of the gun that was trying to fire it, hence the reliance on a weaker charge and the high arc the shell followed.

Fuses had improved greatly in the first two decades of the nineteenth century, when Paixhans designed a gun that could fire a large shell on a flat trajectory. He believed his development could greatly increase a warship's destructive power, and in 1824 he was able to test it against a decommissioned eighty-gun ship of the line. It took just sixteen shells to demolish the veteran.

The shell gun proved as effective in combat. In 1838 a squadron of French frigates equipped with Paixhans shell guns opened fire on the castle of San Juan de Ulúa at Veracruz, one of the strongest forts in the New World. The castle surrendered in a day. The Duke of Wellington, who was no naïf in such matters, was astonished that so impregnable a works had fallen to naval guns alone.

More than developing a way to effectively bring the shell to sea, Paixhans saw clearly the largest consequences that would follow. By introducing a projectile that did not merely pound, but that exploded and burned in the midst of a nest of wood and rope and tar and gunpowder, he knew that he had closed an era. Henceforth, he said, sail must give way to steam, and wooden warships to iron ones.

The speedy capitulation of the Mexican fort had impressed military professionals; the Battle of Sinope astonished the world.

Late in 1853 a Russian squadron closed on a Turkish one defending Sinope, a port on the Black Sea. The Turks had seven frigates, the Russians six ships of the line. Nobody expected the Turkish force to fare well in the unequal encounter, but the disparity of losses was nearly unbelievable: 37 Russian dead as against 2,960 Turks.

The Turkish gunners fought hard and bravely, but they were firing solid shot. The Russian squadron had equipped itself with shell guns. Only one small Turkish ship escaped.

England and France, the leading European naval powers, took heed and started work on the two inaugural iron vessels — *La Gloire* and HMS *Warrior* — that Mallory would try to buy.

THE SHELL GUN REPRESENTED A decisive advance in weaponry, but artillery remained more an art than a science. No seasoned artillerist in 1820 knew more about what went on inside one of his guns than any fifteenth-century alchemist could have figured out from common sense.

The greatest force of the explosion had to be felt by the breech when the gunpowder ignited. This was both obvious and true. But once the projectile began its journey down the barrel, what happened?

Nobody knew. An eighteenth-century cannon is aesthetically pleasing partly because of the ring of built-up metal around its mouth: it makes the piece look good in the same way that a church bell or a trumpet does. That ring was there because of the assumption that the point where the shot is blasted from the muzzle into the air must experience extra violence.

In the early 1840s an American officer named George Bomford set about trying to discover if the long-held beliefs about gun manufacture were true. He devised a pleasingly comprehensible test.

Bomford had a horizontal line of holes drilled along the length of a cannon, an inch or two apart, and in each inserted a pistol barrel charged with a bullet. When the experimental cannon was loaded and fired, the pistols shot their balls into pendulums, which recorded the strength of the impact. The results surprised him. The force of the explosion in the breech was far greater than anyone had imagined, and far less as the shot went down the barrel. There was no increase whatever as it left the muzzle.

Bomford was the chief of the US Army Ordnance Department, and the Army paid the most attention to artillery. That was strange, for land forces had several other weapons in their arsenal—cavalry, musketry—and the Navy had only one: the ship's gun. But naval weaponry was loosely managed, with the captain of each ship deciding how much or little practice was required.

At least one Navy man, however, was paying close attention to Bomford's experiments and Paixhans's writings.

John A. Dahlgren started out with no particular interest in ordnance. Like every other young naval officer, he wanted sea duty, where all glory and preferment in the service lay.

Born in Philadelphia in 1809, as a boy he liked to haunt the city's Navy yard, where he was greatly impressed by the 140-gun three-decker *Pennsylvania* (which would end its days in flames at Gosport). Commissioned a midshipman in 1826, he further sharpened an already keen mathematical mind on coast survey work. In 1843 he got to sea aboard the new frigate *Cumberland*. He had charge of four shell guns, and despite his shipmates' distrust of them, the weapons made a strong impression on him. After his tour on the *Cumberland* ended, he asked for sea duty aboard a "shell vessel." When that didn't come through, he applied for a post in the ordnance department in Washington. He was accepted and reported for duty with little joy: "My main purpose in seeking ordn. duty was to fit myself more fully for sea service."

In fact, he had found his life's calling, but that was far from evident at first. His boss, Lewis Warrington, the chief of the Bureau of Ordnance and Hydrography, had not been told of the new man's appointment and wanted nothing to do with him. Dahlgren found that his post, in the Washington Navy Yard, consisted of a foothold in the plumber's shop where shells were prepared, and, in a wooden shed, the press that packed propellant into rockets. These were the missiles whose red glare had shone down on the defiant star-spangled banner in Francis Scott Key's ballad of the defense of Fort McHenry during the War of 1812. They had never been an important part of British artillery practice, nor were they of American.

Dahlgren surveyed his shabby little domain and went to work improving it. His energy and intelligence began to tell almost at once. He added machinery and sent off new equipment to the Home Squadron, then blockading the Mexican coast under Commodore Matthew Perry. The commodore wrote Warrington a letter full of praise. Completely won over, Warrington gave Dahlgren command of all ordnance in the yard.

He began testing cannon, compiling systematic tables recording their performance. Late in 1849 he spent his birthday testing a 32-pounder. All went well until midafternoon when, he wrote, "I said 'Fire'—An unusual explosion took place instantly, the Battery was filled with smoke, and a great crash of timber was heard— Behind me I heard the ground ploughed up and of the things that fell, something grazed my heels, which afterwards proved to be part of the Breeching. Much stunned by the noise & the confusion, my attention was at first attracted by the cries of a lad; but seeing that he would not be much hurt, I turned to the Battery—amid the smoke, yet lifting slowly, the first object [I saw] was the body of the unfortunate Gunner stretched on the deck & quite dead."

The chase of the gun—the entire barrel from the trunnions to the muzzle—had snapped off and dropped to the ground. The breech had burst, throwing an iron fragment weighing a full ton eighty-one feet.

Dahlgren started to design a burstproof gun. He believed the best way to do this was to build up the back and slim down the front. The result was a cannon of an entirely new shape, bulbous at the breech, and tapering abruptly to a mouth with no built-up rim around it. His early plans excited the predictable ridicule: it was the "bull-frog gun," the "soda-bottle gun." One of the inspectors sent to oversee the casting of Dahlgren's new weapons complained to him about the ugliness of the "pot bellied monsters." The inventor replied, "The guns are as you say not sightly; they do not conform to our conventional notions in such things. But if the workmen who find them ugly had had one of the prettiest flying about their ears, and killing somebody close by, as befel me, it is probable that they would find the beauty of such things to lie in their fitness."

And the guns were superbly fit. Dahlgren had trouble selling his nine-inch one, and more with an eleven-inch version. He was putting in eighteen-hour days, for he was not only promoting a new weapon; he was also studying metallurgy and rationalizing a system for training the seamen who would work the guns. At one low point he wrote, "Job with all his amiability would have lost character in 1855." But, like Job's, his trials finally ended. When the *Merrimack* was commissioned, she was armed with Dahlgren guns that could fire both shell and solid shot. On her show cruise to England, knowledgeable observers believed the ship's armament more than compensated for the shortcomings of her steam plant. One visiting artillerist said that her guns alone made the *Merrimack* the "equal of a line-of-battle ship in everything but name."

Britain paid Dahlgren's gun a subtler compliment by trying to steal its plans. One day a Captain Cox of the Royal Artillery visited the Boston foundry that was casting Dahlgrens. The inventor—and the only recently persuaded US naval command—wanted the gun kept secret (the arms race has never changed). So when Cox asked if he could see the plans, Henry Wise, a lively and observant ordnance inspector who was showing him around, politely evaded the question. Then Wise was called away to some crisis in the machine shop and returned to find that Cox had got hold of the drawings for the eleven-inch gun. The Briton seemed only to be looking them over, but when the two men went out later for a drink Wise noticed that Cox had cut a series of small notches in his swagger stick. Understanding at once that this was a sort of code, Wise deployed another American secret weapon—"the beguilement of Mint Juleps," as he put it—and while his guest was nodding off at the end of the evening, Wise took out his penknife, shaved off Cox's notches, and replaced them with a random assortment of his own.

Despite the foiled mission, Britain remained generous in its assessment of what Dahlgren had accomplished. The *London Morning Post* said, "To no one—not even to Paixhans himself, it may be—is the naval shell system more indebted than to the author whose able and interesting work now lies before us."

A few years before Dahlgren's guns would be turned against Confederate vessels, Stephen Mallory wrote of the inventor, "I really don't know of any living man who has done so much to make our naval ships formidable, nor one who more decidedly merits his country's approbation and reward."

John Dahlgren had built the finest naval gun in the world.

BUT NOW, IN MID-1861, STEPHEN Mallory wanted a better one.

Once again, he turned to Brooke, whose duties kept expanding. He had lately been charged by Jefferson Davis to design a uniform for the Confederate Navy. President Davis specified that it be gray, a color, said Brooke, "universally despised in the navy." That Navy might be brand-new, but the traditions it drew on were not, and no Southern sea officer ever imagined John Paul Jones walking his quarterdeck in a gray coat. Blue was the proper color: there's good reason that to this day it is known as *navy* blue—or simply *navy*.

President Davis, however, prevailed, and Brooke helped design, he said hopefully, "something that certainly will not be objectionable on the ground of display." In November, at Mallory's directive, Brooke drew up regulations for the uniforms. They began, *"For a Flag Officer*, shall be a frock coat of steel grey cloth, faced with the same and lined with black silk serge, double breasted, with two rows of large navy buttons on the breast, nine in each row, placed four inches and a half apart from eye to eye at top . . . ," and so forth, for another two thousand words.

While Brooke was coping with this, he got another order from Mallory: "Rifled cannon are unknown in naval warfare, but those guns have attained a range and accuracy beyond any other form of ordnance, both with shot and shell." They would allow the South to give the enemy a "technical surprise."

Rifling is a spiral groove cut inside a gun barrel that puts a spin on the projectile, giving it greater accuracy and power. Dahlgren was working on rifling his guns, but all that had been produced so far, excellent though they might be, were smoothbores.

In November, Brooke wrote in his diary, "By order of the secretary I designed two rifled cannon of 7-inch caliber for the *Merrimac*—one of them had been cast and is now nearly bored." As Dahlgren had, Brooke built up the breech, but not in the casting; rather, he circled it with thick iron bands. When his new gun was tested, it could fire a hundred-pound shell nearly five miles.

Brooke's rifles were fine guns and became standard in the Confederate Army and Navy, but they did not eclipse Dahlgren's smoothbore, and Brooke specified that the ironclad should mount Dahlgrens along with his new rifled cannon. The *Merrimack* would receive the first two of the hundreds of Brooke rifles that Tredegar made.

While all this modern armament was being forged, the *Merri-*

mack also received a weapon from antiquity. The forward-looking Mallory for once turned to the past and said he wanted his ironclad to have a ram.

The ram as a naval weapon went back two thousand years. The principle couldn't be simpler: put a sharp metal point low on the bow of your ship and drive it into an enemy's hull. Rams had been used on the Roman galleys that fought at Actium, but once cannon had vastly widened the circle of destruction a warship could scatter, the ram became useless.

Realizing that steam and iron were remaking the naval world, and always aware of the shortage of gunpowder that would bedevil the South throughout the war, Mallory said, "Even without guns the ship would be formidable—as a ram." He was right.

The initial planning called for a ton of iron protruding from the *Merrimack*'s prow well beneath the waterline. But once again materials were lacking or tardily sent, and when the giant dagger was mounted, it weighed only fifteen hundred pounds and was perhaps a yard long, its flared base bolted to the ship and tapered to a six-inch-wide point.

A Gosport ship-fitter, swinging his hammer to nail it to the bow, cracked the flange that held it there. With more time, the accident would have been corrected; but there was no time, and once it seemed that the ram would stay in place, the workmen moved on.

John Porter seems initially to have resisted the idea of the ram, Brooke to have pushed for it. The two men were more and more at odds as a swarm of unforeseen difficulties beset them.

One of the most irritating tactics in any organization is to go over your superior's head, and Porter wrote that "Lieutenant Brooke was constantly proposing additions to her [the ship] to the Secretary of the Navy, and as constantly and firmly opposed by myself."

Porter's feelings would hardly have been assuaged when Brooke turned out to be right. Brooke called for additional gunports at the bow and the stern to widen the vessel's field of fire. He worried that the rudder chains were too exposed and demanded they be relocated farther inboard. But each of Brooke's sound ideas meant more work for Porter, and further galled the constructor.

Both men were harassed by the calendar: the first day of 1862 found the ship two months behind schedule and rumors were beginning to seep down from the North about something called an "Ericsson battery" being built to counter his vessel. In the second week of January the Gosport blacksmiths, who had earlier held things up by going on strike, had a patriotic change of heart and signed a public pledge "to do any work that will expedite the *Merrimac*, free of charge, and continue on until eight o'clock every night." The ship was keeping fifteen hundred workers busy, some hammering its iron hide, others cursing over the intractable engines in the dimly lit hold and extending the stern to better protect the rudder, and five women—Elizabeth Fitzgerald, Eliza Young, Elizabeth Young, Theodosia Bunn, and Indiana Shanahan—earning a dollar a day making mattresses and running up curtains for the wardroom.

The oil finally arrived from Richmond on February 7, and four days later stores were being stowed aboard. On the thirteenth the ultimate question of whether the ship could float was answered. Forrest had the dry dock flooded, and the reconfigured *Merrimack* did not founder.

Still, she was far from finished when Forrest ordered her launched. The ceremony took place on February 17—only it was no ceremony at all. William Cline, a Southern private who would serve aboard the ship, was surprised by the lack of pomp that attended her launching: "There were no invitations to governors and other distinguished men, no sponsor nor maid of honor, no bottle of wine, no brass band, no blowing of steam whistles, no great crowds to witness this memorable event."

The spectators preferred to watch the ship venture out into the Elizabeth River from the granite security of the dry dock's walls. Only four nervous marines and their corporal were brave enough to stand on the deck as this impossible craft, this great metal warehouse, shuddered and tilted beneath their feet, all its untried joints rasping, and settled into the river to ride upon its surface.

Soon she would reveal a host of new flaws, but Porter's detractors had already been proved wrong: the *Merrimack* floated, and she would be able to fight once she shipped her guns. Tugs nudged her toward the wharf where tall cranes—hastily chopped down by the retreating Yankees; just as hastily restored by their successors—would hoist them aboard. By then, the sparse crowd of onlookers had long since dispersed.

That quiet launch is curious; it should have been celebrated with more pageantry than a corporal's guard. That the beleaguered South, struggling to supply vast quantities of ironwork to a would-be nation that had never before much cared about heavy industry, could successfully put such a ship in the water—and (after the blacksmiths relented) do it only two weeks behind schedule—is not much less remarkable than the reunited country's putting people on the moon a century later.

Plenty is worthy of celebration here: Mallory's clear and vigorously pursued vision, Williamson's audacity in believing that the remnants of a burned frigate might be the embryo of a new war-fighting machine, the contentious but effective partnership between Brooke and Porter.

But nobody crowed. As soon as Porter had satisfied himself that his child wasn't going to sink, he left the proceedings without speaking to anyone. Years later his granddaughter wrote, "He walked quietly home . . . habitually reserved in a world of his own thoughts, he passed easily among the citizens of Portsmouth that fateful day with his lunch pail at his side."

CHAPTER 8

The Power of Alliteration

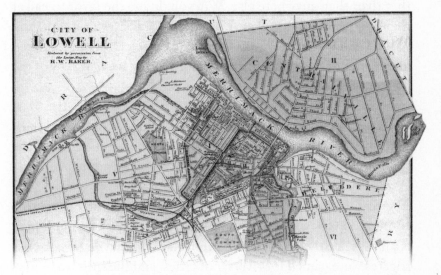

The river—with its *k*—on a mid-nineteenth-century map.

Sometime between the marines uneasily taking their posts on her deck and Porter's quiet departure, the *Merrimack* changed names. She became the Confederate States Ship *Virginia*. But no vessel ever saw such short service amid a greater tangle of nomenclature. What to call her deserves some consideration.

In 1954 a lawyer and Civil War historian named Edward E. Barthell published a book with the enticing title *The Mystery of the Merrimack*. If it is something of an anticlimax to discover that the "mystery" alludes only to the proper spelling of the ship's name, Barthell pursues it with verve and an indefatigable zeal that seems to have led him to read almost everything published in mid-nineteenth-century America.

He begins a decade before his subject's keel was laid, with an amiable invitation sent by that stalwart New Hampshireman Daniel Webster to the New York City politician and diarist Philip Hone in the spring of 1844. "Dear Sir: — On leaving Boston on Saturday I happened to bring along with me a salmon from Merrimack River. We Merrimack men think this fish a little better in that river than anywhere else. Will you do me the favor to call at the Astor [House Hotel] at five o'clock tomorrow (Tuesday) and pass a candid verdict on the subject?" Hone came and rendered his judgment: "The Merrimack salmon proved itself worthy of the high encomiums of the 'Merrimack man.'"

So far, so good; but then Barthell quotes "Frederic Austin Ogg, Ph.D. and Professor of History" saying that Webster had been born in a New Hampshire town "so located that it included the spot where the Merrimac River is formed by the confluence of the Pemigewasset and the Winnipiseogee."

Ah! The *k* has been dropped from the river's name, causing confusion even before the Civil War enters the discussion. There is a Massachusetts town named Merrimac, but the *Merrimack*-class frigates were named for rivers, not cities, and the river was carrying its *k* as early as the 1600s. But when the frigate was launched, we find the *Boston Daily Evening Transcript* reporting, "At precisely 11 o'clock the 'Merrimac' commenced moving from the first ship house, and in fifteen seconds the noble vessel rested proudly on her 'destined element.'"

And so it has gone ever since. Barthell cites some two hundred books that omit the *k*, and the Southern press nearly always referred to the ship as the *Merrimac*. Barthell is firmly on the side of the *k* and is early and authoritatively backed up by a brief letter the chief of the Bureau of Construction sent to the Boston Navy Yard on September 23, 1854: "Sir: The Steam Frigate now in the process of construction at the yard under your command will be called the 'Merrimack.'"

Barthell concludes his book with a defense of what might be considered a finicking project: "It may be noted that the preceding exposition has been concerned solely with the question of the proper spelling of *Merrimack*—a question which normally would be considered as purely moot were we concerned only with usages that, in the course of time, have gradually produced changes in the spellings of many words, and proper names also. However, in our case, we are dealing with a definitely christened name; and we can not help but think that the *Merrimack*, even now in her salty grave, would properly resent being called the *Merrimac*, with as much displeasure as a Lee of Virginia might feel were his name publicized as Le*a*."

There is a larger question about the ship's nomenclature. In the 1980s *American Heritage* magazine ran an article on the fight between the *Monitor* and the *Merrimac* (*sic*). An irritated reader responded, "The *Merrimac* did not do battle with the *Monitor*, nor indeed with any other United States ship in the American Civil War. . . . The Confederate states resurrected her, redesigning everything except the keel, and then christened, launched, manned, and fought her as the Confederate States Ship *Virginia*. To call that ship the *Merrimac* is like saying the British sank the Argentine ship USS *Phoenix* during the Falklands War."

The *Phoenix*, a light cruiser launched in 1938, fought a long, hard war from Pearl Harbor to Leyte Gulf, earning eleven battle stars. The war over, she was decommissioned and sold to Argentina in 1951. Her new owners christened her the *General Belgrano*, and under that name she was sunk by a British submarine in 1982 during the Falklands War.

Captain Edward L. Beach, who fought a long Pacific war of his own as a sub skipper and later enjoyed a career as a novelist and a naval historian, disagreed. The US Navy had sold the *Phoenix* to Argentina; it most definitely had not sold the *Merrimack* to the Confederate Navy. Captain Beach believed that the outcome of the Civil War had decided, along with greater matters, the proper name of the ironclad.

The opposing view was most eloquently stated by William Norris, the chief signal officer of the Confederacy and the head of its secret service, who had been on hand while the *Merrimack* was built and who saw her fight the *Monitor.* "*Virginia* was her name, not *Merrimac*, which has a nasal twang equally abhorrent to sentiment and to melody, and meanly compares with the sonorous sweetness of Virginia. She fought under Confederate colors, and her fame belongs to all of us; but there was a peculiar fitness in the name we gave her. In Virginia, of Virginia iron and wood, and by Virginians she was built, and in Virginia's waters, now made classic by her exploits, she made a record which shall live forever."

Yet even when she was fighting under her new name, many of the men who worked the *Virginia*'s guns called her the *Merrimack*; one of her engineers said he had been "ordered to the *Merrimac* now called the *Virginia*, but except in official communications, ever called by the former name." The alliteration—*Monitor* and *Merrimack*—has only grown more firmly fixed over the years. Regardless of the right of the issue, history and time are powerful editors.

CHAPTER 9

The Entrepreneur

The savvy lobbyist Cornelius Bushnell
was there when Welles needed him.

In the midst of the roiling work of establishing a blockade, Gideon Welles had made his first distracted mention of an ironclad, in his initial report to Congress, submitted on the shattered Independence Day of July 4, 1861. He spent most of the document reviewing his efforts to buy blockade ships, but toward the end he added, "Much attention has been given in the last few years to the subject of floating batteries, or ironclad steamers," then concluded with a mumble: the present time "is perhaps not one best adapted to heavy expenditures by way of experiment." He went on to ensure that nothing at all would be done for at least a generation by recommending "the appointment of a proper and competent board to enquire into the matter."

He found even that temporizing measure difficult to achieve. In his early days on the job, this man who would play so decisive a role in preserving the Union struck many of his contemporaries as curiously insubstantial. The California senator John Conness said Welles "did not have a tangible shape, and that one's arm could sweep through his form."

To be fair, Welles was shouldering his way through a storm of distractions (the state of Massachusetts, for instance, had suddenly decided it wanted a navy of its own). The North was not blind to the promise of ironclads, and ideas were buzzing about even before Lincoln took office. In January 1861 a wealthy Boston railroad lawyer named Elias Derby had proposed slapping one together to relieve Fort Sumter, and Donald McKay, the most celebrated shipwright of the era, the creator of the famous clipper *Flying Cloud*, wrote that "the times for line-of-battleships are over. . . . No ships constructed on the old system are capable of sustaining fifteen minutes' fight" against one of the new iron "monsters without being blown to pieces." He offered to bring America up-to-date by building an ironclad that, he wrote Welles in April, is "a necessity for us . . . regardless of the higher cost, if we do not want to lose all prestige on the seas." McKay's "higher cost" came to a million dollars, and Dahlgren sent a reply regretting "to perceive that this Congress is not likely to make any appropriation for constructing an Iron plated ship."

By the time the reborn *Merrimack* was ready to come out and fight, the US Navy had received more than a hundred proposals for ironclads (and one for a *rubber*clad—alas, never pursued—that would bounce away cannonballs as an umbrella does raindrops). These plans had to be considered by a half-deserted Navy Department: every employee of the Bureau of Ordnance and Hydrography had gone South, with the two forlorn exceptions of the draftsman and the messenger. Hardly surprising, then, that the departed chief's replacement said, "It would be hazardous to rely upon new models of vessels, however plausible."

That was the opinion throughout the department: at a time when the US Navy was scrambling to acquire ferryboats, building a new type of ship—and out of metal!—bordered on the absurd.

Welles might have agreed had he been in charge of the Bureau of Ordnance and Hydrography. He had no inherent fondness for radical technology, but he was responsible for the entire Northern naval effort.

He had made his wan suggestion that Congress consider forming an ironclad board the same week Mallory had ordered an actual ironclad into existence. The public nature of the *Merrimack*'s building that bothered Brooke manifested itself in other forms than newspaper celebrations of the titan-to-be. Long before there was talk of an Emancipation Proclamation, slaves understood that in this war, although so far prosecuted only by white men, their better chance lay with the North.

Their masters knew that too. Small boats started patrolling the Norfolk waters to keep slaves from getting word of the *Merrimack*'s resurrection through the battle lines. But one, Mary Louvestre, who belonged to a local ship chandler, wrote down specifications of the ironclad and managed to sneak them through to Washington. The idea of a uniquely powerful enemy fighting ship took on more urgency for Welles. He began to worry about the Confederate vessel, and even more about where it was being built.

The blockade he was struggling to impose began at Chesapeake Bay and ran south all the way to the tip of Florida, but no part of it was so crucial to the Union as its most northern. Who held the Chesapeake held the key to naval victory. As long as Federal ships kept on station there, they could strangle the ports in Virginia, which were the Confederacy's most crucial. To maintain the blockade, they also had to control Hampton Roads, and they did, so far.

The *Merrimack* could change that. Days after his July Fourth presentation, Welles had become eager to get Congress to establish his ironclad board, but he was still too green to know how to initiate legislative action. One of his impressive qualities was that his high if unsought office never planted in him any delusions of omniscience. He wasn't too proud to seek out advice. So, just as the ship his tardy agitations would eventually produce defined modernity in its era, he turned to a man who can also be described as modern.

DURING HIS CONNECTICUT NEWSPAPERING DAYS, Welles had become friends with Cornelius Bushnell, a New Haven venture capitalist—although that now-ubiquitous term was still far in the future—who though barely out of his twenties had made himself one of the richest men in his state.

He came from an old local family—Bushnells had been in Connecticut for eight generations—but not a particularly prosperous one. He left school at fifteen to work on a coastal ship. A year later, he had command of a sixty-ton schooner, and at twenty-one he founded a wholesale grocery business in New Haven. Within a decade it was the largest such concern in the state, and Bushnell's acquisitive spirit turned toward the great wealth generator of the age, the railroad.

In 1858 he bought a single share of New Haven & New London stock and used this tiny lever to pry his way into a stockholders meeting. The strong personality that had elevated him from deckhand to ship's master in months got him the presidency of the road. In two years he pushed his line through a barricade of regulations to have his trains rolling across the Connecticut border into New York City. This brought him into conflict with the powerful New York & New Haven, which refused to sell tickets for Bushnell's road, or even check baggage on it.

Bushnell fought his far larger competitor up to the state Supreme Court and won. But any line that wanted to assure its profitability needed contracts to carry the mail, and this brought Bushnell to Washington. There he not only swiftly acquired the skills of a successful lobbyist, but also saw the Civil War begin. He went to the Senate chamber to hear Jefferson Davis give his farewell address to the United States and was in the city when

Sumter surrendered. In the tense days between the declaration of war and the arrival of Massachusetts troops to defend the capitol, he patrolled the streets with a rifle, part of a hastily improvised force that never saw action.

During that time he met Commodore Hiram Paulding, just back from his brief, unhappy command of Gosport. He told Bushnell that what the Navy needed were "iron batteries," and that Bushnell should try to see that they got built.

Bushnell was both businessman and patriot. He owned a shipyard in Mystic; here was a chance to virtuously combine his own interests with those of his nation. He knew no more about ironclads than did any other railroad man of his time, but he knew Samuel Pook, a highly regarded Boston shipbuilder. At the time he met with Bushnell, though, Pook was equally ignorant about ironclads. The two set about designing what would become the *Galena*, a well-built but wholly ordinary two-hundred-foot schooner with iron plates laid horizontally along her sides.

With the *Galena* under way, Bushnell returned to Washington, and there sat down with Gideon Welles amid the cigar smoke and genial pandemonium of the Willard Hotel, where much of the business of Congress seemed to get done. Bushnell knew the secretary of the navy would make a desirable ally; and Welles understood that there could be no better training in how to manipulate a legislature than having emerged victorious from railroad wars.

Welles explained that he had just "called the attention" of Congress to the dawning epoch of iron fighting ships, but "without effect." Did Bushnell think he might get a bill establishing an ironclad board through Congress? If so, Welles would draft it that very afternoon. Bushnell said he'd be glad to help.

In a few hours the two were back together, Welles with his bill, Bushnell ready to put it in the hands of the head of the House Naval Committee.

Bushnell worked fast and shrewdly. On August 3 Congress approved "An Act to provide for the construction of Floating Batteries." A loose term: a *floating battery* could mean anything from the waterborne iron shed that had bombarded Fort Sumter to a new kind of ship of the line. Welles was "authorized and directed to appoint a board of three skilful [*sic*] naval officers to investigate the plans and specifications that may be submitted for the construction of iron or steel-clad steam ships or steam-batteries."

For the enterprise, Congress allocated "the sum of one million five hundred thousand dollars." That was less than the cost of just one of the ships England was already building to join HMS *Warrior*, but in a time when the average annual American household income was about $300, it was still a lot of money.

Lincoln signed the bill into law the same day Congress approved it.

Welles assembled his board within a week. As its chairman, he picked an old friend, Commodore Joseph Smith. A Navy man for more than half a century, Smith had entered the service in 1809, had been wounded during the War of 1812, and had served aboard the frigate *Constitution* during America's second war with the Barbary States. He had taken the post he still held, chief of the Bureau of Yards and Docks, in 1846, the same year Welles became head of the Bureau of Provisions, and the two men had quickly gained one another's confidence. Hiram Paulding, who had suggested Bushnell turn his efforts to ironclads, joined the board, as did Commander Charles Davis, who was perhaps the most leery of the three about armored warships.

The board members took on their new task with humility. At the outset the committee wrote, "Distrustful of our ability to discharge this duty . . . we approach the subject with diffidence, having no experience and but scanty knowledge in this branch of naval architecture."

The confident Bushnell had already commissioned two ironworks to make the plates for his *Galena* when he brought his plans to the board. They were received with the caution evident in the members' declaration of inadequacy. The board did not turn Bushnell down outright, but warned that their "objection to this vessel is the fear that she will not float her armor . . . and have stability enough for a sea vessel. With a guarantee that she will do these, we recommend on that basis a contract."

Guarantee was a big word. Bushnell didn't know how to offer one. But back in the high-level freemasonry of Willard's, someone introduced him to Cornelius DeLamater, who owned an ironworks in New York City. Bushnell at once steered the conversation to iron ships and to the difficulty he was having persuading the Ironclad Board that his was viable.

DeLamater said he knew someone "whose opinion would settle the matter definitely and with accuracy." That was when Bushnell first heard the name of John Ericsson.

He was a Swede, DeLamater said, a good friend of his and a brilliant engineer who knew more about iron ships than anyone else. *He lives in Manhattan; go see him.*

Bushnell went the next morning. He took what railroad passengers still called "the cars" to New York City, made his way downtown to Franklin Street, and knocked at the door of number 95.

A housekeeper opened it and showed him into an office, where he was soon joined by a strong-looking man of middle height and soldierly bearing, apparently in his later fifties, neatly but quietly dressed, balding and heavily furred with side-whiskers.

They exchanged names. Bushnell showed the engineer the plans for the *Galena* and said that he—and the Ironclad Board—wanted to make sure it would float. Ericsson said he needed time to work out the necessary calculations and asked Bushnell to leave his plans and return tomorrow.

Back in the office the next day, Bushnell looked uncomprehending on pages of mathematical notations while Ericsson explained what they had revealed. "She will easily carry the load you propose and stand a six-inch shot at a respectable distance."

This might not have been good news for the hypothetical crewmen of the hypothetical *Galena*—Southern ironclads were bound to carry heavier weaponry than six-inch guns—but it greatly pleased Bushnell at that moment: the board wasn't asking about vulnerability, just seaworthiness.

As Bushnell thanked his host and rose to head back to Washington, Ericsson produced a dusty cardboard box and asked his guest if he'd like to see a model of his own vision of a floating battery, one that would scarcely feel a six-inch cannonball or any other one because it was "absolutely impervious to the heaviest shot and shell."

Bushnell said he would.

CHAPTER 10

The Inventor

John Ericsson at about the time he moved to America.

John Ericsson is a puzzling figure in the pantheon of American inventors. He turned the course of a whole war, he wrote about what he was doing with spirited precision, and he had a career filled with the highs and lows that we like to ascribe to our struggling geniuses. Yet he is not remembered as being in the front rank of nineteenth-century innovators. Possibly his personality is in part to blame. He could make strong, close friendships—Bushnell was to name one of his nine sons Ericsson—but from first to last he had a rebarbative nature, always angry when things didn't go his way and often when they did.

He was angry when he produced that cardboard box: angry at

the US Navy. And the Navy was, with far less justification, angry at him.

Ericsson was born in 1803 in Langbanshyttan, a Swedish mining town whose pits had provided a livelihood for four generations of his forebears. His father, Olaf, a mathematician and mine inspector, encouraged John's early interest in machinery, even when the boy melted down his mother's silver spoons for the metal necessary to build a little windmill. He early established himself as a prodigy. At the canal era's dawn, his father got a job supervising the building of one across the entire nation. Young John was helping survey the route while he was still so small he had to stand on a box to reach the eyepiece of his transit, and by the time he was sixteen he had charge of six hundred workers as well as all the lock machinery.

At seventeen he joined the army, where he drafted impeccable maps of Sweden's military installations up near the arctic circle on the country's northern frontier. By this time machinery had wholly taken over his imagination. Convinced that heat was a more efficient power source than steam, he developed what he at first called a "flame engine." This was a steam engine without the steam; hot air pushed its pistons, and it worked well, at least on a small scale.

He had just begun to gain recognition for the device when he embarked on an unusually complex personal life by impregnating a young woman named Carolina Lilljeskold. He was on one of his surveying trips, staying at the house of Carolina's father, a retired army captain from a noble family. Ericsson was solidly in love with Carolina, wrote her fervent poems, and planned to marry her.

The captain would have none of that. Ericsson came from perfectly respectable stock, but this was the early 1820s. "Never will I give my daughter to a commoner without a future," declared Captain Lilljeskold, and sent her away to Stockholm to bear her child.

It was a boy. The Lilljeskolds arranged for him to be adopted by strangers. Carolina never saw John again, but she defied her father to the extent of secretly getting in touch with Ericsson's mother and placing the infant in the family of John's sister Carolina.

John sent money to support his son, but refused to contact him directly. The two would not meet for more than half a century.

The broken romance drove Ericsson away from Sweden forever. He decided to immigrate to England, where, given his interests, he would surely have gone sooner or later, for the machine age was being born there in its iron crucible.

He borrowed money, got a leave of absence from the Swedish army, and arrived in London in the spring of 1826. He came with his hot-air engine, which caught the interest of the Institution of Civil Engineers. Steam engines had been at work in Britain for more than a century, and here was the possibility of simplifying the mechanical equation by doing away with water. A trial was arranged.

The wood with which Ericsson had fired his engine in Sweden put out heat quickly, good for getting it going, and then moderately, good for keeping it going. Coal, England's fuel, burned slowly at first, then hotter. When Ericsson fired his engine with it, the device started slowly and, after the heat rose, made a few spasmodic jerks, came close to melting, and seized up into immobility.

Despite that outcome, the demonstration brought Ericsson into contact with a successful British engineer named John Braithwaite, who was so impressed by the twenty-three-year-old Swede that he went into partnership with him. Together they produced the world's first successful steam fire engine. The king of Prussia bought one, but it was too novel to win a following in England. They turned their attention to the newcomer that was just beginning to pose a threat to Britain's highly evolved canal system.

Railroads, like the steam engine itself, were the children of mines. Once you tunneled very far underground, especially in rainy Britain, your works were likely to fill with water. The first great, cumbersome, gasping steam engines sucked that water to the surface. And long before there was anything but human and animal muscle to propel them, carts rolled along rails drawing the mined coal to the nearest navigable river.

With steam pumping water, it was only a matter of time— although a lot of time—before the powerful vapor was put to use moving locomotives. By the second decade of the nineteenth century several had lumbered onto the scene. They were still so primitive that there was no certainty they could replace the steam-driven windlasses that had come into use pulling trains along their tracks with cables. Like most new things, the locomotives ignited strong passions. When in the 1820s backers proposed to use them on a railroad line to be laid between Liverpool and Manchester, quarreling about it—fomented by the canal and stagecoach companies—reached Parliament.

The Liverpool & Manchester went forward, revealing itself to be a work never before attempted on such a scale: viaducts to be built, and sixty-three bridges, three tunnels bored under the city of Liverpool, and, at Mount Olive, a seventy-foot-deep notch hacked through a sandstone mountain.

What would give this costly road its life? The Liverpool & Manchester's directors announced a competition, open to anyone who could build a locomotive; the reward was £500 and a commission to supply the line's engines.

Ericsson got word of the contest late. He said that he wouldn't have been giving a thought to railroads "but for a letter from a friend, at the end of July, 1829, informing me, merely as news, that a 'steam race' was expected."

Not only expected, but imminent. In just seven weeks the meet was to be held at Rainhill, a rare stretch of the L&M offering a run of flat right-of-way.

Braithwaite and Ericsson went to work at once. What they built closely prefigured the *Monitor* that awaited Ericsson thirty years in the future: nowhere near enough time; no rails to test the engine on, so it would have to prove itself in its first action; and a creation lighter and more nimble than anything of the kind that had preceded it.

Fifteen thousand people gathered at Rainhill on October 6, 1829, to crowd along the tracks and watch five locomotives battle it out. One was wrecked on the way to the trials. A highly optimistic inventor named Thomas Brandreth entered the Cycloped, which lived up to its *-ped* suffix by being powered by two horses trudging side by side on the short treadmill that turned its wheels. It showed little promise even before, as the *London Times* reported, "one of the horses working Mr Brandreth's carriage fell through, we understand, the floor, but was extricated without much injury."

That left three. Two of them, the Sans Pareil and the Rocket, were heavy, weighed over four tons, and pulled their fuel behind them in tenders. The third, fittingly named the Novelty, weighed half as much and was entirely self-contained.

This was Braithwaite and Ericsson's entry. It was equipped with an iron bellows that forced the air through the firebox, ensuring flames hot enough to keep the steam pressure up: the higher the speed, the greater the draft. The more efficient heating allowed for a slimmer boiler: the Sans Pareil's was four feet across, the Novelty's just thirteen inches.

The Rocket opened the show. The only entrant to be built in an actual locomotive factory, she had been tested weeks before, and she proved a crowd-pleaser, racketing along at twenty-four miles an hour and finishing her sprint amid cheers. Next came the Sans Pareil, which also acquitted itself well.

Then it was Novelty's turn. Ericsson and Braithwaite had shipped their engine north from London completely untried: they—and all those spectators—would be the first to see how fast she could go, if she could go at all.

The two men climbed aboard. One of them cracked the throttle, and the correspondent for *Mechanics' Magazine* reported, "Almost at once, it darted off at the amazing velocity of twenty-eight miles an hour, and it actually did one mile in the incredibly short space of one minute and 53 seconds! . . . It seemed, indeed to fly, presenting one of the most sublime spectacles of human ingenuity and human daring the world ever beheld."

The *Liverpool Chronicle*'s reporter said, "The *Novelty* passed the spectator with a rapidity which can only be likened to a flash of lightning." As they churned by the grandstand, Braithwaite and

Ericsson lifted their hats to the "fair occupants" who "acknowledged the compliment by cheers and waving of handkerchiefs."

The two builders found that moment just as fine as it sounds, and it was the last good one they had at Rainhill. Their forced draft turned out to be too violently forced: the bellows broke down, and although the judges were lenient in allowing the inventors time to repair their machine, it kept failing them. The Rocket won.

The public failure of the Novelty added a few more thorns to Ericsson's haughty, volatile temperament. He said he would be a rich man had "not the Englishmen's devilish intentions put me to Hell," but he had no desire to go back home. He overstayed his leave, and when the king of Sweden looked leniently on the deserter and reinstated him in the army as a captain, Ericsson resigned from the service but kept the rank: for the rest of his life he referred to himself as Captain Ericsson.

The promotion did not help with his debts. Two years after the Rainhill trials he owed £15,000 pounds—an almost unbelievable £5,000 of it in tailor's bills—and in the spring of 1832 Ericsson went to debtors' prison. The incarceration seemed to focus his mind, and he turned his thoughts from land to sea propulsion.

He believed the universally used paddle wheels that powered steamships were already archaic and began work on a device that would drive a ship from its stern. Success has a thousand fathers, but it is entirely possible that John Ericsson invented the modern propeller.

He mollified his creditors and not only got himself out of jail, but married.

His bride was Amelia Byam; like Ericsson's son, she was illegitimate, the child of an adventure between a member of the English gentry and a Spanish woman. They were married in October 1836, and Ericsson assessed the fate of the match when he wrote thirty years later, "I have not been in a church since March, 1826, except once in London, when on a certain morning I committed the indiscretion of not only going inside the holy room, but of also appearing before the altar and there giving a promise difficult to keep."

His fortunes were improving. The year of the Rainhill trials, Ericsson met Francis Ogden, the American consul in Liverpool, who knew a great deal about steam engines (a decade earlier he had made one that no less an authority than James Watt had called "beautiful"). Ogden believed in Ericsson and backed him. In 1835 the two men patented a sounding device that sold by the thousands, and two years later Ericsson built his first screw-driven ship, the *Francis B. Ogden*. Designed as a tug, it could steam along at ten knots.

Ericsson and Ogden hoped to sell the propeller to the Royal Navy and invited representatives of the Admiralty to a demonstration. In the summer of 1837 the tug towed a barge containing four sea lords along the Thames from the Admiralty quarters at Somerset House to Greenwich, six miles away, and back, maintaining its ten-knot speed throughout.

Ericsson's guests thanked him politely and turned him down: the Admiralty was not yet ready to embrace the propeller.

The *Francis B. Ogden* did impress one visitor. Its namesake brought a fellow American named Robert Stockton to see the boat and introduced him to the man who had built it. Stockton was to have a powerful impact on Ericsson's life, and America's.

CHAPTER II

The Peacemaker

A Currier & Ives lithograph of the *Princeton* disaster
correctly shows the Peacemaker bursting on its left side.

A decade after he met Ericsson, Commodore Stockton was in command of the US forces in California and the territory's governor. Although he had left a spectacular calamity behind him in the East, he seemed highly satisfied: "My word is at present the law of the land. My person is more than regal. The haughty Mexican Cavalier shakes hands with me with pleasure, and the beautiful women look to me with joy and gladness."

One of Stockton's officers, Lieutenant Henry Watson, thought otherwise: "Commodore Stockton ... is at times at least in conduct a crazy man. He is pompous, inflated, phlegmatic, morose and not infrequently coarse and vulgar in his manners and conversation, wrapped up in his own importance, he is totally regardless of the feelings of others, vain beyond belief, he is even unable to utter a sentence without revolving every thing down to I Bob Stockton."

Ericsson would come to know well both the figure in that

radiant self-assessment, and the one Lieutenant Watson saw. Handsome, rich, possessed of great gifts and the incubus of a greater vanity, Robert Stockton was the product of six generations of New Jersey gentry. In 1808, at the age of thirteen, he entered the College of New Jersey, as Princeton then was known; his great-great-grandfather had been a founder of the school, which was built on Stockton land. He studied law there, but was drawn to the sea and left the college after a year to join the small American Navy in time to see action in the War of 1812 and then to serve against the Barbary pirates off the North African coast.

Back on American soil, he married a wealthy South Carolina woman and within a decade was the richest man in New Jersey and president of the Delaware and Raritan Canal.

The British Admiralty might not have liked the *Francis B. Ogden*, but Stockton did. He decided his canal needed a propeller-driven vessel, and that John Ericsson should build it. "I do not want the opinions of your scientific men," he told Ericsson after a run up the Thames on the *Ogden*. "What I have seen this day satisfies me."

He commissioned two screw streamers, promising the inventor that "we'll make your name ring on the Delaware as soon as we get your propeller there." Ericsson got only one of the ships built, but under the name *Robert F. Stockton*, it handily crossed the Atlantic—the first propeller ship to do so—and went into service on the Delaware and Raritan.

Stockton had broader ambitions. Back in England, he gave Ericsson another commission, this one for an enormous twelve-inch cannon, to be forged in the coal fires of the Mersey Ironworks in Liverpool under Ericsson's direction. This would be the largest naval gun ever made, and Stockton planned to mount it on a new kind of warship.

Stockton's heart had remained with the Navy, and with the heft of New Jersey's two senators behind him, he had gained a rank that allowed him to make his will felt.

In 1841, President John Tyler appointed as secretary of the navy one of those driving spirits who have, from time to time, remade the service.

Abel Upshur proposed a number of reforms—better pay for officers, better conditions for seamen, new bureaus to manage an increasingly complex enterprise—and, above all, better ships. He wanted a steam navy.

Upshur asked for $7 million. Today, when a sufficiently prosperous and motivated enthusiast can spend that much on an automobile, the sum sounds not so daunting. In 1841 it was the largest military appropriation ever sought in peacetime.

Upshur got the money, and some of it went to Robert Stockton. He and the Navy secretary were in perfect agreement about creating a modern fleet, and Stockton pressed hard for the ship he envisioned to mount Ericsson's cannon. He got Congress to support his vessel, and just as impressive, he talked Ericsson into coming to America to design it. The inventor moved to Manhattan in 1839; he would live there for the rest of his days.

The ship, which began to take shape in the summer of 1841, was the first propeller-driven war vessel designed from the keel up by any navy. Ericsson created the engines that Benjamin Isherwood would spend many sweaty months tending. The ship's furnaces glowed in the steady iron breath of a forced-draft system—an Ericsson invention evolved from his work on the Novelty—that was far more efficient than any stack, and they used clean-burning anthracite coal, leaving no telltale smudge of smoke to be spotted by hostile eyes. Stockton named her after his hometown: the *Princeton*.

She was launched on September 5, 1843, christened not with the traditional bottle of wine broken across her bows, but with a flask of American whiskey. Stockton, who always sought good press, got plenty, and he shared the praise with Ericsson. On the day of the launching, Stockton declared he'd "been all over the world in search of a man who could invent a complete ship of war. He is my friend, here at my side." After the *Princeton*'s thoroughly satisfactory sea trials—she was the fastest steamship in the world—Stockton called Ericsson "the most extraordinary genius of the present day."

This goodwill did not last. Already Stockton's vanity was telling him that his designer was getting too much recognition. The first glimpse of Stockton's dissatisfaction came with his decision to build a gun of his own.

The *Princeton* already had Ericsson's twelve-inch cannon, but Stockton commissioned one that would be a foot greater in diameter, and "forged of American iron." Embracing the military fondness for euphemism that a century later would turn the War Department into the Department of Defense, he named his weapon the Peacemaker.

In overseeing its construction, Stockton had closely copied Ericsson's plans, but he had a poor understanding of the metallurgy involved in such an immense cannon. When it came glowing and fuming into the world at the Hamersley Works in New York, the Peacemaker was not only the world's biggest naval gun, it was, at fifteen tons, the largest single piece of iron ever forged. Certainly the weapon *looked* sound enough.

Ericsson was uneasy about the Peacemaker, even though he had been there when the barrel was bored out. Off Sandy Hook, New Jersey, he had fired his cannon more than 150 times with up to thirty-five pounds of powder. That was an enormous charge for that era, and the gun developed tension cracks. Ericsson repaired them by shrinking three-inch-thick iron bands around the breech. This meant taking a near-molten ring of iron from the forge and sliding it over the barrel, there to cool and contract and hold the breech in a powerful grip. With this reinforcement applied, the gun gave no further trouble however heavy the charge.

Stockton too had built up his barrel, but by welding rather than shrinking on red-hot iron—which turned out to be the difference between putting a cotton sock or an Ace bandage on a sprained ankle.

Nor had Stockton run extensive tests on the Peacemaker, firing it just five times before declaring it ready for duty. Ericsson the engineer was honestly troubled by this, but perhaps it was Ericsson the rival—for he had no small share of vanity himself—that expressed his reservations by saying that Stockton's assistants did not have "sufficient knowledge for the planning of a common wheelbarrow," and "as for Captain Stockton, he never made a plan in his life."

Stockton took the *Princeton* up the East Coast before heading to the Potomac and a series of promotional galas paid for out of his own pocket. He had told Ericsson he'd pick him up near his Manhattan home. On the appointed day, Ericsson was waiting on a Wall Street pier in a sharp February wind, his luggage at his ankles. The *Princeton* came into view, approached, and sailed serenely past. The inventor could see her two great guns as she went by, his pointing its muzzle at the ship's wake, Stockton's Peacemaker at her bow. She steamed downstream and out of sight.

On February 18, 1844, Stockton welcomed some three hundred members of the House and the Senate and several cabinet officials, piped aboard the *Princeton* by a Marine band. The day could not have gone better with the focus of Stockton's campaign, President Tyler.

As the ship made its way down the Potomac and the time came to demonstrate the Peacemaker, the gun roared its symbolic defiance at the navies of the world, the 225-pound shot bounced for miles along the river like a skipped stone, and pungent smoke darkened the deck. Stockton was all rhetorical flourish: "It's nothing but honest gunpowder, gentlemen; it has a strong smell of the Declaration of Independence, but it's none the worse for that. That's the kind of music when negotiations fail."

President Tyler returned to the White House and drafted a letter asking Congress to authorize several ships built on the same new principles as the *Princeton*, but larger and even better-armed.

Stockton would have done well to leave his party-giving, with his goal accomplished. But he was a showman; he had to follow up a big success with a bigger one. On February 28 a crowd of 350 came aboard. President Tyler was there again, squiring his fiancée, Julia Gardiner, and Abel Upshur, now secretary of state, and Thomas Gilmer, who had replaced Upshur as Navy secretary. . . .

The entire cabinet save for the secretary of the treasury embarked that morning.

Once again the Peacemaker frightened and delighted its audience, who then retired below for lunch and champagne, a drink the President was known to favor. When Upshur stood to toast him with it, he picked up a bottle that turned out to be empty and, smiling, said that the "dead bodies" must be removed before the toasts could begin. Stockton laughed. "There are plenty of living bodies to replace the dead ones," he said, passing Upshur a fresh bottle.

Sometime during the toasts that followed, Gilmer, the new Navy secretary, asked to see the Peacemaker demonstrated one more time. The guests returned to the deck; one later said that Tyler had been going to join them when his son-in-law remembered a song (everyone was singing by then) that the President had liked in his youth—something about the glories of 1776—and he remained below to hear it.

On deck the guests, perhaps a hundred of them, watched sailors drive home the charge and the ball, and Stockton took hold of the firing lanyard. He gave it a sharp tug.

Senator Thomas Hart Benton of Missouri wrote, "I saw the hammer pulled back, heard a tap—saw a flash—felt a blast in the face, and knew that my hat was gone: and that was the last I knew of the world, or of myself, for a time."

George Sykes, a New Jersey congressman, also was first aware of hats: the smoke lay thicker along the deck than after any earlier firing, and unable to see through it, he glanced over the rail and noticed a dozen hats bobbing in the water by the ship's side. Then he looked back into the prickling, lifting blue-white fog and was "astonished to find that every man between me and the gun was lying prostrate on the deck—and about 30 or 40 men lying in heaps indiscriminately and promiscuously round the gun either killed, wounded, or knocked down and stunned by the concussion."

Below, the party rattled happily along; the President wrote that the gun's report did not "arrest the song and merry jest."

The singing stopped only when the guests realized the cries they heard coming down through the hatchways were not cheers.

The Peacemaker had burst its left side a yard down the breech, blasting chunks of wrought iron weighing as much as a ton through the group of onlookers. Upshur and Gilmer had died instantly and unmarked, but Virgil Maxcy, a prominent Maryland lawyer and the American chargé d'affaires in Belgium, had been dismembered; his corpse fell apart in the hands of the sailors who tried to move him. David Gardiner, a former member of the New York State Senate, father of the President's fiancée, died soon, but "very hard." His daughter was being kept below by those who had seen the riven deck. Six were killed, among them Tyler's personal servant, a slave whose name has come down to us only as Armistead. All were men; of the 150 women aboard that day, none—not even the one who was flung up into the *Princeton*'s rigging—suffered serious injuries.

Stockton had been behind and to the right of the blast when he pulled the lanyard. As soon as Senator Benton regained consciousness, he saw him, "hat gone, and face blackened, standing upright, staring fixedly at the shattered gun." Accounts differ—of course they would—but evidently Stockton, having been taken briefly below, where he said, "Would to God that I alone had been slain and all my friends been saved," returned to the deck and took command. He coolly and effectively saw to it that the wounded were helped and did his best to restore order. Less than half an hour later a steam tug was taking the passengers off the *Princeton*.

Stockton had behaved well in the hours after the catastrophe; in the days and weeks that followed, he behaved about as poorly as possible, at least to his sometime partner.

John Ericsson learned about the *Princeton* disaster in the New York newspapers. Already angered by Stockton's abandoning him on the pier, he was enraged by his reemergence into the captain's memory. Although Ericsson had been on hand while the warship was designed and built, Stockton said, he was only a nuisance: This "mechanic of some skill thrust himself upon me . . . to my surprise and annoyance. . . . I did not employ him, but permitted him, as a particular act of favor and kindness to superintend the construction of the Princeton." The warship was all Stockton's doing—save for the Peacemaker, which was Ericsson's sole contribution.

President Tyler immediately declared Stockton a "brave and distinguished commander," and in no way responsible for the disaster.

Stockton asked for a court of inquiry, which was quickly convened and just as quickly—three weeks after the explosion— exonerated him. Ericsson, summoned to testify, wrote on March 1, "How different would I have regarded an *invitation* from Captain Stockton a week ago! I might then have had it in my power to render good service and valuable counsel. *Now* I can be of no use." The restrained but direct response infuriated Stockton.

All the more reason to lay the gun's failure on Ericsson. And Stockton didn't let it rest there: for the rest of his life he campaigned to keep the inventor from being paid for his work on the *Princeton*. Time and again, Ericsson submitted his bill to Congress, which naturally was more likely to respond to a request to withhold money than act on one to spend it. In 1856 the Court of Claims awarded the inventor $13,930. Two years later, Stephen Mallory, who valued Ericsson's work, urged Congress to pay him: "The *Princeton* [was] made at great cost to Captain Ericsson. He exhausted every dollar he had on earth making the experiment. . . . The quality which the *Princeton* had we have translated into every vessel, but we have never excelled her. . . . I ask you, when the country has reaped these great advantages, is it just, is it magnanimous of the American people to refuse him this paltry compensation?"

Congress proved neither magnanimous nor just. Stockton made clear that his successful obstruction of the payment was driven by personal animus. He remained angry about Ericsson's refusal to testify on his behalf after the explosion: "If Ericsson hadn't been such a damned coward, there would have been no trouble about his getting his money for the vessel." He did finally get it, but not in his lifetime: Congress paid it to his estate.

Just days after the Peacemaker burst, the House Committee

on Naval Affairs cut off funding for propeller-driven warships. Instead, the board commissioned three side-wheelers.

The Navy would get its screw steamers in time, but Stockton's gun delayed their advent for years.

The calamity did not end his career; he commanded the Pacific Squadron in the war with Mexico and was largely responsible for wresting what is now California into the Union. But that bombastic tribute he paid himself as governor hints at an uneasy defensiveness.

He got into squabble after squabble with his superiors, retired again from the service, ran for president in 1856 on the unsavory Know-Nothing ticket decrying Catholics and immigrants in general, and eventually retired to a seven-hundred-acre estate he called Sea Girt because it stood high on the New Jersey shore.

He liked being near the ocean and spent a lot of time gazing out over it, nursing his disappointment that the one thing he most wanted, command of a modern American Navy, had been lost to him by that day on the *Princeton*. From his aerie he might well have watched the *Monitor* making its slow way south to Virginia. He died in 1866, having seen the ship's designer, whom he had done his best to disparage as a mere "mechanic," become more famous than this most determined fame-seeker had ever been.

CHAPTER 12

Perfect Protection

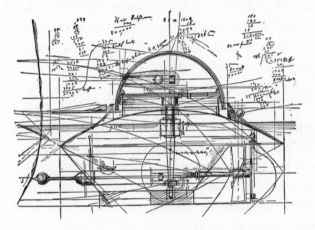

One of Ericsson's early sketches of what would
evolve into the *Monitor*'s turret.

Throughout, Ericsson remained a hard and steady worker. His
intense powers of concentration made him endlessly prolific;
they also blighted his marriage.

In the spring of 1840, while he was designing the *Princeton*,
Amelia crossed the Atlantic to join him. Ericsson liked his new
country and would proudly become a citizen of it in 1848. "I am
well satisfied with America," he wrote. "The people are much better than the travel books told me." His wife, however, detested
it and found New York gaudy, flashy, and vulgar. And lonely: Ericsson, constantly at his drafting table, complained that she was
"jealous of a steam engine." She stayed only five months. She came
back to Manhattan two years later and once more quickly returned
to England, this time for good. Ericsson never saw her again.
He found a bleak advantage in the separation, writing a quarter

century later, "Fate by this misalliance, made it possible for me to devote twenty-five years of undivided, undisturbed attention to work, which would not have been so if I had lived in what is called a happy marriage."

Perhaps not entirely undivided and undisturbed. In his will drafted in 1878 he left lifetime pensions to a Miss Sarah Thorne and a Miss Mary Austin, both of Manhattan, and bought Miss Austin a house. He once wrote, "Evening calls of the most pleasant nature are made frequently, since Eve's kinfolk has prerogatives and can make claims before which even the constructor of caloric engines and Monitors has to yield."

The "caloric engine" was what he was by the 1840s calling his flame engine, and nothing—not the Novelty nor the propeller nor the *Princeton*—kept him from trying to perfect it.

He believed heat not only a superior motive power to steam, but a far safer one. Boiler explosions were distressingly common during the first half of the nineteenth century, both on land and, often with much worse results, at sea. As late as 1865 the side-wheeler *Sultana* blew up on the Mississippi near Memphis, killing more than seventeen hundred Union soldiers in what remains the worst maritime disaster in American history. When, in the early 1850s, Ericsson began planning a full-size vessel to be powered by his caloric engine, one of his backers was a line owner named Gazaway Lamar, who had lost his wife and six of his seven children when one of his ships exploded off the Carolina coast in 1838.

The *Ericsson* (he chose the name) was launched in 1852. Weighing two thousand tons, 250 feet long, she was a side-wheeler, for her machinery was far too large to fit in the bottom of the hull where a propeller shaft had to lie. Her four massive pistons, fourteen feet across, fascinated the visitors who rode on top of them during their leisurely six-foot rise and fall. But for all the engine's heroic scale, and its frugal use of fuel, it was too weak to drive the ship faster than eight knots. With the speed of the average steamer of the time nearly twice that, the *Ericsson* was a failure. Its inventor defended it for the rest of his life. In 1878 he wrote,

"There was more engineering in that ship than in ten *Monitors*. I regard the hot-air ship as by far my best work, it was simply a mechanical marvel." But he never tried to build another.

He did, however, keep working on his caloric engine, which, reduced to a far more modest size, proved highly successful. When Ericsson began to market it, in 1858, he sold three thousand in three years, and as late as the 1920s one could buy a household fan spun by an elegant little hot-air engine powered by a teacup-size alcohol burner.

So when Bushnell showed up on Franklin Street with his plans for the *Galena*, Ericsson, although still galled by his failure to collect on the *Princeton*, had not been financially inconvenienced by the bad faith of Congress.

Nor had any of the reverses he'd suffered damaged his essential self-confidence by the time he lifted the lid off his dusty box to show Bushnell the ship model inside. His visitor recognized it as a ship only because Ericsson had said it was. What Bushnell saw was a smooth cardboard cigar with a bump in its middle. That bulge, Ericsson explained, was designed to contain a cannon—just one, but a monster with a twenty-inch bore. The model was not of an ironclad, exactly, for the iron would not merely be cladding. The vessel wouldn't have armor laid over a wood frame; it would be entirely iron, stem to stern. No masts, no sails—just a steam-driven metal hull that would run nearly submerged save for that turret, which rose above the surface to revolve and train its single cannon on an enemy no matter which way the ship itself was heading.

Bushnell had never seen anything like it. Only a few dozen people in the world had.

Ericsson told his guest the idea went back a long way. In 1846 a congressional committee on naval affairs sought suggestions on the "practicality of rendering an iron-vessel shot-proof." Ericsson had been thinking about such a ship for years: "The great importance of what I call the sub-aquatic system of naval warfare strongly presented itself to my mind in 1826." That was back in Sweden, when he had seen the behavior of low-lying lumber rafts in lake storms that nearly capsized taller ships. "I found that . . . the raftsman in his elevated cabin experienced very little motion, the seas breaking over his nearly submerged craft."

Ericsson had sent the naval committee plans for a vessel that largely lived beneath the surface because "a conventional iron ship so thickly armored would sink."

His proposal went in just two years after the Peacemaker exploded, and the Navy didn't want any more experimental warships from John Ericsson. He got no answer.

Next he tried Napoléon III. At least he got a polite response this time, although a discouraging one: "Monsieur: The Emperor has himself examined with the greatest care the new system of naval attack which you have submitted to him. His Majesty directs me to have the honor of informing you that he has found your ideas very ingenious and worthy of the celebrated name of their author; but the Emperor thinks that the result to be obtained would not be proportionate to the expenses or to the small number of guns that could be brought into use."

There the matter rested for eight years, until Ericsson saw the Ironclad Board's advertisement, issued on August 7, 1861, which ran in all the Northern newspapers, calling for bids to build "one or more ironclad steam vessel of war . . . for either sea or river service to be no less than ten or sixteen feet draught of water. . . . The smaller draughts of water . . . will be preferred." The vessel was also "to be rigged with two masts, with wire rope standing rigging, to navigate at sea."

Three weeks later Ericsson sent—not to the Navy Department, but directly to "His Excellency Abraham Lincoln"—a letter that reveals both his dedication to the Union cause and the conviction of infallibility that so often made him believe he held a stronger position than he actually did.

"Sir: The writer, having introduced the present system of naval propulsion and constructed the first screw ship of war, now offers to construct a vessel for the destruction of the rebel fleet at Norfolk and for scouring the Southern rivers and inlets of all craft protected by rebel batteries." He sought "no private advantage or emolument of any kind. Attachment to the Union alone impels me to offer my services at this fearful crisis—my life if need be—in the great cause which Providence has called you to defend."

Why choose him to build the ship? Simple: He "possesses practical and constructive skill shared by no engineer now living."

The letter apparently never got to Lincoln, but it did make its way to Benjamin Isherwood, who rejected the idea out of hand. Once again, Ericsson received from Washington nothing but silence.

That was about to change. As Ericsson explained his ship, the quick, canny, enthusiastic Bushnell took it all in and was immediately convinced. He urged the inventor to go to Washington with his model and present it to the Ironclad Board. Ericsson, several times burned by officialdom, refused. *All right*, Bushnell told him, *I'll do it*.

Good for Bushnell! He still wasn't sure whether his *Galena* would be built, and in promoting Ericsson's ship, he might well be working against his own interests. His entrepreneurial instincts weren't completely extinguished by patriotism; he proposed a partnership with Ericsson, which the inventor immediately accepted. A mutual trust that would last all their lives had grown between the two men in a few hours. Still, Bushnell would have been safer backing only his own ship. But he had seen in Ericsson's pasteboard model the germ of a war-winning weapon, and set off at once.

Not to Washington, though. Gideon Welles was at his home in Hartford, the first time he'd been back to Connecticut since taking up his cabinet post in March, and Bushnell went to see him first.

With fine salesman's bluster he walked into the Navy secretary's home, brandishing Ericsson's plans and declaring that they meant not only trouble for the South but—Bushnell knew Welles was at the moment fretting about the possibility of Britain entering the war—that the President "need no further worry about foreign interference," because Bushnell had "discovered the means of perfect protection."

CHAPTER 13

Something in It

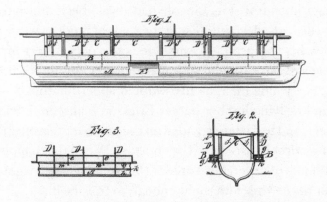

Abraham Lincoln submitted this drawing with his patent application
for a device to lift stranded boats off riverbeds.

A braham Lincoln had, like Welles, been thinking about iron-clads. William O. Stoddard, who served as one of the President's wartime secretaries, witnessed an early discussion of the subject. Thirty years later Stoddard wrote a memoir called *Inside the White House in War Times.* He tells it all in the present tense with a jocose sprightliness that makes some of what he reports seem dubious. But he was there.

Speaking of the bustling early weeks of Lincoln's White House tenancy, Stoddard writes, "All sorts of people come upon all sorts of errands, and the broad-shouldered, plain-looking fellow sitting there seems to have his lap full of joiner-work, painted black. It reminds one of Noah's arks he used to get at Christmas, only that it is low and wide, and has no procession of wooden animals. There are toy cannon, too, looking out of the windows, instead of giraffes. That man was in to see the President yesterday, and they sat down

together and discussed Western steamboats and flatboats and gunboats, and they turned that thing inside out. It has been here a
good while, sitting on the mantel. It is the first model of a 'tin-
clad' gunboat, for use upon the shallow waters of the West, and
the President has had more to do than most are aware of with the
beginnings of the Mississippi flotilla."

That's not surprising. Lincoln had always been drawn to technology; he had a deep interest in the tools of modern warfare, and
he knew his way around rivers. He is the only American president ever to have sought and received a patent, and it involved
ships. As a young man, he had worked aboard flatboats—much
like the low-lying lumber barges Ericsson had seen defying bad
weather—and had been stranded on the sandbars heaved up by the
always-restless Mississippi River bottom. When that happened, it
meant hours of miserable work for the crew, lugging freight to the
bank until the vessel was light enough to free itself.

While Lincoln was still a freshman congressman in 1848, he
began working on what would become registered patent No.
6,469: "Be it known that I, Abraham Lincoln, of Springfield, in the
county of Sangamon, in the State of Illinois, have invented a new
and improved manner of combining adjustable buoyant air chambers with a steamboat or other vessel for the purpose of enabling
their draught of water to be readily lessened to enable them to pass
over bars, or through shallow water, without discharging their car-
goes." The "air chambers" were waterproof bladders attached to
the hull that could be inflated to boost the vessel off the obstacle
that had grounded it. At the time, the patent office required not
only drawings and a description of an invention, but a model of it
as well. Lincoln's law partner William Herndon remembered that
"occasionally he would bring the model into the office, and while
working on it would descant on its merits and the revolution it was
destined to work in steamboat navigation. Although I regarded
the thing as impracticable I said nothing, probably out of respect
for Lincoln's well-known reputation as a boatman."

That practicability was never tested, but the patent office

accepted Lincoln's invention, and his interest in new mechanical solutions to old problems never waned. When he had been a circuit-riding lawyer back "in the ante-railway days," a fellow attorney remembered, "and we would stop at a farm-house for dinner, Lincoln would improve his leisure in hunting up some farming implement, machine or tool, and he would carefully examine it all over, first generally and then critically."

His friend did mean "critically." Lincoln would take the implement, "turn it over and around and stoop down, or lie down, if necessary, to look under it; he would stand off and examine it at a little distance; he would shake it, loft it, roll it about, upend it, overset it, and thus ascertain every quality and utility which inhered in it, so far as acute and patient investigation could do it."

Lincoln's grasp of machinery, and of how it might be applied to potential technologies, could approach the visionary. In 1858 he imagined devices that are just now beginning to reveal their largest possibilities. "Of all the forces of nature, I should think the *wind* contains the largest amount of *motive power.*" In his native Illinois, "all the power exerted by all the men, and beasts, and running-water, and steam, over and upon it, shall not equal the one hundredth power of what is exerted by the blowing of the wind over and upon the same place." That power had never been fully exploited: sailing ships, of course, but "add to this a few windmills, and pumps, and you have about all. . . . As yet, the wind is an *untamed*, and *unharnessed* force; and quite possibly one of the greatest discoveries hereafter to be made, will be the taming, and harvesting of the wind."

He was fascinated by every kind of technology that could reduce human labor. In 1859 he said, "I have thought a good deal, in an abstract way, about a Steam Plow."

He thought in a concrete way too. Much of his first prosperity in Springfield came from his patent cases. To argue them, he taught himself both to understand machinery and to explain it to people who didn't. In an age of increasingly sophisticated agricultural implements, he found himself in a courtroom facing several different models of reapers. As he went from one to another telling how they worked, the jurors left their seats to crouch down for a better look. After a few minutes of this, the opposing counsel conceded, "I guess our case has gone to hell; Lincoln and the jurors are on their knees together."

Now, as a war president, Lincoln sought out martial objects to examine, from breech-loading rifles to the incipient machine guns that would grow to devastating adulthood in the next century. He had both taken up by the Union Army.

In his survey of novel armaments, Lincoln most enjoyed his visits to the Washington Navy Yard, for that was John Dahlgren's domain. Lincoln had formed firm friendships with two men in the Navy Department, and the closer of them was Dahlgren.

The gunnery expert had a difficult time meeting his commander in chief. When Lincoln first came to Washington, Dahlgren said, "The throng that gathered about the President was impenetrable." A month after his inauguration, Lincoln paid a surprise visit to the Navy Yard. Dahlgren was chief ordnance officer there, and Franklin Buchanan, although holding Southern sympathies, was commandant. Lincoln wanted to meet Dahlgren, but he was away, and Captain Buchanan showed the presidential party around.

Dahlgren was disappointed again to miss the chief executive, but his feelings were soon repaired. Lincoln had agreed to give away Buchanan's daughter at a wedding to be held the next night at the commandant's quarters. The ordnance officer had been invited, and someone brought him over to meet the President, who warmly took one of Dahlgren's small hands in his two big ones.

Lincoln saw what a Washington newspaperman described as "a light complexioned man of perhaps forty years of age, slight, and of medium height; pale and delicate features. His countenance is exceedingly thoughtful and modest, and expresses complete unconsciousness of being observed; while his eye is inevitably keen and his nostrils expand as he talks, with a look of great enthusiasm."

Much of that enthusiasm was for the federal Union. The day before, Buchanan had assured the President of his own loyalty to the United States. Lincoln, who didn't miss much, may have smelled something pro forma in the irreproachable declaration. He saw none of the merely dutiful in Dahlgren, and that initial conversation, which lasted a full half hour, was the birth of an enduring friendship.

On April 17, 1861, Dahlgren wrote, "It has now leaked out that Virginia seceded . . . secretly in order to grab the public property that is within her borders. . . . Everyone believes too that a body of men are on the way to take Washington and the alarm is intense."

Five days later he received a note from Welles ordering him to "assume temporary command" of the yard, and to "discharge all suspected persons upon satisfactory evidence of their disloyalty to the Government, and place the yard in the best possible state of defense." A few hours later Captain Buchanan arrived and handed Dahlgren a letter: "As I have this day resigned my Commission as a Captain in the Navy, and consider myself only temporarily in command here, you will . . . superintend the defence of the yard when necessary. I shall not take any part in the defence of the Yard from this date." Buchanan was going South. As at Norfolk, so were others. "The officers of the Washington Navy Yard . . . ," Dahlgren wrote, "abandoned their duty, to join the standard, of what they considered their paramount allegiance; and the command of the most important position thereby devolved upon [me], who alone had remained faithful to his trust."

Dahlgren found himself in charge of one of the Union's most crucial installations, the Washington Navy Yard's facilities even more valuable now that Norfolk was gone. With secessionists all about him—Rebel flags were blossoming a few miles away in Alexandria—he not only had to run an immense manufacturing facility, but also to defend it. He assembled his own little navy, mounting guns aboard three steamers. The Potomac Flotilla kept the river open, disposing of Confederate mines and exchanging fire with newly installed shore batteries.

Meanwhile, Dahlgren stepped up production, running piping for gaslights into workshops so that their business could proceed at night. Soon his ordnance department was producing two hundred shells and thirty-five thousand bullets every day.

"The President often comes to the Yard," Dahlgren wrote in his diary, "and treats me without reserve." Lincoln came not only in his capacity as leader of the national war effort, but also because he enjoyed seeing all that machinery going through its revolutions. One observer wrote, "The Navy Yard here seems a favourite lounging place for Old Abe and his wife, who are here almost every day."

Gideon Welles wrote that Dahlgren was "always attentive and much of a courtier" to the President, by which Welles meant something of a toady: "He is intensely ambitious, and, I fear, too selfish." Still, Welles admired Dahlgren, believed he would "gallantly sustain his chief anywhere," and encouraged the friendship he saw the ordnance man so sedulously cultivating.

That friendship was already secure. In July, with the crisis past, when Dahlgren's vest-pocket navy was guarding the Potomac and his factories spinning out munitions, some captains took note of a law passed in 1804 that forbade anyone below their rank to be in charge of a Navy yard. Dahlgren was only a commander, and they wanted his job. Lincoln refused. "The Yard shall not be taken from [Dahlgren]. He held it when no one else would, and now he shall keep it as long as he pleases." Days later, Congress repealed the 1804 law; Dahlgren called that "the best compliment I ever received."

THE OTHER NAVAL OFFICER TO have gained Lincoln's trust and friendship was Gustavus Vasa Fox, whose emergence in the war's early days was a stroke of good fortune both for the President and for Welles.

A Massachusetts man just turned forty, Fox had entered the Navy in his teens, been in the war with Mexico, then left the service during the promotion-starved 1850s to help run one of his native state's many mills.

He married the daughter of a New Hampshire judge who had

wed another of his girls to Montgomery Blair, holder of the post-master generalship that had eluded Welles. Of all the members of Lincoln's inchoate cabinet, Blair had pressed the most strongly to relieve Fort Sumter. Lincoln liked his spirit and, at Blair's suggestion, sent Fox to assess the situation at Sumter while it was still in federal hands.

Fox returned saying he thought the garrison ready to fight but believed the commander, Anderson, reluctant. Fox would have made his report with persuasive eloquence. He was a social man, equally at ease with civilians and his fellow sailors, amusing, determined, and so self-assured that he grated on many of his military colleagues.

Not Lincoln, though. When war seemed imminent, the President put Fox, although still a civilian, in command of a force to relieve Fort Sumter. Fox and his ships arrived in time to hear the bombardment, but their only role was to ferry Anderson and his surrendered garrison up to New York.

Sumter was gone, but Fox was there to stay. Using his mysterious genius for combining the oblique with the direct, Lincoln forced him on Welles in an entirely new position: assistant secretary of the navy. Welles soon discovered that he had gained a valuable ally in this man, who today would be called chief of staff. Everything Welles didn't know about naval matters, Fox did. Just as important, the two became friends. With the war over and Fox resigning his post, Welles summed up their years together: "I regret to lose him from the Department where, notwithstanding some peculiarities which have raised dissatisfaction with a few [actually, a good many] he is of a most invaluable service. He has a combination of nautical intelligence and common sense such as can hardly be found in another, and we have worked together with entire harmony, never in a single instance having had a misunderstanding."

Fox would be won over to ironclads, but at the war's outset he was no more enthusiastic about them than was the rest of the US Navy. Lincoln, the landlocked Illinois lawyer, saw before Fox did what they promised. The President had been thinking about armored fighting ships a good fifteen years before he met the assistant secretary. In 1848, during his single term in Congress, Lincoln took up the cause of an inventor named Uriah Brown. Since 1814, Brown had been trying to develop a steam-driven ironclad that, with its sloping sides, would have been similar to the one Mallory commissioned. The Mexican War brought Brown as close as he would ever come to getting his idea funded. Lincoln promoted it, but the war soon ended, and with it Brown's chance of being remembered as a naval innovator.

Lincoln's understanding of the challenges posed by ironclads took Fox by surprise during one early conversation between the two men.

Lucius Chittenden, register of the treasury, was far removed from naval matters. But he and Fox had become friends, and the assistant secretary liked to take him along when he dropped in on the President. On one of these visits, soon after Sumter, Lincoln brought up Anderson's account of the iron-faced floating battery in Charleston Harbor and asked whether the Union should build armored warships. Years later Chittenden recalled, "Mr. Fox replied, in substance, that the subject was under active consideration in the Navy Department, but that it was novel; it was very important, and though generally impressed with the practicability of such vessels, he was not yet prepared to commit himself to any fixed opinion. The President, somewhat earnestly, observed that 'we must not let the rebels get ahead of us in such an important matter,' and asked what Mr. Fox regarded as the principal difficulty in the way of their use." Fox said he feared that their heavy armor would sink them almost as soon as they were launched.

"But is not that a sum in arithmetic?" the President asked. "On our Western rivers we can figure just how many tons will sink a flatboat. Can't your clerks do the same for an armored vessel?"

"I suppose they can. But there are other difficulties. With such a weight, a single shot, piercing the armor, would sink the vessel so quickly that no one could escape."

Lincoln didn't think much of this answer. "Now, as the very

object of the armor is to get something that the best projectile cannot pierce, that objection does not appear to be sound."

Fox repeated that armored ships were being considered, and Lincoln let the matter drop. He took it up again in September when, Stoddard wrote, "there came another sort of man to sit here and wait his turn to see the President. He was a massive, vigorous fine-looking man, and he said his name was Bushnell. He brought, to show to the President, a model of a strange, altogether new sea-going war-monster, devised by another man named Ericsson."

It didn't happen quite that way. Bushnell knew better than simply to show up in the Executive Office with a cardboard model of a wholly unprecedented ship and expect a hearing. He'd had no difficulty selling Ericsson's idea to Welles, who sent him off from Connecticut to Washington to begin proselytizing, saying he'd follow shortly. "Mind you, this was Friday," Bushnell wrote, "and I had not had the plans in hand twenty-four hours, but I started Saturday evening, arriving in Washington Sunday morning." He knew what levers to pull once he was back in the capital, and he got an interview with Secretary of State Seward. Like Welles, Seward was persuaded, and it was "the very nice note" he gave Bushnell that got him in to see Lincoln.

The entrepreneur had polished his pitch by then, and he found a receptive listener. One can catch a glimpse of what made Bushnell so persuasive—an intimate, unforced understanding of the person who needed to be sold, an easy sense of humor—in his brief recollection of part of the meeting. Lincoln, not a man given to boasting, volunteered right off that he knew nothing of maritime matters save for flatboats. Bushnell said, "And as the little boat or model {I} showed him was as flat as need be, he understood the good points from the start."

After hearing out his petitioner, Lincoln told Bushnell he'd have to present his plan to the Ironclad Board. The President explained that although he had no power over that body, he would attend the meeting. Bushnell was delighted, knowing the chief executive's presence would be a strong vote in his favor.

Lincoln was as good as his word. The next day, at eleven in the morning, he came into the room where Fox and the board members Joseph Smith and Hiram Paulding, along with a crowd of interested but superfluous naval observers, were waiting to see what this new thing might be.

Bushnell began, he said, "big with hope." He spoke smoothly, and although "compelled to listen to nothing but disparaging criticism from all the old and young officers of the Navy," he believed he'd interested Smith and Paulding. Lincoln kept a deferential silence throughout. After an hour during which Bushnell fielded a lot of professional skepticism, Smith nodded politely to the President and asked what he thought of the "novel little plan." Lincoln raised himself out of the low chair he'd been occupying and made the remark that is always cited during the story of the *Monitor*'s controversial birth. Over the years, it has become bowdlerized to insipidity and near meaninglessness: the President felt "a good deal as the girl [sometimes with the inane addition that she was a "Western girl" or a "fat girl"] did when she stuck her foot in a stocking, that there was something in it." Chittenden wasn't there, but the words he attributes to Lincoln ring far truer: "As the darky said, in putting on his boot, into which someone had put a Canada thistle, 'I guess dar's something in it.'"

Bushnell was right in perceiving he'd impressed Smith and Paulding, but they didn't want to make a final decision until Davis, the board's most junior member, had his say. Would Bushnell come back tomorrow?

Of course. Giving no sign of having been wearied by his trying round of implorings, Bushnell made his pitch to all three board members. Then nods, handshakes, and would he come back one more time?

Again, yes, "and I went back to my hotel quite sanguine of success."

But the next day could hardly have gone worse, "for during the hours following the last session, I found the air had been thick with croakings that the Department was about to father another Ericsson failure."

Startled but now cowed, Bushnell told the board they were being distracted by a myth. "Never was I more active than now in trying to prove that Ericsson had *never* had a failure. That, on the contrary, he had built for the Government the first steam war propeller ever made." He brought up the unfortunate caloric ship *Ericsson* and claimed it failed only because the science of metallurgy had not yet caught up with its builder's genius.

"I succeeded at length in getting Admirals Smith and Paulding to sign a report advising the building of the third battery, *provided* Captain Davis would join with them." Davis rendered his judgment in scriptural terms. Gesturing to the much-traveled model, he paraphrased a passage from Exodus: "You may take that little thing home and worship it; it would not be idolatry, since it was made in the image of nothing that is in heaven above, or that is in earth beneath, or that is in the water under the earth."

Bushnell, not a man easily discouraged, tasted discouragement now. "All was dark about me," and "with a sad heart I reported to Secretary Welles." But Welles "cheered me up by saying that some influence could be brought to bear on Davis."

Bushnell "caught the idea." He had "never met a man with more power to magnetize and carry his audience with him than Captain Ericsson. He got capitalists to put their money into that caloric ship just as freely as water, although it was only an experiment."

So the entrepreneur decided he had one shot left in his locker, although it was—like those early shells—an unstable and dangerous one. During their morning together Ericsson had told Bushnell all about the Peacemaker explosion and its aftermath, and "I told Secretary Welles that Ericsson had bound himself under oath never to come to Washington until he had been paid by the United States Government his long overdue engineering bill for the *Princeton*."

On Tuesday Bushnell reembarked on his triangular odyssey— New York, Connecticut, Washington, New York—and boarded the cars for Manhattan fretting about Ericsson: "How in the world can I get the man to go, with the state of facts I have to relate?"

The answer came to him while the train jolted through Baltimore. Along with Napoléon III's polite refusal to adopt the subaqueous vessel, the emperor had given its inventor a consolation prize. "Then I remembered," Bushnell wrote, "the flash in [Ericsson's] eye and the brightening up of his countenance when he showed me a beautiful gold medal that Louis Napoléon had sent him."

As the low brick row houses jerked past, Bushnell thought, "I will get him through his vanity." How to do it? Lie.

After a few hours of sleep at the Astor House, Bushnell knocked on Ericsson's door at nine o'clock Wednesday morning. He was heartened that the engineer "did not wait for his girl Ann to come and let me in, but came himself to the door."

Ericsson asked, "What are the results?"

Bushnell beamed. "Magnificent!"

"Well, what?"

"Paulding says that your boat would be just the thing to punish the Rebels at Charleston."

As it had when he displayed the gold medal, Ericsson's "countenance lit up." Thirty years later, telling the story to the Connecticut Navy Club, Bushnell said, "I knew then that I had him."

Bushnell dispensed more fictitious praise: "You have a friend in Washington, Commodore Smith; he worships you. He says those plans are worthy of the genius of an Ericsson."

"How about Davis?"

"Oh, Davis." Bushnell waved Davis aside like a housefly. "He wanted two or three explanations in detail which I could not give him, and so Secretary Welles proposed that I should come and get you to come to Washington and explain these few points to the entire Board in his room tomorrow."

"Well, I'll go," said Ericsson. "I'll go tonight."

"Mind you," Bushnell recalled years later, "*I* didn't go." He was an audacious man, but he had his limits. He knew how much Smith would enjoy learning that he worshipped the author of the *Princeton*, and how the engineer was likely to respond to Davis's Bible lesson. Bushnell "remained in New York, just not fancying the presence of Captain Ericsson when he should first meet Captain Davis."

Davis was the first board member Ericsson met. Bushnell wrote that the inventor introduced himself and said, "I have come down at the suggestion of Captain Bushnell"—the honorific *captain* seems to have been pretty freely thrown around in those days—"to explain about the plan of the *Monitor.*"

That name still lay in the future, but whatever Ericsson may have called his prospective vessel, Davis knew what he was talking about. "I was very coldly received," Ericsson wrote, "and learned to my surprise that said Board had actually rejected my plan."

"Coldly" and "surprised" don't come close. When Davis realized what this visitor was after, he exclaimed, "What, the little plan Bushnell had here Tuesday; why we rejected it *in toto.*"

Ericsson might have done anything just then. But fortunately he was so taken aback that his surprise overcame his temper.

"Rejected it? What for?"

Smith, who had arrived by then, said the board didn't have faith in the vessel's stability.

"Stability! No craft that ever floated was more stable than she would be; that is one of her great merits."

Now it was Ericsson's professional pride that trumped his temper. He asked for a couple of hours to go to his hotel and "prepare the proof."

Smith, Paulding, and the recalcitrant Davis were in Welles's office when Ericsson returned at one o'clock. Given that he'd expected to come to Washington to receive accolades and a contract, he put on a remarkable performance. Bushnell said the man was "a full electric battery in himself," and he had been thinking about this particular project for years. He was forceful, comprehensive, and idiomatic—at one point he declared, "She will float upon the water and live in it like a duck!" Bushnell wrote Welles years later, "You remember how he thrilled every person present in your room with his vivid description of what the little boat would be; and that in ninety days' time she could be built; although the Rebels had already been four months or more on the *Merrimack* with all the appliances of the Norfolk Navy Yard to help them."

Those ninety days weighed heavily in Ericsson's favor. The board was going ahead with Bushnell's *Galena* and had also approved another ironclad. This vessel, which would be called the *New Ironsides*, was closest to the British *Warrior*: a big conventional steam frigate protected by four-and-a-half-inch iron plate, with her guns running the length of the ship in the traditional broadside arrangement. But neither she nor the *Galena* would be ready soon.

The board was also swayed by Ericsson's answer when Welles asked the cost: $275,000. That was $40,000 more than the *Galena*, but a third the price of *New Ironsides*.

Most important, though, was the clarity of Ericsson's explanation of why his ship would stay afloat. When he had finished, Paulding told him, "Sir, I have learned more about the stability of a vessel from what you have said than I have ever known before."

The Ericsson bumptiousness came through only at the end, when he concluded his talk with a demand rather than a request: "Gentlemen, after what I have said, I consider it to be your duty to your country to give me an order to build the vessel before I leave this room."

He did leave the room orderless, though, sent away while the board conferred. Late in the day he returned to Welles's office. The secretary of the navy told him, "Go home and start her immediately and send Bushnell down next week for the formal contract." Bushnell always liked to remember that the ship was already under construction "just eight days after the plans were first shown me and placed in my hands."

THE BIBLICAL CAPTAIN DAVIS WAS quite right about being offered something never before seen under heaven.

Ericsson called it "a fort on a raft," and it has been described as being two ships, composed of what were referred to as the "upper vessel" and the "lower vessel." The former, 172 feet long by 41 wide and tapering to a point at both ends, sat on the latter like the lid on a shoebox. Its framing of seven-inch-thick pine planks, supported by oak beams ten inches square, was covered by two layers of half-inch iron plate. This was the deck; as Bushnell had said, it was flat as could be, the surface interrupted only by the gun turret, the stack, which could be struck down before battle, and the pilothouse, a four-foot iron cube up at the bow. (The Ironclad Board's specifications had called for masts and sails; Ericsson ignored this stipulation, and as far as we know, nobody ever raised the issue again.)

The lower vessel, the hull, contained the ship's complex workings, and its crew. Fifty feet shorter than the upper vessel, it was made of iron only a half inch thick, but protected by the overhang of the upper vessel. The stern half held the engine. It had two cylinders, although their yard-wide pistons faced each other in a single long tube set crosswise to the hull. The steam entered at either end, and the pistonheads were separated by an iron wall. Capable of putting out 320 horsepower (its inventor claimed; later Navy tests showed less), it was fed by twin boilers whose furnace fires were accelerated by a sophisticated descendant of the forced draft Ericsson had pioneered in the Novelty. The blowers he designed could suck in seven thousand cubic feet of air a minute and kept the working spaces of the ship livable. Without a constant flow from the air intakes, the iron rooms would fill with lethal gases. Flanking boilers and engine, the coal bunkers held one hundred tons, enough for eight days' steaming.

The forward half of the ship was given over to the powder magazine on the port side and the shot lockers on the starboard. Crew and officers lived between the explosives and the missiles they propelled. The crew got a space sixteen by twenty-five feet, where they ate, stayed when off duty, and slung the hammocks they slept in. The officers enjoyed opulence, on a tiny scale. Ericsson had agreed to fit out his ship "complete in all parts and appointments for service." He took this seriously; along with designing everything else he found time not only to equip the officers' quarters with black walnut paneling, but also to see that each tiny stateroom received a soap dish, a slop jar (chamber pot), and a china washbasin ennobled with the ship's name in bright gold. One of the future occupants was happily surprised to find these touches of luxury when he reported for duty: "Capt. Ericsson fitted our rooms up at his own expense & has been very liberal. I have been on board nearly all the vessels that have left the yard since I have been here & seen no room as handsomely fitted up as ours."

Between the living quarters and the engine room a massive bulkhead divided the ship. It supported the most significant feature of the entire revolutionary vessel.

The idea of a revolving gun turret was no more new than that of an ironclad fighting ship. An American named Theodore Timby had patented one in 1843, and although his was designed for land use, Ericsson's partners—to his great annoyance—later insisted on giving Timby a $5,000 royalty for every turret installed on one of their warships (they thought better of it after making only three payments).

A Royal Navy captain named Cowper Phipps Coles proposed to take the turret to sea. He had seen the balky ironclad French vessels bombard the Kinburn batteries during the Crimean War and set to work improving maritime armor. In 1855 he came up with a plan for a man-of-war that, rather than mounting broadside guns, had a single turret holding a 68-pounder. The turret didn't move, so the ship had to maneuver to point the gun. Four years later Coles had refined his idea and was promoting "shotproof hemispherical screens" resting on turntables. The drawback of a turret ship was that it could mount far fewer guns than a broadside vessel. Coles held that the number of cannon no longer mattered: what counted was their power and the strength of their shielding. No need, he said, to drench an enemy in shellfire, but merely to stand up to whatever is thrown at you while delivering a few decisive blows.

Coles eventually got to conduct a test, and it went well. His turret survived thirty-three hits from 68-pound smoothbores and 110-pound rifles, bravely rotating and able to return fire all the while. Lord Palmerston, the prime minister, was convinced, stating, "Comparatively small iron-cased ships armed in this way . . . and without any portholes and low in the water, will prove formidable ships of war."

Palmerston said that on September 24, 1861, three days after the Ironclad Board told Ericsson they had awarded him his contract. Later, Mallory would rather petulantly claim, "Coles is entitled to the paternity of the *Monitor.* I studied his views attentively in 1855 and again in 1859." Ericsson maintained that he had "perfected the invention more than seven years before Captain Coles brought out his abortive scheme in England."

Coles's turret might have withstood a friendly pummeling; Ericsson knew his would be up against the efforts of a determined and highly capable enemy.

The initial plans he'd put before the board called for a ship armed with self-designed weapons he poetically named "hydrostatic javelins" and a hemispherical turret shaped like an inverted grapefruit half. Such esoteric refinements disappeared under the hammer of necessity: now he wanted two of the biggest guns made and the most easily built housing to protect them. "Every part of the *Monitor* is straight or curved in one direction only, no compound curves," said Ericsson of his simplifications.

That midships bulwark had to be strong for it supported a structure that weighed 120 tons even before the guns were added to it.

Ericsson designed a cylinder nine feet high and twenty in diameter. Coles's tests had shown that four layers of inch-thick plate could not stand shocks so well as a single four-inch plate, and just days after getting his ship approved, Ericsson wrote Commodore Smith—from whom he was soon to get more advice than he wanted—that he had the "expectation of obtaining rolled plate 4 inches thick to form the outer half of the turret." A year before the war, the South had produced 26,000 tons of iron and steel to the

North's 450,000 tons; but despite such industrial preeminence, no four-inch plates were to be had. The turret would have to be built up with layers—Ericsson called for eight of them—of the one-inch plates he found he could get "at once, 5 feet square, at the rate of 140 tons per week." Smith, having no choice, agreed.

The turret's top was crisscrossed with two-inch bars under-girded by six-inch ones, the interstices of the grid set closely enough to (it was hoped) keep out shell fragments while allowing the gunners sufficient light to see. The floor was also a grating, pierced by two hatchways that allowed men and munitions to enter.

In action, the whole heavy structure rested on an iron spindle nine inches thick that was rotated by its own steam engine, which could be run by a single operator. For most of the vessel's life it would sit on a bronze ring so closely machined that the turret's weight alone made the seal watertight.

The basic elements of the ship were attended by a thousand de-tails. Toilets, for instance. Ericsson designed the first marine heads set below the waterline. Their pumps and cutoffs were tricky to work and would be for another eighty years: during World War II a German submarine captain lost his U-boat by mishandling the mechanisms of its head.

ONCE, IN THE SUNNY DAYS before Sumter, Ericsson's friend DeLamater had suggested that the two of them visit Niagara Falls. Ericsson wanted to know why: "Is anything the matter with them?"

A joke, but like most jokes based on a truth. The fixity of pur-pose the inventor brought to any job, the total absorption that had made his wife "jealous of a steam engine," served him and the Union well in this most demanding of tasks.

He got an extension of the original deadline. Or, rather, Bush-nell did, arguing that "the whole vessel with her equipment will cost no more than to maintain one regiment in the field 12 months, and each are experiments to be used to save the Government and

Union; should ours prove what we warrant it, will it not be of infinitely more service than 100 regiments?" This eloquence won Ericsson less than two weeks, giving him one hundred days to finish his ship.

The inventor said with his customary bombast that he had embarked on "such herculean labor . . . as is not on record in the history of engineering." The boast has a good deal of truth: the *Monitor* was the most complicated machine that had ever been built. The *Merrimack* generated just one patent—for its submerged hull—but the ship Ericsson was working on may have incorporated upward of forty inventions. In the heat of his efforts, the inventor never took the time to patent any of them. He had to do everything on the fly. The ship began without a complete set of working plans, and the engineering drawings never did quite catch up with the job.

This troubled Smith. He believed in Ericsson, but he fretted. Another "Ericsson failure" would be a Smith failure as well.

The beleaguered inventor began to get messages such as this: "I understand computations have been made by expert Naval Architects on the displacement of your vessel." He must have been as irritated by the phrase "expert Naval Architects" as he was by the sentence that followed, for the experts had concluded that "she will not float with the load you propose to put upon her and if she would she could not stand upright for want of stability."

Ericsson had heard enough about stability. Replying to "these absurd statements relating to the battery," he wrote ". . . that there is no living man who has tripped me on calculations or proved my figures wrong in a single instance in matters relating to theoretical calculations."

This self-assurance never quit the inventor. But he couldn't do it all by himself. His initial trust in Robert Stockton might have been misplaced, but he'd chosen a solid partner in Bushnell, and Bushnell knew he needed more partners.

CHAPTER 14

No Battle, No Money

Civil War ordnance being loaded aboard ship at West Troy, New York.

The steady little Hudson River city of Troy, New York, is not generally remembered as a cradle of maritime activity, but it played a crucial part in the creation of the *Monitor.* By the mid-nineteenth century Troy had become a center of iron founding, and Bushnell had a couple of business friends there, John Winslow and John Griswold. They were partners in two of the largest foundries in the Northeast, Rensselaer Iron Works and Albany Iron Works, the latter the nation's leading maker of railroad iron. Bushnell had contracted with them to provide plate for his *Galena.* As soon as Ericsson entered his life, he telegraphed them both and asked them to meet him in Washington.

When Griswold and Winslow arrived, Bushnell took them out in a carriage; he felt Willard's too public a place for him to make his proposition. During the ride he told them about Ericsson and his warship and said that if they could help the project get approval, a partnership supporting it would benefit them and their country.

Both men were on friendly terms with Secretary of State Seward and through him had arranged Bushnell's meeting with Lincoln. The two were in the room when the President attended the Ironclad Board meeting.

Once the board gave its approval, Bushnell formed his partnership: Winslow and Griswold would share a half interest in the ship, he and Ericsson the other half. Ericsson would be in charge of the design; Winslow would contract out the iron; and Griswold, who was president of the Troy City Bank, would see to the financing.

The four men had no written contract among themselves. Winslow said, "It was simply a verbal agreement, and nothing more, and acted upon in good faith throughout." This accords with the speed and compression of the whole enterprise. What doesn't is Winslow's claim that he and Griswold alone had come up with all the capital; but he said that many years later.

The Ironclad Board might have given Ericsson the go-ahead, but his payment would only come in $50,000 increments, the first not to appear until the Navy Department determined that $50,000 worth of work had been done. That meant the partners were responsible for all the initial financing. They apparently put up $10,000 each, and Griswold started to raise more money while Winslow began his contracting.

Every element of the ship's hurried birth was supplied by civilian contractors. Winslow quite naturally turned first to the Rensselaer Iron Works because he and Griswold owned it.

The plate forging went to H. Abbott and Sons in Baltimore, the largest rolling mill in the nation. The factory immediately began making armor for the Union ironclad, while Tredegar, just 130 miles to the south, was doing the same for the Confederate one.

New York was then a city filled with heavy industry, and most of the manufacture took place near Ericsson's home. Cornelius DeLamater, who had sent Bushnell to Ericsson's door, got the contract for the engines. The Phoenix Foundry, on the East River, had made many of the components of the *Princeton* twenty years earlier. DeLamater was a clerk there then; now the old Phoenix was the Cornelius H. DeLamater Iron Works, and its owner had become such close friends with Ericsson that DeLamater was one of the few who addressed him by his first name.

The lower vessel went to the Continental Iron Works, across the river from DeLamater in Greenpoint, Brooklyn. The all-important turret was the responsibility of the nearby Novelty Iron Works. This operation sounds as if it might have made children's mechanical banks, but in fact it was New York's leading producer of marine steam engines, and the only factory with machinery heavy enough to bend Abbott's plates to the turret's curvature.

Welles had told Ericsson to start work immediately, and he did, writing later that "while the clerks of the department were engaged in drawing up the formal contract, the iron which now forms the keel plates of the *Monitor* was drawn through the rolling mill."

He was already well along when he got a nervous letter from Smith saying that the commodore would "be subjected to extreme mortification if the vessel does not come up to the contract in all respects."

But not nearly as much as Ericsson, as it turned out.

Early in October, Bushnell went to Washington to receive the contract and take it to his partners to sign. Welles had drafted it himself. Much of the document was fine, describing the ship-to-be, and containing the usual language about the necessity for good workmanship and the finest materials. The $275,000 price tag was in place, the money to be paid in stages, with a stiff but not unreasonable 25 percent held back until the ship proved itself.

That too seemed innocuous: a "test of the qualities and properties of the vessel" that "shall be made as soon . . . as practicable," and definitely within ninety days.

Then it dawned on Bushnell just what that test entailed.

Smith had not been entirely sly about it. On September 30 he wrote Ericsson to say that his vessel "is novel and because it is so, the Government requires the designer to warrant its success." That didn't merely mean sea trials and calculation of fuel consumption and the like, but "placing the vessel before an enemy's batteries."

The whole idea was so new, the Ironclad Board held, that its validity could be demonstrated only in battle. If the fight went against the ship, the backers would lose not just their final 25 percent, but also have to pay back every dollar the government had spent on it. This was a warship contract unique in history.

BUSHNELL UNHAPPILY WENT TO ERICSSON to break the news. Surely he expected a volcanic outburst, for it is difficult to imagine an arrangement more likely to remind the inventor of how badly he'd been treated over the *Princeton.*

Here we see most clearly Ericsson the professional, Ericsson the supremely self-confident, and Ericsson—it is not too strong a word—the genius.

Bushnell witnessed no fury at all. Instead the inventor looked up from his plans and called the draconian stipulation "perfectly reasonable and proper." He had done the work, had designed the first ship to be built solely by an engineer, and he had complete faith in the integrity of his calculations. He believed he should pay the price for any error: "If the structure cannot stand this test, then it is indeed worthless." He signed the contract on October 4.

The other two partners were not nearly so stoic. Griswold was hesitant, but Winslow (who would later preen about having shouldered the entire risk) was appalled. He refused to sign unless Bushnell could come up with backers to post bonds guaranteeing that they would pay if the government didn't.

Bushnell persuaded a Connecticut friend to shoulder some of the potential debt, then approached the New York financier Daniel Drew to take on the rest. Drew is seen today as perhaps the most ruthless and venal operator in that buccaneering age of finance capitalism, but it should be remembered that he agreed to enter this deal with little to gain and a good deal to lose.

Ericsson paid scant attention to Bushnell's negotiations. He was wholly occupied with his ship, and with placating Smith, which he did with uncharacteristic patience. The commodore kept pestering him, almost daily sending messages such as "The more I reflect upon your battery, the more fearful I am of her efficiency."

Mostly, Ericsson made palliative replies—"Rest tranquil as to the result; success cannot fail to crown the undertaking." But now and then he showed a spark of temper, as when he told Smith that because the Navy had "thrown the entire responsibility, as to practical success, on the contractor, you will I respectfully submit permit him to exercise freely his own judgment in carrying out the mechanical part of the work."

To Smith's credit, this sort of sharp retort didn't rile him. Once he wrote Ericsson, "I make suggestions, offer objections which are only intended for your consideration but is nowise to control your action. The responsibility rests with you and I would not change it if I could. Excuse my interference thus far if I have annoyed you, & I will be silent in future."

The placatory message would not have given the inventor much relief. He was fortunate that most of the work was being done close by, for he had to inspect it daily. Thomas Rowland, the owner of Continental Iron Works, who had hundreds of men busy on the hull, wrote that "Mr. Ericsson was in every part of the vessel, apparently at the same moment, skipping over planks and gangways, up and down ladders, as though he were a boy of sixteen. It seemed as though a plate could not be placed or a bolt struck without his making his appearance at the workmen's side."

Ericsson's energy was coupled with the physical strength that all who knew him commented on. During one of his visits to Rowland's, he barked his shin on a log of bar iron that had been left in a heavily trafficked part of the yard. He told two workers standing nearby to move the obstruction. Both men shook their heads: *No, sir; too heavy.* Ericsson scowled but said nothing more. Instead he stooped, picked up the bar, carried it to a scrap heap, and dropped it there.

At their noon break, the two workers recruited a couple of friends, and together they took the bar to one of the big shop scales. It weighed six hundred pounds.

That would have happened on a morning visit; by noon Ericsson had made his way to the foot of East Twelfth Street where the turret was taking shape at Novelty. The men assembling it lacked an advantage enjoyed by their Southern rivals: they could not probe with drill bits to find the right place to seat a bolt. All the holes had been punched before the iron got to Novelty, and all had to align perfectly or there'd be no turret. Ericsson's job was one of precision unparalleled in this new industrial epoch, and it sent him back to his drafting table at Franklin Street every evening.

So far, the turret was fitting together properly; it would be completed in the Novelty yard to prove that it *could* be, but it was far too large to move intact. The plates had to be disassembled and freighted to where the titanic jigsaw puzzle would come together again on top of the upper vessel.

Smith might momentarily have been quiescent, but Ericsson was about to receive another visitor, and their encounter offers both a look at the engineer's temperament, and the pressure he was under.

Commander David Dixon Porter was down South fitting out a fleet of mortar ships that were to help open the Mississippi when "I received orders from the Navy Department to make a critical examination of the vessel and report my opinion of her capabilities."

A few days later Porter appeared in Ericsson's drafting room and showed him his orders. Did the engineer welcome this influential officer, offer him a drink, or at least a chair? Not at all. This wasn't Commodore Smith, and Ericsson thought he had no business there. Porter wrote that his host opened the conversation with a burst of sarcasm: "Well, you are no doubt a great mathematician, and know all about the calculations which enter into the construction of my vessel. You will have many papers to examine; help yourself and take what you like best."

If Commander Porter was put off by this reception, he didn't show it. "I'm no great mathematician," he said, "but I am a practical man, and think I can ascertain whether or not the *Monitor* will do what is promised of her."

The affable response only served to anger Ericsson. "Ah, yes! A practical man! Well, I've had a dozen of those fellows here already, and they went away as wise as they came. I don't want *practical* men sent here, sir. I want men who understand the higher mathematics that are used in the construction of my vessel—men who can work out the displacements, horsepower, impregnability, endurance at sea in a gale, capacity to stow men, the motion of the vessel according to the waves, her stability as a platform for guns, her speed, actual weight—in short, everything pertaining to the subject. Now, young man [Porter was forty-eight], if you can't fathom these things, you had better go back where you came from. If the department wants to understand the principles of my vessel, they should send a mathematician."

Ericsson paused to take a breath, and Porter put in mildly, "Well, although I am not strictly what you would call a mathematician, I know the rule of three, and twice two are four."

This stoked the inventor's mounting rage. Porter wrote, "Ericsson looked hard at me, his hair bristled up, and the muscles of his brawny arms seemed to swell as if in expectation of having to eject me from the room."

Instead, he treated Porter to a further tirade. "Well! I never in my life met with such assurance as this. Here the Government sends me an officer who knows only the rule of three and twice two are four, and I have used the calculus and all the higher mathematics in making my calculations. My God! Do they take me for a fool?"

Had Ericsson been speaking to, say, Gideon Welles, that outburst might have put an end to the *Monitor* before her keel touched water. But Ericsson was fortunate that his guest was as confident a man as himself and had nothing to prove. His father, David Porter, had been a famous frigate captain in the War of 1812, and Porter's adoptive brother was David Farragut; Porter came from the closest thing to a naval dynasty America ever had. Just as important for this particular assignment, he possessed a sense of humor.

"Well, Mr. Ericsson," he said, "you will have to make the best of a bad bargain and get along with me as well as you possibly can. I am perfectly willing to receive instruction from you."

"Ah, ha!—That's it, is it? And so you think me a schoolmaster to teach naval officers what I know? I'm afraid you're too bad a bargain for me; you must expect no instruction here. Take what you like from my shelves, but you can't have my brains."

Porter suggested that Ericsson show his plans "and, if you won't explain them, let me see what I can make of them."

The incredible colloquy continued, "Ah, young man! With your limited knowledge of simple equations you will run aground in very short time. Look at this drawing and tell me what it represents."

Porter studied it carefully. "It looks to me like a coffee mill."

Ericsson leaped from his chair. "I am a fool to waste my time on you. That is the machinery that works my turntable for the turret. I have spent many sleepless nights over it, and now a man who only knows a little of simple equations tells me it's a coffee mill!"

He thrust a small wooden model into Porter's hands. "Now what do you think of that?"

Porter said he "regarded the model with a critical eye, holding it upside down. 'This,' I remarked, 'is evidently the casemate'—passing my hand over the bottom—'and this'—pointing to the turret—'is undoubtedly where you carry the engine.'"

Ericsson groaned and swore until Porter said he fully understood the vessel and "proposed to the inventor to go and examine the Simon-pure article, and we crossed the ferry to Greenpoint."

Once at the ship, Porter took off his coat and, followed by Ericsson, made his way through the dark iron chambers. After an hour he climbed from the hold into winter daylight and said, "Now, sir, I know all about your machine."

"Yes," the inventor said for a final time, "and you know twice two are four, and a little of simple equations."

Porter regarded him coolly. "Now, Mr. Ericsson, I have borne a good deal from you today; you have mocked at my authority and have failed to treat me with the sweetness I had a right to expect. I am about to have satisfaction, for on my report depends whether your vessel is accepted by the department, so I will tell you in plain terms what I think. . . ."

"Say what you please," said Ericsson—"glaring at me like a tiger ready to spring."

". . . I will say this to the Government—in writing, too, so that there can be no mistake."

"Go on, sir, go on! You will run on a rock directly."

"Well, then, I will say that Mr. Ericsson has constructed a vessel—a very little iron vessel—which, in the opinion of our best naval architect, is in violation of well-known principles, and will sink the moment she touches the water."

Porter was talking about John Lenthall, chief of the Bureau of Ship Construction and Repair, an able man but one whose entire experience was with sailing ships. He liked to disparage what he called "Ericsson's iron pot." Ericsson summarized Lenthall for his guest: "Oh, he's a fool!"

Porter pressed on, "But I shall say, also, that Mr. Ericsson has constructed the most remarkable vessel the world has ever seen—one that, if properly handled, can destroy any ship now afloat, and whip a dozen wooden ships together if they were where they could not maneuver so as to run her down."

Ericsson gaped at Porter, grabbed his hand and shook it, and emitted a rare laugh. "My God! And all this time I took you for a damned fool, and you are not a damned fool after all!"

Porter laughed too. He wrote years later that he and Ericsson "have been the best of friends ever since."

Porter went to Washington and delivered his favorable report. His faith in the coffee mill and its creator never flagged. He wrote, "Had Ericsson been listened to on the first breaking out of the war, and his plans adopted, the United States Government would in one year not only have been able to take possession of all the Southern ports, but to have bid defiance even to the great fleets of

England and France in case either nation felt disposed to meddle in our affairs."

IF PORTER'S VISIT HAD PROVED unexpectedly heartening to Ericsson, it still left him with much to worry over. There was trouble about the guns.

Along the way from solid shot to shell, cannon had developed a new nomenclature. For centuries they had been named for the weight of the shot they fired— 6-pounders, 9-pounders, the big 68-pound carronades carried by ships of the line—but now guns were coming to be known by the size of their bore, which conformed to the size of the missile they threw. Those with the largest bore fired the biggest shot, and Ericsson wanted fifteen-inch ones. He couldn't get them and had to settle for twelve-inch. Supported by four huge beams, their carriages rested on brass rollers so nicely balanced that in a calm sea a single crewman could push one forward to the gunport. When fired, the recoil would be damped within six feet by an arresting mechanism similar, Ericsson specified, "to that applied to the United States Steam Ship *Princeton*." He hadn't forgotten the *Princeton*, and now that he had a contract, he didn't mind referring to this naval bugaboo. "You will not doubt my ability to handle the gun," he wrote Smith with a note of defiance, "if you call to mind the facility with which the 12 inch guns of the *Princeton* were worked with my carriages and friction gear."

The cannon would point their muzzles out of vertical oval ports protected by iron shutters, hung on pivots at their tops, that could be swung up when a gun was ready to fire and dropped while it was being reloaded.

And there would be only two guns. That the Navy Department had agreed to this armament is another reflection of Ericsson's persuasiveness. No major warship since the dawn of naval gunnery had put to sea with just two cannon.

Four days after signing the contract, Ericsson asked for the specifications of the Dahlgren.

The plans arrived quickly. The cannon did not. There is an irony (and a reminder of how quickly technology was advancing a century and a half ago) in that the Dahlgren gun, whose inventor had struggled so hard just a decade earlier to get it accepted, was now a precious commodity. The Navy didn't want to risk even two of them on some civilian's contrivance. An ordnance department officer declared that Dahlgrens "will never be used on *her.*"

Winter had shut down, a cold one for the Union, whose sap had sunk as low as it would get. Even during the awful Wilderness fighting of 1864 that cost the Union 17,500 casualties in two days, the North had the memory of big victories to warm it. But there was no Gettysburg or Vicksburg to offer reassurance as snow began to fall on the still-scattered components of Ericsson's experiment.

In October the battle of Ball's Bluff, the second large engagement of the war, had ended in a Confederate victory so complete that some in Congress believed the outcome was the result of a conspiracy. Three weeks later, in Missouri, a Federal force had been driven from the field after the Battle of Belmont. Abraham Lincoln thought the initial advance had shown spirit and formed a good opinion of the commander, Ulysses Grant. Still, it was another defeat.

George Templeton Strong, the New York lawyer whose diary is as fascinating as it is voluminous, reflected the national temper when he wrote on December 23, "Vile weather, cold, wet, blowy, rainy, sleety. Walked uptown through it this afternoon in a cantankerous frame of mind, though I was buying Christmas presents." Nor had his mood improved by the turn of the year. On the thirty-first, he wrote, "Poor old 1861 just going. It has been a gloomy year of trouble and disaster. I should be glad of its departure, were it not that 1862 is likely to be no better."

John Ericsson was doing his best to brighten Strong's New Year. As the short gray days came and went, he drew and drew and drew.

CHAPTER 15

The Tardy Patriot

Franklin Buchanan, the thoroughly
intimidating captain of the *Merrimack*.

Franklin Buchanan founded the US Naval Academy, but he is better known for the command he held just a few days.

He was born in Baltimore in 1800, the son of a successful physician (his name, unlike that of the hapless future president, was pronounced "Buck-annon") who died when the boy was seven. Four years later the War of 1812 began, and Franklin was drawn to military service. His mother encouraged him to join the Navy.

He enlisted at the age of fourteen. He was a schoolboy, and his school was to be the ships he served abroad. There was as yet nothing like a naval academy, and officers learned the ropes (an idiom that is with us still) at sea. In the fall of 1826 Buchanan, now

141

a lieutenant, realized every young sea officer's dream by getting command of a fine new frigate, the *Baltimore*. Like all dreams it didn't last long, for the twenty-six-year-old captain's sole duty was to sail from the Chesapeake to Rio de Janeiro and turn the ship over to its Brazilian purchasers. No maritime glory was to be had, but Buchanan did take the *Baltimore* safely through a gale, and he had held command.

He'd held it harshly. The great corrective in the Navy then was flogging, and as the officer responsible for discipline on his ship, Buchanan believed in the lash. He applied it so lavishly that he became the object of a most unusual protest.

In 1831, at the end of a three-year cruise as first lieutenant on the frigate *Constellation*, Buchanan debarked and boarded a boat to take him to Baltimore. Dozens of the sailors from his frigate had also bought passage. When he came up on deck to take the air, a fellow passenger wrote, "The seamen gathered around him, and gave vent to their feeling in blasphemous oaths."

Buchanan, who didn't scare easily, showed no fear as the men cursed and threatened. "There he stood," wrote the witness, "in statue-like repose, not a word escaping his lips. He seemed rooted to the deck. For a full five minutes or more he braved the tempest, but not a man dared lay the weight of his finger upon him." Then he turned and walked through the group to his cabin.

That was no act. Buchanan's righteousness had nothing to do with querulous self-satisfaction; he stood on the side of virtue. That so many sailors with eighteen months of sea duty behind them should have squandered money and shore leave to express their anger did not give him the least pause.

Buchanan's time on land ended more pleasantly than it began, for he went to Talbot County, Maryland, to visit a young woman he'd met at the wedding of a fellow officer. She was Ann Catherine Lloyd—"Nannie"—a daughter of Edward Lloyd, former Maryland governor and senator, and the owner of hundreds of slaves who worked a fiefdom more typical of the great plantations of the Deep South than of a border state.

Lloyd's domain was a sort of independent principality. Frederick Douglass, who had spent his childhood as a slave there, wrote, "It was generally supposed that slavery in the State of Maryland existed in its mildest form . . . but there were certain secluded and out-of-the-way places . . . where slavery, wrapt in its own congenial darkness, could and did develop all its malign and shocking characteristics, where it could be indecent without shame, cruel without shuddering, and murderous without apprehension or fear of exposure or punishment. Just such a secluded, dark, and out-of-the-way place was the home plantation of Colonel Edward Lloyd."

Buchanan saw no darkness there, only a ratification of his view of how the world should work: an orderly, sharply defined hierarchy maintained by tradition and the whip.

Engaged by the summer of 1833, Nannie and Franklin got married in Annapolis early in 1835. He was not so keen to get to sea now and tried to wangle short cruises and shore duty. A good stretch of the latter began in the summer of 1845. With the country growing, and its fleet with it, George Bancroft, then secretary of the navy, chose Buchanan to establish a permanent institution to educate midshipmen in a regimen more systematic than putting them aboard a ship and hoping for the best. Knowing that most Navy men would resist abandoning the tutelage that had formed them, Bancroft picked Buchanan because of his service-wide reputation as a man who believed in order, who was energetic enough to establish it down to the smallest detail, and who was hardhanded enough to enforce it.

Bancroft had not chosen merely a noisy taskmaster. Drawing on the curriculum of West Point, Buchanan set about creating at Annapolis a Naval Academy teaching "English grammar and composition; arithmetic, geography, and history; navigation, gunnery, and the use of steam; the Spanish and French languages." He took over an old army post, acquiring professors (twenty-two, at $1,200 per year) and iron bed frames (eighty, at $8 each), and he had his school up and running in four months.

In the spring of 1847 Bancroft decided that the Naval Academy had gained a sound enough footing to spare its founder, and Buchanan, who had been petitioning to serve in the war with Mexico, went to Norfolk to take command of the sloop of war *Germantown*.

Mexico had no fleet to speak of; save for chasing privateers, the American Navy waged this war on land. Buchanan left the *Germantown* to attack a Mexican stronghold three miles in from the coast on the Tuxpan River. At the head of 150 sailors and Marines, he stormed the works and drove off their defenders. He would have preferred a sea battle, but his victory was decisive, and he had several Mexican cannonballs stowed aboard his ship as a memento.

The rising officer went on to serve as Matthew Perry's flag captain aboard the frigate *Susquehanna* when the commodore used a blend of tacit threat and delicate entreaty to persuade Japan to accept Western trade. Buchanan wrote that Perry was "the most industrious, hard working, energetic, zealous, persevering, enterprising officer of his rank in our navy." A few years later Buchanan accused this paragon of "ungenerous, unjust, and wanton abuses of authority." The change of outlook, as complete as it was abrupt, reflects Buchanan's Manichaean view of everything. He perceived his fellow creatures as, to use two of his favorite terms, either *high toned* or *worthless*. Perry had put himself in the larger camp over a question of discipline.

Certainly there had been a grave breach of it. Coal heaver William Thompson, chafing under shipboard strictures on the *Susquehanna*, shouted at Lieutenant John Duer, "Come on, you son of a bitch; you would not let me go ashore and want to treat me like a dog!" He then made for Lieutenant Duer with an extraordinary little arsenal that included an auger, an eyebolt, and a musket. This was a capital offense; the hastily convened court-martial found Thompson guilty, and Buchanan ordered him "hung by the neck until dead to the fore-yard arm of the United States Frigate *Susquehanna*."

Perry intervened and commuted the sentence to life imprisonment. Buchanan thought that showed contemptible softness, but what permanently damned Perry in his eyes was the commodore's having the decision read to the officers and crew of the *Susque-*

hanna. Buchanan saw that as a public humiliation, and he would not let it drop. Back in America he petitioned the secretary of the navy for redress, writing that Perry had "overstepped bounds of his privilege and propriety by addressing the conduct of the Court in language as illogical as untrue, and impugning my Character as a Member of the Court, to which I cannot submit in silence as a man of Honour."

He got no satisfaction; the Navy Department was not about to censure the man who had just brought off the most successful diplomatic mission of his generation. Buchanan's disgruntlement with the Navy deepened with the appointment, in 1857, of a new secretary of the navy, the Connecticut-born Isaac Toucey, who was in the "worthless" camp: "Our Sec'y is a Yankee through."

A ready hater, Buchanan was becoming ever more angered by "the rascally Northern interference with the institution of slavery." Despite his growing disaffection, he was pleased and surprised the next year to be made head of the Washington Navy Yard. This was better than almost any sea command and put him at the very top of his service.

Soon after, whatever satisfaction he felt was tarnished by Abraham Lincoln's election. When the returns were in, Buchanan wrote a friend, "We can never again feel as proud of the flag we sail under." In April, the Sixth Massachusetts marched through Baltimore on its way to reinforce the capital. A mob formed, threw stones, then bullets; the troops returned fire; twelve civilians and four soldiers died. The townspeople had shed the "patriotic gore / That flecked the streets of Baltimore," in "Maryland, My Maryland," the most bellicose of all our official state songs and the only one to bear a 150-year-old grudge ("She is not dead, nor deaf, nor dumb— / Huzza! She spurns the Northern scum!").

The anthem echoes Buchanan's feelings. He'd always been loyal to the Navy, but he took everything personally, and to him Maryland was more personal than the Union the Navy was sworn to defend. He believed his state was bound to secede, and that he must follow her.

On April 22 he went to see Gideon Welles. Just six weeks into the job, the Navy secretary knew his visitor's reputation as a valuable officer and got to his feet to greet him.

Buchanan said he was there for "the most unpleasant duty I have ever performed." He was resigning.

Welles said he was sorry to hear it. Buchanan wanted to explain himself. "Under the present circumstances," every Marylander had to stand by the state "when the blood was flowing in the streets." He went on to assert that he was leaving the Navy Yard in good order and had given orders that it must be defended.

Welles offered him neither sympathy nor gratitude, saying only, "Every man has to judge for himself."

Buchanan left and went to turn over the yard to John Dahlgren.

Maryland did not secede. When it became clear that wouldn't happen, Buchanan wrote Welles withdrawing his resignation. New to his job though Welles was, and important though the penitent was, the secretary met his request with a curt, unambiguous reply: "By direction of the president, your name has been stricken from the rolls of the Navy."

The affront fed Buchanan's wellsprings of rancor. He wrote a nephew, "My intention is to remain neutral, but if all law is to be dispensed with . . . and a coercive policy continued which would disgust barbarians, and the South literally trampled upon, I may change my mind and join them."

His change of mind—if it had not already occurred—was hastened by an incident that might have been designed to enrage him, the national crisis boiled down to a personal insult. In June, a party of New York volunteers sent to remove all ordnance from a nearby armory noticed on the gatepost of Buchanan's home the souvenir cannonballs he had captured at Tuxpan. The soldiers took those too.

The lost round shot, the imperiled institution of slavery, dismissal from the Navy, all fermented together in Buchanan's mind. Speaking of the war more truly than he knew, he declared, "The Negro is the cause of it all." A "war of *races*" was shaping up.

His anger simmered into paranoia: now he saw a Federal conspiracy to foment a slave insurrection, "to cut the throats of their masters, the land to be given to northerners."

Late in August, he acted. Transferring his property to Nannie, so that Yankee predators could not confiscate it, he headed for Richmond. He first went to Stephen Mallory's office, and the secretary immediately commissioned him a captain in the fledgling Confederate Navy, making him chief of the Bureau of Orders and Detail. That was the highest office in the service, but the "detail" in the title proved all too accurate. Buchanan was responsible for enlistment records, contracts, steam-plant maintenance, provisions, supply. He found himself responding to requests for oil to keep binnacle lamps burning.

Like Ericsson, he spent the fall and winter bent over a desk. Then, on February 24, 1862, orders came from Mallory. Buchanan was to take command of his nation's already famous ironclad. "The *Virginia* is a novelty in naval construction," Mallory wrote him, "is untried, and her powers unknown, and the Department will not give specific orders as to her attack upon the enemy."

Mallory understood that French Forrest wanted to be given the ship he had done much to shepherd into existence, and that by rights of seniority he should have it. Mallory, though, knew Buchanan not only as able, but combative. He wanted a man of violence.

"Her powers as a ram are regarded as formidable, and it is hoped that you may be able to test them. Like the bayonet charge of infantry, this mode of attack . . . will commend itself to you in the present scarcity of ammunition."

Days earlier, Confederate troops had lost the western strongholds of Forts Henry and Donelson, leaving Tennessee vulnerable to an advance along the Cumberland and Tennessee Rivers. Mallory concluded his orders with "The condition of our country, and the painful reverses we have just suffered, demand our utmost exertions, and convinced as I am that the opportunity and the means of striking a decisive blow for our Navy are now for the first time presented, I congratulate you upon it, and know that your judgment and gallantry will meet all just expectations."

Despite that cumbersome sentence, the final words are a bugle call: "Action—prompt and successful action—now would be of serious importance to our cause."

Captain Buchanan left his wearisome paperwork and headed for Norfolk the next morning.

CHAPTER 16

Trial Run

The Rebel ironclad comes out to fight in a print
published a quarter century later.

The superseded French Forrest was not happy to see Buchanan, and neither was Catesby ap Roger Jones (that hiccup of an *ap* is a Welsh patronymic meaning "son of"). Jones too had wanted command of the *Merrimack* and had reason to expect it. He had been with the ship from the beginning, in both its incarnations.

Born in Virginia in 1821, he joined the Navy at fifteen and in a decade became so capable an artilleryman that he spent three years as John Dahlgren's chief assistant on the development of his gun. Jones had a bad brush with the Retirement Board, not through any professional failings on his part, but because of rumors about his fondness for young men. That trouble was behind him when the *Merrimack* was launched in 1855, and he sailed as ordnance officer on her maiden voyage. He immediately distrusted her engines, and her whole design: he said she "rolled very deeply—rolled badly." The test firings of her Dahlgrens, however, went without a hitch.

Jones would get to know the ship far better than he had on her inaugural cruise. He left the Union with his state and, as a captain in the brand-new Virginia Navy, which was soon to be absorbed into the Confederate service, got to Norfolk in time to see the smoke rising from the burning yard.

Put in charge of the Jamestown Island defenses, he worked closely with John Brooke during the tests on the *Merrimack*'s armor (David Dixon Porter said he particularly regretted the loss to the US Navy of Brooke and Jones). In November, Jones was made executive officer—second only to the captain—of the ironclad, largely on the strength of Brooke's recommendation to Mallory. Jones inherited a plague of troubles.

The *Merrimack* had not only surprised many detractors by fulfilling its primary function of floating; it floated all too well. Jones wrote Brooke, "The ship will be too light, or I should say, she is not sufficiently protected below the water. Our draft will be a foot less than was first intended, yet I was this morning ordered not to put any more ballast in fear of [its breaking through] the bottom. The eaves of the roof"—that is, the iron skirt protecting the ship's wooden hull—"will not be more than six inches immersed which in smooth water would not be enough; a slight ripple would leave it bare except the one-inch iron that extends some feet below. We are least protected where we most need it, and may receive a shot that would sink us; a thirty-two pounder would do it. The constructor should have put in six inches where we now have one."

Brooke was as annoyed as Jones to discover the *Merrimack* needed to be much heavier to find her proper waterline, saying later, "Mr. Porter stated to me that he had accidentally omitted in his calculations some weight which was on board the [original] ship, in consequence of which she did not draw as much water when launched as he anticipated."

Given the tense relationship between Brooke and Porter, this seems an unlikely statement for the constructor to have made, and it was not repeated. Porter had apparently forgotten to include in his calculations the weight of the vanished masts and rigging. If so, he never admitted it.

Jones appended one hopeful note to his denunciation of the

design: "We have yet to take on our powder, and most of the shells, and 150 tons of coal which is thought will weigh it down a foot or more." He knew this was graveyard whistling; as the shells were fired, and the coal burned, the lightening ship would rise to expose her vulnerable underside.

The guns wouldn't help, as they were already aboard. They had begun to arrive in November: six 9-inch Dahlgren smoothbores and four of Brooke's rifles: two 6.4-inch and two 7-inch. The former weighed five tons, the latter, seven.

The cannon had got there on time; their ammunition was more problematic. They could fire both shells and solid shot—bolts—which had far greater penetrating power, but the overstrained resources of Norfolk and Tredegar couldn't supply both at once. Brooke and Jones, working in the easy mutual trust of a long partnership, talked it over and agreed that shells should have priority. After all, the targets would be wooden ships.

The only solid shot taken aboard was meant for them too. These were balls for the nine-inch Dahlgrens, destined to be hot shot, an effective weapon but a tricky one to handle: the cannonballs had to be heated to near incandescence in the boiler furnace—they'd been cast slightly smaller than usual to allow for expansion—and hoisted sizzling to the gun deck.

The time had come to recruit the men who would work the guns. There had to be a lot of them; each of the four rifles required a crew of 26, and the ship's complement would be about 320.

As head of the Bureau of Orders and Detail, Buchanan had a hand in manning the *Merrimack*, but most of the work fell to Jones and Forrest. The wardroom presented no problem. The Confederacy had reaped so fine a harvest of officers that it had too many capable men for the available berths. For his lieutenants, Jones signed up John Taylor Wood, grandson of President Zachary Taylor and another gunnery expert who, though born in Iowa territory, went with the South; Charles Simms, who had helped capture three Union ships the past June; John Eggleston, barely out of his twenties, but a Navy man from the age of fifteen; Hunter

Davidson, who in the coming battle would continue to serve one of his guns after its muzzle had been blown off; Walter Butt, just returned from spending two months as a prisoner after he'd refused to take an oath of allegiance to the United States; Robert Minor, who had served aboard the *Susquehanna* with Buchanan and had been with Simms at the capture of those Union ships. John Brooke petitioned to be aboard, but Mallory said he couldn't spare him.

William Williamson was the most likely choice for the ship's chief engineer. He knew the *Merrimack*'s balky engines better than anyone else, but he was also chief engineer of the Confederate Navy, and the demands on him were heavy. The post went to Ashton Ramsay, who, although only twenty-four, had come to know and loathe the steam plant while serving aboard the *Merrimack* before the war.

Ramsay had been first assistant engineer aboard the USS *Niagara* in the middle of the Indian Ocean when the 1860 election took place. "We were so far from home," he wrote, "that many could not give serious thought to these matters." When the *Niagara* returned to Boston the following April, the pilot came aboard with a sheaf of newspapers. "The Union is smashed and gone to hell," he said. "See for yourself."

Ramsay saw and left the ship. He traveled in civilian clothes to Richmond, and like many other seamen joined the Army in hopes of getting into the fight right away. But he'd caught Mallory's eye and was ordered to Norfolk to help Williamson revive the *Merrimack*'s engines. Williamson's second had just been dismissed for being "insubordinate and disrespectful," and Ramsay quickly proved himself an able replacement.

He had no faith in the ship's power plant, and not much in the ship itself. "I was . . . fully cognizant of its shortcomings, which I set to correct as far as possible, with the limited means at my command." A fellow officer, posted south from Norfolk, offered him a somber farewell: "Goodbye, Ramsay, I shall never see you again; she will be your coffin."

If Jones had little trouble assembling an excellent wardroom, the crew was not so easily achieved. Forty years later, Eugenius Alexander Jack, third assistant engineer on the *Merrimack*, wrote, "There was no difficulty in finding men, for there were many old salts around Norfolk and Portsmouth ready and glad to go in the great ironclad, and of landsmen there were many volunteers from the military companies garrisoned around."

This is a proud old veteran casting the warmest possible afterglow on his service in the brave days of '61. He strays from the truth. Some of the *Merrimack*'s crew arrived in shackles.

Then as now, the war was perceived largely as a land affair. Unlike the officers, the majority of US Navy seamen had stayed with the Union, and most of those who hadn't joined the Confederate Army. Naturally, the Army wanted to keep them.

"Naval rendezvous"—recruiting stations—set up in Richmond and Norfolk offered landsmen $12 a month and those with sea experience $18 to ship aboard the *Merrimack*; all would get four cents a day to pay for their liquor ration. When these incentives drew a meager response, French Forrest, who was helping with the effort, wrote, "I have reconsidered the matter in regard to the bounty to be given to the men who are to be detached for the *Merrimack*." He would pay $20 up front to every able seaman who signed on. That didn't work either, and in January, Jones sent Lieutenant Wood to drum up volunteers. Wood visited Yorktown and the headquarters of Brigadier General John Magruder, who with thirteen thousand men was guarding the Virginia Peninsula.

Magruder, making a show of being helpful, offered two hundred volunteers, from whom Wood picked eighty. The recruits who arrived at Portsmouth, however, were, Wood angrily reported to Buchanan, "certainly a very different class of men from those I selected. . . . I find but two of the men selected by myself were sent; the others are men I did not see, nor even visit their encampment."

After Lieutenant Minor reviewed them he wrote, "Some of the 'so-called' volunteers had bad characters from their commanding officers, who could not manage them, and were brought on board in double irons."

One was fresh from twenty days' hard labor; several were notorious malingerers; others had been insubordinate.

Jones knew that he must do his best with what he could get. Minor said, "He immediately had their irons struck off, and that if they wished to remain they could do so and start fair with the other men." Lieutenant Jones had been a good choice for his job. "This course proved eminently judicious, as some of them were the best men on board."

Other crewmen trickled in, one, William Burke, with the dubious qualification of having been in civilian life a "comedian." But Wood also got trained gunners from the Carolinas, Alabama, Louisiana, and Virginia regiments. None of them needed to learn how to splice a rope or reef a sail; the *Merrimack* had to survive on its engines, its shield, and its firepower.

As the crewmen gathered, they were trained and retrained to load and fire cannon. Dahlgren and Brooke had done much to advance the technics of artillery, but tending a gun still demanded, as it had for centuries, the most relentless human labor.

Bridges and buildings aside, few things look less mobile than a nineteenth-century naval gun. Throughout most of any voyage, the guns had to stand still as park statues, with much of the crew's effort given over to making sure they stayed put no matter how much the weather might toss the ship about. But in action, they were in constant motion, leaping, bucking, swiveling.

Working them involved a choreography at once swift and ponderous. It began with pushing a flannel bag full of powder down the barrel, and following it with the shot. Shells came strapped to a *sabot*—literally, a "wooden shoe," from the French; it was a French invention—that held the fuse facing forward away from the powder, whose explosion would light it.

Eighty years earlier, a gun had been fired by pouring fine-grained priming powder into a touchhole—the vent—that led to the charge and putting a match to it. This was a fussy, frustrating business, as the priming could easily blow away. By the time of the Civil War, cannon were equipped, like enormous muskets, with locks: hammers that, at the yank of a cord, snapped down on a percussion cap, a copper cylinder filled with fulminate of mercury. Its small explosion when struck touched off the far larger one.

That fired the gun and initiated a host of additional actions, beginning with sponging out the barrel to make sure no smoldering remains of the previous cartridge were waiting to set off the new one when it was driven home.

By 1850, calculations put a crew's number at one man to every five hundred pounds of gun. A 32-pounder required fourteen men, and a boy—the powder monkey—who carried the charges up from the magazines. The first captain was in charge, attended by a sponger, an assistant sponger, the loader, tacklemen who hauled on the ropes that ran the gun out, and "crowmen," who strained at handspikes to lever the beast into position.

Only the gun captain and the second captain looked toward the enemy; the rest stood facing the piece. As action neared, the first captain would order, "Cut loose the battery," and the crew would unmoor the gun. The charge went home, the percussion cap got set, and the captain, standing behind the breech, gestured with his hands (spoken orders often could not be heard in battle) until the gun was pointing where he wanted it, when he shouted, "Well!" Then he stood clear of the path of recoil, and his second said, "Ready." The captain raised and dropped his arm and called, "Fire," as he tugged the lanyard.

Noise, smoke, and the cannon bounded back from the gunport (the only thing it did to help with the routine), while the spongers set to work as the powder monkey offered a fresh charge.

Most of the *Merrimack* volunteers had never seen the guns they would be serving and wouldn't until she went out to fight. With workers crowding the ship night and day, the recruits had to train on the outmoded armament of the USS *United States*. She had captured HMS *Macedonian* in her glory days during the War of 1812 and had been left undamaged at Norfolk through sentimentality.

Now she was a receiving ship, a rotting waterborne barracks where the men also lived.

The old frigate's guns, small and obsolete though they were, could not get enough powder for the training exercises. As the February days passed and pressure mounted, not enough of anything was on hand. On the twenty-seventh, Forrest wrote Major General Benjamin Huger, in command of the Department of Norfolk, "The *Virginia*"—Forrest had just begun calling the ship by her new name—"is now detained for powder. When it will arrive I am unable to say, and in the present expediency I write to suggest that if you feel authorized to make the transfer of the necessary ammunition, it would relieve us greatly." He concluded the letter with the thin promise that "when the powder for the ship arrives it will be delivered . . . to you, to replace that which you may be able to spare me to meet the present emergency."

To another Army officer Forrest wrote, "I have to inform you that I consider it of vital importance that the Virginia be furnished with as much powder as you can possibly spare. I require 8000 pounds, of which I have received 1000 from Richmond." He added that "it will take three days to fill the powder bags." And "the messenger is instructed to wait for your reply."

John Porter had somehow got word and reported that the Northern ironclad would be launched on February 1. He was wrong, but not by much, and his anxiety only added to his labors, as Mallory immediately wrote him demanding daily progress reports.

Progress was slow, and worse. The iron shutters to protect the guns turned out to be inadequate. Forrest was further annoyed by the behavior of the locals. They'd been full of fire and approbation the past fall; now, though, "I have been not a little surprised by the apathy or rather the lack of patriotism of the citizens of Norfolk and Portsmouth in aiding the Government to protect their firesides. Why can they not contribute to the building of an iron-clad for the harbor defense?"

Jones, tormented alike by citizen indifference and lack of gunpowder, wrote Brooke, "Somebody ought to be hung."

Jones didn't say it, but he may have wished Franklin Buchanan among those hung. The captain had visited Norfolk just once, on December 4, when he gave the *Merrimack* a cursory glance in dry dock. He probably knew then that he would be getting command of the ship, and he had helped make sure it received the best officers. But when Jones, sweating through the endless daily problems, said "the want of interest and energy in completing the *Merrimack* is disheartening," he was indicting Buchanan. "Her Captain should be here," he told Brooke, "and so I wrote him a month ago."

Yet when the captain did finally come, on February 25, Jones was downcast, writing wistfully, "Until he was ordered, I was listened to, but of course that cannot happen now."

The other officers were glad to see Buchanan. To them, the angry vigor that had won him so many enemies among the deckhands seemed a valuable weapon. Ramsay said he was "one of the grandest men who ever drew a breath of salt air," and that his appointment was "hailed with great satisfaction by all of us." Lieutenant Eggleston put him in the highest naval fraternity: he was "as indomitably courageous as Nelson, and as arbitrary. I don't think that the junior officer or sailor ever lived with nerve sufficient to disobey an order given by the old man in person."

Buchanan saw his ship afloat for the first time. She looked shorter than her 270 feet because, as Brooke had intended, her hull was submerged and only her iron casemate showed above the water. To Third Assistant Engineer Jack, she was "a curious looking craft. The sloping sides of the shield sinking below the water about two feet and inclining upward pierced with gun ports looked like a sloping Mansard roof of a house, but a sight of the black mouthed guns peeping from the ports gave altogether different impressions and awakened hope that ere long she would be belching fire and death from those ports." The roof was canted at a thirty-six-degree angle to deflect shot, and although it represented only part of the vessel, it dwarfed the two wooden steamers that were fretting and jostling alongside it. These were the *Beaufort* and the *Raleigh*, warships, but only barely; the former mounted a single 32-pound rifle, the latter two 6-pounders. At the moment, the two ships were serving as tugboats—as, indeed, the *Raleigh* had been before her martial rebirth.

They were part of the grandly named James River Squadron. To soothe the feelings of the officers over whose heads he had jumped Buchanan, Mallory had appointed him a commodore, and thus in charge of a fleet rather than a single ship. Along with the *Beaufort* and the *Raleigh*, his squadron included the side-wheelers *Patrick Henry* and *Jamestown*—each carrying a battery of one 64-pound smoothbore, six eight-inch smoothbores, and two 32-pound rifles— and another former tug, the *Teaser*, mounting one 32-pound rifle. Buchanan could hoist his flag on any of them, but of course he picked the *Merrimack.*

She was not a tidy ship. To overcome her stubborn buoyancy, Porter had combed the Navy Yard for every heavy piece of scrap iron he could find. When the threat of this ballast's breaking through the hull became acute, the rest was dumped on the decks before and behind the casemate. There are no known photographs of the *Merrimack*, and none of the many artists' imaginings of her suggests that she went into action disfigured by tons of rubbish strewn on her topside.

The crew had joined the ship by the time Buchanan arrived and were not liking it. As on the *Merrimack*'s Northern counterpart, the space above the guns was covered with an open iron grid; rain fell in and seeped through the gun deck below to drizzle on the berth deck, still dank from its immersion, where the men slept. A few days earlier Jones had written Mallory, "We are living aboard, and are as uncomfortable as possible—there has not been a dry spot aboard her, leaks everywhere—mechanics are at work on a thousand things which should have been done months ago." They weren't at work on the new gun shutters, though, because these hadn't arrived from Tredegar—and wouldn't.

Buchanan did not greatly care. He wanted to take the ship out as soon as she had enough coal and powder aboard to fight the Union vessels in Hampton Roads. He hoped for a combined operation with the army, the *Merrimack* attacking the Federal ships while Magruder took the shore batteries and Fortress Monroe. On Sunday, March 2, Buchanan wrote the general, "It is my intention to be off Newport News early on Friday morning next unless some accident occurs to the *Virginia* to prevent it. You may therefore look out for me at the time named. My plan is to destroy the frigates first, and then turn my attention to the battery on shore. I sincerely hope that acting together we may be successful in destroying the enemy."

Just as Magruder had initially offered Lieutenant Wood choice troops, so did he agree to support Buchanan's attack. A couple of days later, though, the captain heard from Mallory that "it will be impossible for General Magruder to act in concert with or render you any aid in the plans agreed upon to attack the enemy at Newport News."

Magruder's reason was a hard recent rain that had made the roads impassable. In fact, the general seems to have welcomed that rain with all the relief of a drought-parched Kansas farmer because he had little faith in the *Merrimack*. As he put it to the Confederate War Department, "I am . . . satisfied that no ship can produce such an impression upon the troops at Newport News as to cause them to evacuate the fort."

But at least, on March 5, the Army at last turned over enough powder to fill the *Merrimack*'s magazines. Buchanan, who had officially taken command of the ship the day before, issued orders to Commander John Tucker, captain of the *Patrick Henry* and head of the James River Squadron: "It is my intention . . . to appear before the enemy off Newport News at daylight on Friday Morning next (March 7). You will, with the *Jamestown* and *Teaser*, be prepared to join us. My object is first to destroy the frigates *Congress* and *Cumberland* if possible and turn my attention to the destruction of the battery on shore, and the gunboats. You will, in the absence of signals, use your best exertions to injure or destroy the enemy. Much is expected of this ship and those who cooperate with her by her Countrymen, and I expect and hope that our acts will prove our desire to do our duty, to reflect credit upon the Country and the Navy. . . ." Buchanan finished by telling Tucker to keep an eye on the *Merrimack*'s signal flags: "No. 1 signal hoisted under my pennant indicates, 'Sink before you surrender.'"

Despite Buchanan's determination, March 7 found the *Merrimack* still tied up to her wharf, delayed by more bad weather. The captain wanted to set out that evening, but when darkness began to fall, Jones wrote in disgust, "The pilots, of whom there were five, having been previously consulted . . . all preparations were made, including lights at obstructions . . . claimed they could not pilot the ship during the night." It is hard to blame them for not wanting to coax that twenty-two-foot-deep hull through a twisting, partially blocked channel in darkness, especially because—as Major Charles Norris, the Confederate secret service agent who had been with the ship for the past few days, observed—"she was a little more manageable than a timber-raft."

The extra day gave Buchanan the opportunity to enjoy another communication from General Magruder justifying his refusal to help: "The *Merrimac* will make no impression at Newport News."

AND THEN IT WAS SATURDAY morning, March 8. Spring can come early to Virginia, and this was a perfect spring day, with all the clouds gone from a mild sky, and gentle winds barely troubling the surface of Hampton Roads.

Buchanan had his flag officer's red pennant run up and ordered the engines started. That was no easier a task than all the other cosseting they required. They first had to be coaxed into life with a warming bath of steam while the black gang (as the engine-room crew was known; a term that referred to the miasma of coal dust in which they worked) put their shoulders to iron bars and levered the crankshaft around. Chief Engineer Ramsay cracked open the condenser injection valve and edged the throttle forward. The black gang stood back as the crankshaft gathered momentum. The propeller began slowly to revolve.

The ubiquitous mechanics started to leave the ship while she lay throbbing at the dock.

Among the last preparations, the casemate had been basted all over with "ship's grease," which could be almost anything oily: pork fat cooked off in the galleys, beef lard. Jones believed the slimy coating would help deflect shot; all was so untried on this vessel that she would be bringing into battle the silly along with the brilliant.

Buchanan had told his plans for the shakedown cruise only to Jones, Lieutenant Minor, and the captains of his squadron. His crew were expecting a "trial run," but that was sufficiently interesting to have drawn a crowd of onlookers even before a signal gun cracked at eleven o'clock and line handlers cast off the ropes holding the *Merrimack* to the dock.

A few tardy workmen leaped across a widening slice of water while the ship turned her bow downstream. Plates and beams creaked as the vessel, dim in the coal smoke pumped skyward by the engines' mounting struggle, headed out into the Elizabeth. The *Beaufort* and the *Raleigh* joined her.

Buchanan stood forward, exchanging terse remarks with Hezekiah Williams, the pilot, his blue uniform (the unwelcome gray had yet to be issued) perfectly visible to the crowd, collecting cheers. From time to time Williams left the captain's side, climbed down from the casemate, and waded thigh deep in water to cast overside the lead-weighted sounding line, which, drawn back up, told him how much room he had beneath the keel. Not a lot: the rudder often rasped along the bottom.

Applause grew as the ship passed Norfolk, but it wasn't universal. A midshipman wrote, "We found the wharves crowded with people, men and women cheering us on our way, and many of the men with serious countenances. One man, I remember, called out to us, 'Go on with your old metallic coffin! She will never amount to anything else!'"

Buchanan sent the crew to lunch, then tipped his hand to Ashton Ramsay, calling the chief engineer up from his machinery.

Ramsay came on him "pacing the deck with a stride I found it difficult to match, although he was then over sixty and I but twenty-four."

"How about your engines?" Buchanan asked. "They were in bad shape in the old ship, I understand. Can we rely on them? Should they be tested by a trial trip?"

"She will have to travel yet some ten miles down the river before we get to the Roads. If any trouble develops, I'll report it. I think that will be a sufficient trial trip."

Buchanan liked that answer. He had another question: Could the engines stand the shock if the *Merrimack* rammed?

Ramsay doubted his engines, but not their moorings. "They are braced tight. Though the boilers stand fourteen feet, they are so securely fastened that no collision could budge them."

Buchanan liked that answer too. He called the crew to their battle stations.

The mess steward tapped the engineer's elbow. "Better get your lunch now, Mr. Ramsay. It will be your last chance. The galley fires must be put out when the magazines are opened."

Ramsay went to his meal knowing this was no trial trip and realizing the sailors must have sensed the same thing. "Passing along the gun deck after the ship was cleared for action, I was particularly struck with the countenances of the guns' crews, with set lips unsmiling, contrasting with the careless expression of sailors when practiced at 'fighting quarters' on a man-of-war."

When he reached the wardroom, Ramsay found his fellow officers eating at only one end of the long table. At the other, Assistant Surgeon Algernon Garnett was setting out his blades and bone saws. When the fighting started, the wounded would be brought there.

"I had no appetite, and merely tasted some cold tongue and a cup of coffee."

Sounding strangely modern across 150 years, Ramsay tells us, "This was the real thing."

At half past one, Buchanan assembled the ship's company on

the casemate. Engineer Jack wrote, "The officers grouped upon the shield top abaft the smoke stack and the men forward. . . . The Boatswain piped all hands to muster and I placed myself touching elbows with my brother officers on the starboard side of the shield top. The men were arranged in line opposite. We knew that we had been mustered to hear the address of Captain Buchanan before we entered the fight."

A history of the Confederate Navy published in the 1880s reported the address this way: "Men, the eyes of your country are upon you. You are fighting for your rights, your liberties, your wives and children. You must not be content with only doing your duty, but do more than your duty! Those ships"—Buchanan pointed forward to where the Union fleet lay—"must be taken, and you shall not complain that I do not take you close enough. Go to your guns!"

Jack heard something quite different. In a navy, word travels as quickly as it does in any other hermetic society. "All were curious," Jack wrote, "to know how [Buchanan] would meet the insinuations that had been made against his loyalty to the Southern cause. It had been said that after he had resigned from the United States Navy to take up arms with the Confederacy, he had petitioned to be taken back again."

Jack recalled a more personal exhortation: "I heard when I came to the command of this vessel aspersion upon my loyalty and doubt of my courage and zeal. I promise you that when this day's work is over, there will be no more cause for any such unjust suspicions." Buchanan sent his men back to their fighting quarters.

Smelling like a butcher shop, steering like an oxcart, gleaming dully and potent with radical menace, the *Merrimack* steamed into Hampton Roads. "The narrows of the river were passed," wrote Jack, "and away in the distance the hulls of the enemy's squadron began to loom up."

CHAPTER 17

The Prisoner Takes Command

John Lorimer Worden did not hesitate to
become captain of the untried *Monitor*.

G eneral John Wool, in charge of Fortress Monroe—where
Isherwood had tried so hard to take the *Merrimack*—had
been worried about the ironclad since October. A successful foray
by the *Merrimack*, he wrote Lincoln, "might prove no less fatal to
the Union than to the Administration."

Wool's colleague Flag Officer Louis M. Goldsborough, head of
the North Atlantic Blockading Squadron, warned Welles that the
ship would be "exceedingly formidable," but he was more sanguine
than Wool and had worked out a plan of attack. The frigates *Congress* and *Cumberland*, on station off Newport News, would draw
the *Merrimack* into battle, while the *Roanoke* and the *Minnesota*

moved out from the protection of Monroe's guns to catch the Rebel ship between two broadsides and cut off its retreat. Although Goldsborough was eager to have the Union ironclads get launched and, as he put it to Gustavus Fox, "drive the Confederates to the moon," he thought his several wooden warships could overcome the single iron one.

The Northern press, hot with what Walt Whitman called "a fever of doubtful news," was about equally divided between Wool's pessimism and Goldsborough's confidence.

In November the *New York Tribune* said the *Merrimack*'s massive metal roof would sink her before she got near any Union ship. The *Boston Advertiser*, remembering a kind of sea warfare already invisibly slipping into obsolescence, was sure that if Northern sailors could gain as much "footing as would serve for a cat" on her deck, they would capture the ship by boarding.

The *New York Times*, though, worried that the *Merrimack* would make short work of lighter vessels such as troop transports, and "even the men-of-war themselves would be lucky if they escaped receiving a disabling shell through their great tempting timber hulls." The popular *Frank Leslie's Illustrated Newspaper* cautioned those who were jeering at the Southern ironclad that "some cool morning, we may have occasion to laugh out of the other side of our mouths."

To this stew of boastful anxiety the South added a sophisticated campaign of what decades later would be called disinformation.

On February 6, a Norfolk newspaper, the *Day Book*, reported that a grave miscalculation of how much armor the *Merrimack* could carry meant she had to be entirely rebuilt. The *Richmond Whig* said the failed warship might at least be used as a floating battery like the one that had been towed into place to shoot at Fort Sumter.

In North Carolina, the *Wilmington Journal* deplored the effort "being bungled away on the *Merrimack* and some other ruined hulks." The first reports were deliberate fabrications, but the editor of the *Journal* later admitted he had been "nicely taken in."

So was much of the North. The *New York Post* announced that the *Merrimack* had reemerged as a "sort of marine hybrid" combining the least valuable qualities of a "steam-ram and Noah's Ark. They have overloaded the hull, and the machinery of the *Merrimack* is utterly unfit for the propulsion of this marine monstrosity. If she ever appears in Hampton Roads our navy will be glad to secure her as a curiosity of marine construction."

The editor of the *Wilmington Journal* might have been misled, but Gideon Welles did not think the *Merrimack* a negligible threat, and neither did Ericsson or John Dahlgren, who wanted obstructions placed in the Elizabeth River to keep her from coming out. Commodore Smith was definitely scared. In early December, having learned that the turret was still a month away from completion, he wrote Ericsson, "I beg of you to push up the work." He reminded the engineer—who scarcely needed reminding—"You have only thirty-nine days left." And "I shall demand heavy forfeiture for delay over the stipulated time of completion." Ericsson didn't need to be reminded of that either.

Given that nothing like Ericsson's battery had ever before been built, work was actually coming along with impressive speed. On November 15, three weeks after the keel had been laid, the Navy's building superintendent allowed that $50,000 worth of progress had been made. Just a month later, the figure had risen to $150,000.

Alban C. Stimers was certifying the stages of completion. Thirty-four years old, he had joined the Navy as a third assistant engineer in 1849. An instinctive grasp of machinery helped him rise quickly to become chief engineer in less than a decade. The last US Navy man to have charge of the *Merrimack*'s impossible engines, he'd been posted to the frigate *Roanoke* when the war began.

That first generation of steam engineers was a contentious lot. Stimers's competence, like Isherwood's, came accompanied by a self-assurance so complete that it annoyed many of his line-officer colleagues. One took a swipe at the entire engineering fraternity when he said Stimers was "smart but coarse—and like all of his kind overbearing and disagreeable." Stimers shared Ericsson's temperament: brusque, touchy, combative. Fortunately for the Union, though, the two got along well and became fast friends. Knowing that on his vessel the engineer would be at least as important as the captain, Ericsson had written Smith in October that as a man "of the highest intelligence will be required for the battery, the success mainly depending on that officer as the whole is machinery, permit me to suggest Chief Engineer A. C. Stimers of the *Roanoke.*" Smith put the request to Welles, who took Stimers off the *Roanoke* and made him "Superintendent of the iron-clad vessel or Battery." In that position, he was the Navy's representative, there to make sure construction went forward properly, and to say when government money could be released. He had complete trust in Ericsson's ship from the start, but he never suspected that he would be commanding its turret in battle.

The same government on whose behalf Smith was threatening Ericsson for not being speedy enough was holding up the work through parsimony. On January 4, Ericsson wrote Smith that of the $150,000 long since approved, he had received just $37,500. Without money for a night shift, the pace began to falter. He had paid out of his own pocket and borrowed from friends to keep the workers on the job.

As the weeks went by, the hundred-day deadline became elastic, depending on how the days were counted. Even in wartime, the Greenpoint yard was silent on Sundays, so Sunday couldn't count as a contractual "day," could it?

For all the governmental fretting, there was no longer any doubt that the ship *would* be launched. The guns weren't aboard yet—or even located—when Fox wrote Ericsson asking him to suggest a name for his vessel. On January 20 the engineer replied, "In accordance with your request, I now submit for your approbation a name for the floating battery at Greenpoint. The impregnable and aggressive name of this structure will admonish the leaders of the Southern rebellion that the batteries on the banks of their rivers will no longer present barriers to the entrance of Union forces. The ironclad intruder will thus prove a severe monitor to those leaders. But there are other leaders who will also be startled and admonished by the booming of the guns from the impregnable iron turret. Downing Street will hardly view with indifference this last [latest] Yankee notion, this monitor. To the Lords of the Admiralty, the new craft will be a monitor.... On these and many similar grounds I propose to name the new battery *Monitor.*"

WHOM TO COMMAND THIS INSTRUMENT of admonition? A midlevel officer whose competent but lackluster career had taken a violent turn when he gained the unhappy distinction of becoming the first prisoner taken by either side in the Civil War.

Born in 1818 to a farming family in Westchester County, New York, John Lorimer Worden joined the Navy at sixteen and learned seamanship on a sloop of war in the South Atlantic. He was promoted to "passed midshipman"—that is, a full-fledged if junior officer—in 1840. Four years later he married and was assigned to the US Naval Observatory. The Observatory had the advantage of being in Washington, where Worden and his wife, Olivia, would live, on K Street, for the rest of their days. The disadvantage was demanding, tiresome shorebound work: scanning ships' logs and compiling charts of the weather they recorded, day by day, month by month. Worden got to sea during the Mexican War on a supply ship, then was sent back to the Naval Observatory. The meteorological drudgery was interrupted by turns of sea duty, his last before the war as the executive officer on a frigate.

He longed for a war, not through any inherent bloodlust, but because what he called "the greatest hope" of his "existence" was to rise in the Navy. War was dangerous and ugly; it was also a wonderful promotion accelerant.

On April 6, 1861, he reported back to Washington "for special duty connected with the discipline and efficiency of the naval service." Dismayed by the vague, drab-sounding posting, "I asked to be relieved from these orders and to be assigned duty afloat, which was granted."

Not right away, though. He had barely settled in on K Street when "that night near midnight I was sent for by the Secretary of the Navy who informed me that he wanted me to go at once to Pensacola with dispatches for Captain Henry A. Adams."

Captain Adams commanded a squadron standing off Fort Pickens, the last, weakly held Union outpost in seceded Florida. Adams had troops aboard his ships, and the Army captain in charge of those men held orders from Washington to put them ashore. Adams refused. In that strange state of inchoate war, a deal had been struck during the last days of President Buchanan's administration. Back in January, the North promised not to reinforce Fort Pickens so long as the South did not attack it. Adams felt he had to honor the agreement, but he didn't like it. He drafted a message to Welles saying he believed the order to land the troops had been issued with "insufficient authority" to justify "the fearful responsibility of an act which seems to render civil war inevitable." Then, giving his superior a respectful nudge, he went on to say that he stood "ready at all times to carry out whatever orders I may receive from the honorable Secretary of the Navy."

He entrusted the message to one of his officers, Washington Gwathmey. Lieutenant Gwathmey proved to be a man of honor; his sympathies lay with the Confederacy, but he smuggled the message North hidden under his shirt (in the tinderbox mood of the time, its discovery could have provoked a war as surely as landing the troops), delivered it to Welles, and, his last Federal duty done, resigned his commission and headed back South.

Welles hurried to the White House and told Lincoln he wanted to reinforce Pickens. Lincoln agreed. The Navy secretary wrote in his diary that immediate action was crucial, "but in the general demoralization and suspicion which pervaded Washington, who was to be trusted with this important mission? . . . Paymaster Etting was in Washington, and I sent for him. . . . About five o'clock he reported to me that Lieutenant John Worden had just arrived [in town], and that he would vouch for him as untainted by treason."

Welles summoned Worden and asked him to start for Pensacola at once, telling nobody, not even his wife, what was in the orders he carried. The secretary handed them over, saying that if Worden thought he was going to be searched, he must memorize their contents (which would not be difficult: land your troops now), and then shred and eat them.

Worden boarded the next mail train to begin the long journey down the Eastern Seaboard. He wore his uniform; without it he already stood a good chance of being hanged for a spy. At Atlanta, a raucous group of soldiers boarded the train. They too were headed for Pensacola and clearly weren't bound there on Federal business. Worden ducked into the car's water closet and destroyed the message (we don't know whether he did actually eat it).

When he arrived at Pensacola, four days after leaving Washington, Worden learned he must report to General Braxton Bragg, in charge of the local Confederate troops, before he could visit the Union squadron.

Bragg said, "I suppose you have a dispatch for Captain Adams?"

"No, not a written one," which was true by then, "but a verbal communication."

Bragg later insisted that Worden assured him the message was "of a pacific nature." The general wrote him out a pass; visiting privileges had been established in the January agreement.

A storm kept Worden away from the squadron's flagship for another day, but when he finally delivered his brief message, Captain Adams moved at once, and a company of the Sixth Artillery and 115 Marines joined the Pickens garrison hours later.

Adams ordered Worden back to Washington. The lieutenant feared he would be arrested as soon as Bragg got word of the reinforcement, but Adams assured him he could make the trip in safety, and Worden did until he reached Alabama.

By that time Bragg had received a dilatory communication from the Confederate War Department: "Lt. Worden of US Navy has gone to Pensacola with dispatches. Intercept them."

Too late to intercept the message, but not to seize its bearer. Two days after the batteries opened on Sumter, Worden was taken off the train at Montgomery, still the Confederate capital, marched through an angry crowd, and locked in the city jail. He was not badly treated. His warden was friendly, and the widow of a Navy officer who had known Worden in calmer times sent him baskets of food from Memphis. Still, no Alabama city jail cell was salubrious, and Worden stayed in his for seven months, his health corroding while to the North the Union Army was routed, and the *Merrimack* took shape, and the *Monitor*'s keel got put down.

The early months of the war had no machinery in place for the exchange of prisoners, but in October Flag Officer Goldsborough suggested to the Confederate naval authorities at Norfolk that Worden be swapped for a Rebel officer of equal rank captured during the operation that had taken Hatteras Inlet the past August. Worden left his Montgomery cell and on November 20, under twin flags of truce, was exchanged.

He spent a few weeks recuperating on K Street before he received, on January 11, a message from Commodore Smith. It concerned the *Monitor*. In terms similar to those Mallory had sent Buchanan about the *Merrimack*, Smith wrote, "This vessel is an experiment. I believe you are the right man to command her."

Why was this officer, whose only prominent professional achievement had been incarceration in a Southern jail, given charge of one of history's half dozen most famous warships?

Smith knew and liked Worden; Welles had been impressed by the alacrity with which he accepted his dangerous assignment to convey the Pickens message; and unlike the South, the North had more ships than it did capable men to skipper them.

Olivia Worden urged her husband to refuse the assignment. The *Monitor*'s executive officer later wrote that Worden had been a "sick man" who accepted his command "against the protests of his physicians and the entreatment of his family."

But accept it he did, and enthusiastically. As quickly as he had set off south with the Fort Pickens orders, he headed north to Manhattan, took the ferry to Greenpoint, and first saw his ship, still turretless and standing on solid ground beneath a cold January sky.

Worden understood steam propulsion—everyone in the Navy did by now—but he had never given much consideration to the idea of an iron fighting ship. What might he have thought of this somber metal lozenge that looked like no other vessel any captain had ever seen? Many perfectly brave men in Union service would have rejected it outright.

Not Worden. He immediately wrote Smith, "After a hasty examination of her, am induced to believe that she may prove a success. At all events I am quite willing to be an agent in testing her capabilities, and will readily devote whatever of capacity and energy I have to that object."

He took command of his unlaunched ship on January 16, four days before Ericsson suggested her name.

CHAPTER 18

Paymaster Keeler Comes East

A page from the Keeler family album shows the paymaster in his uniform.

The jail pallor was still on Worden when his paymaster, William Keeler, met him three weeks later and wrote, "Capt. Worden is in the regular service. He is tall, thin & quite effeminate looking, notwithstanding a long beard hanging down his breast—he is white & delicate probably from long confinement & never was a lady the possessor of a smaller or more delicate hand." Rather surprisingly, Keeler goes on to say, ". . . But if I am not very much mistaken he will not hesitate to submit our iron sides to as severe a test as the most warlike could desire."

William Frederick Keeler was a perceptive man, a lively, loquacious Midwesterner whose letters to his wife, Anna, offer not only an intimate look at life aboard the *Monitor*, but also the most immediate record we have of day-to-day service in the Civil War Navy.

Thirty years earlier, Keeler would not have been in uniform. The growing complexity of the Navy had both formed the position of paymaster and brought it up to parity with the rank of lieutenant. A clerical job, it had steadily expanded in importance. As Keeler explained his duties to Anna, "I have charge of all provisions, clothing, stationery, what are called Small Stores, such as Tobacco, Soap, candles, thread, buttons, needles, jack knives, & all the thousand & one little things a Sailor will stand in need of—besides the money. The Arms, ammunition, & Ship Stores, such as sails, cordage & the like, I have nothing to do with. My Steward's business is to give out the men's rations daily & render me an a/c [account]. Clothing, Small Stores & everything but the daily rations I issue myself."

While he was telling Anna all this, he had "not yet seen my iron home & know nothing more about it than what I hear from others, but I conclude that it is a novel looking craft."

Keeler's only previous maritime experience had been rounding the Horn on a journey to the California gold fields that proved unrewarding (but not uneventful: his two brothers died during that violent Western migration). He had, however, learned to keep careful track of a wide variety of objects, and he knew a good deal about machinery.

Born in Utica, New York, in 1821—he was forty when he joined the *Monitor*—he had, one of his sons wrote, "a roving disposition." It first brought him to Connecticut, where he met and married Anna Dutton, then to California, and finally to China before he came back to America and settled in LaSalle, a town one hundred miles west of Chicago on the Illinois River. There he built a trade as—his crowded business card records—"Watchmaker & Jeweller, Dealer in Fine Gold & Silver Watches, Jewelry, Silverware, Clocks, Looking-Glasses, Guns, Pistols, Stationery, Toys, Gilt Mouldings, Fish Tackle, Sportsmen's Materials, of every description, and Fancy Goods of all kinds." By 1857 Keeler had forsaken this commercial Golconda to become the senior partner in the "La Salle Iron Works, Founders & Machinists . . . Manufacturers of Steam Engines, Mill Gearing, Horse Powers, Corn Shellers, Coal Cars, Stoves, Iron Railing & Machinery of all kinds, Brass & Iron Casings . . ." The workings of the *Monitor* would not have intimidated him.

Forty was old to begin a military career, but Keeler thought slavery a "hideous deformity," and his anger at the "traitorous and wretched souls" of the secessionists, coupled with that roving disposition, got him to pull strings—Anna's father was friendly with Cornelius Bushnell—to become an "Acting Assistant Paymaster and Clerk." On January 4, Welles signed orders summoning him to New York.

Eight days later, Keeler sent Anna the first installment of what would become a highly entertaining war-long Iliad.

". . . To begin at the beginning—I took a Sleeping Car at the Rock Island depot, got a good double berth to myself, in a few minutes heard them call out Ottawa, have a very indistinct recollection of something being said about Morris & the next thing of which I was conscious was a vigorous shake" from the porter "with the announcement that we were 'most to Chicago,' accompanied with the modest demand of ten cents for blacking the gentleman's boots."

Keeler got out of his berth "feeling much refreshed & at ½ past 5 found myself in Chicago. I took a ticket for N.Y. via Lake Shore and Erie R.R. paying $24.00, making the fare through $27.00." That was pretty hefty, the equivalent of perhaps $750 today, but Uncle Sam was paying. "At Six we started for New York. In the evening we were at Toledo where we changed cars & went

to Cleveland, changed again—took a narrow top shelf in a sleeping car & on the morning found myself in Buffalo after a good
night's sleep." But he'd missed his connection for New York by half
an hour, and checked into a railroad hotel, "a slow drizzling mist
Keeping me in the house most of the day."

He caught a 7:00 PM train "for N.Y., at Hornelsville laid myself
away on a shelf for the night." By noon the next day he was on
"the Jersey City ferry for N.Y., the boat grinding her way through
masses of floating ice with which the harbor was filled.

"As soon as we landed I made my way across the city & from
there to the [Brooklyn] Navy Yard. . . . At the entrance to the Yard
I was stopped by a guard who demanded my business."

Keeler said he'd been ordered to report to Commodore Hiram
Paulding, who had charge of the yard, and "was referred to the
Sergeant of the guard who told me to pass and directed me to
the Commodore's office which I found filled with men & officers,
getting orders, signing passes, &c." Keeler approached a desk. "I
made my business known to one of the Clerks who entered my
name in two or three different books, then turned me over to another who entered my name again in as many more." The flurry of
record keeping completed, the recorder "endorsed the time of my
reporting on the back of my dispatch, then sent me back to Clerk
No. 1, who told me that the Commodore's signature was needed
on my papers."

Commodore Paulding wasn't there. Keeler, threading his way
through a routine that any junior officer seeking his post in World
War II—or on the eve of Desert Storm—would recognize, finally
got to Commander John Almy, "a frank, blunt sort of sailor man."

Almy glanced over Keeler's papers and said, "Oh, Paymaster
Keeler. Glad to see you, sir. Where are you from, sir?"

Keeler told him Illinois.

Almy, looking "a little surprised," said, "Well, we don't get a
great many sailors from the prairies out there."

Keeler pertly responded that "folks there were doing their duty
on land."

Confederate artillerymen in the Charleston Harbor floating battery during the bombardment of Fort Sumter on April 12, 1861. The iron-faced precursor to the CSS *Merrimack* shed every Yankee shot.

Lincoln's "Old Father Neptune," Secretary of the Navy Gideon Welles. He soon became worried about Confederate ironclads, but at first didn't know how to counter them.

DESTRUCTION OF THE UNITED STATES NAVY-YARD AT NORI

UNITED STATES.   TUG YANKEE.   CUMBERLAND.   MERRIMAC.

DESTRUCTION OF THE UNITED STATES SHIPS AT THE N

Norfolk, the North's crucial Virginia naval installation, commits fiery suicide on April 20, 1861. At top, the ship houses burn; below, much of the US fleet perishes. The three-decker

BY FIRE, BY THE UNITED STATES TROOPS, ON APRIL 20, 1861.

PENNSYLVANIA.

-YARD, BY ORDER OF THE GOVERNMENT.—[SEE PAGE 294.]

[SEE PAGE 294.]

to the right is the 140-gun ship of the line *Pennsylvania*, the largest sail-driven warship ever built in America.

What the Confederates found at Norfolk when they took over the ruined yard. Despite the widespread destruction, they captured a huge amount of matériel and hundreds of heavy guns.

Abraham Lincoln in 1862. As a young man he had learned a lot about the buoyancy of ships while serving as a bow hand on Mississippi River flatboats, and he saw earlier than most the need for Union ironclads.

MAKING GUNS FOR THE NEW MONITORS AT PITTSBURG, PENNSYLVANIA.—Sketched by Mr. Theodore R. Davis.—[See Page 535.]

The evolving monitors demanded ever-heavier guns, and the Fort Pitt Foundry in Pittsburgh made many of them. By war's end the immense works had produced 60 percent of the Union's cannon.

The photographer James Gibson came aboard the *Monitor* in the summer of 1862 and posed her officers in front of the turret. William Keeler stands in the back row, wearing glasses; Lewis Stodder sits at the far left in the second row, Samuel Dana Greene to the extreme right.

John Ericsson was one of the most popular men in the United States when he had this imposing portrait made in a New York photographic studio soon after the battle.

The *Monitor*'s first captain, John Lorimer Worden, seemingly not justifying Keeler's impression that he was "effeminate."

Looking forward along the *Monitor*'s deck: Second Assistant Engineer Albert Campbell, left, and Lieutenant William Fly observe the effect of Confederate shot on the turret. Beyond is the pilot house, newly outfitted with sloping sides.

The crew passes a hot, quiet July day on the James River. One hand reads a newspaper while others pay close attention to a game of checkers.

The galley steams topside preparing a warm-weather lunch; one of the ship's African American crewmen squats in the foreground.

DESTRUCTION OF THE CONFEDERATE IRONCLAD "MERRIMAC," BLOWN UP BY HER COMMANDER, MAY 11, 1862.
FROM A SKETCH TAKEN FROM CRANEY ISLAND.

WORDEN

BANKHEAD

LOSS OF THE "MONITOR" IN A STORM OFF CAPE HATTERAS, DECEMBER 30, 1862.—GALLANT EFFORTS TO RESCUE THE CREW
BY THE "RHODE ISLAND."

The end of the two antagonists. Above, the *Merrimack* explodes off Craney Island, Virginia, on May 11, 1862. Months later, the doomed, sinking *Monitor* struggles to stay afloat in a gale while boats from the side-wheeler *Rhode Island* try to take off her crew.

"Yes, glad to hear it. Ever been to sea?"

Keeler gave him a firm yes, but Almy probably guessed the sea time had been logged as a passenger when Keeler asked if it was necessary to get a uniform; he would feel more comfortable in the clothes he'd brought East with him.

Almy snapped, "Not at all, not at all, get a uniform before you go to sea." Taking pity on the landlubber, he added, "We will let you rest a while before you go."

Yet the Navy had apparently already seeped into Keeler's spirit. After Almy put his name to them, the papers had to further feed bureaucracy's maw with an infinitude of countersignings, and "I was introduced to quite a number of the officers in the different offices I went into & was much pleased with their looks & appearance—'First impressions' are good at any rate. There appeared to be more real earnestness of purpose & less of that swagger & bluster & rowdyism about them than among many of the land officers I have met with."

He had to stop once again at Clerk No. 1's desk before his office round ended, but Keeler didn't mind that at all because the clerk "gave me an order on the Navy Agent in N.Y. for my traveling allowance at the rate of 10 cents per mile. As the distance cannot be less than 1000 miles," he stood to clear nearly seventy-five 1861 dollars on his train trip.

Keeler obediently acquired a uniform (and, to his irritation, a dress sword: "the regulations require it so I had to go to the expense of $16.00 for one of those useless toys"). He would wear Navy blue for the next five years, but at the outset told his wife that although "bright handsome uniforms are so common here that scarcely any notice is taken of them[,] I felt awkward enough at first in mine, it seemed as if everyone was looking at me, but I am getting used to it now." As he became more comfortable in his new clothes, Keeler met his girlish but warlike captain and his fellow officers. "Mr. Green, Our lieutenant is a young man also in the regular service, black hair & eyes that look through a person & will carry out his orders I have no doubt."

Mr. Green was Samuel Dana Greene, and he *was* young, just shy of his twenty-second birthday. A Marylander who had graduated seventh in his class from Annapolis in 1859, he began his naval career on Farragut's future flagship. The sloop of war *Hartford* was in Chinese waters when Sumter surrendered, so far from home that it took her nine months to get back to Philadelphia. Once there, in December 1861, Greene volunteered for the *Monitor.* That he was chosen as her second-in-command so early in his career is another reflection of how thin spread the Navy was just then.

Still, Worden wanted him and told Smith so. On January 23 Smith wrote Stimers saying, "Lt. Green will be ordered today. Lt. Worden applied for him." Then, having expanded the circle of those privileged to hear his ever-renewed doubts to include Stimers, Smith added, "A good deal of wonderment and many surmises are afloat."

Whatever worries Worden may have held about his ship—and he did have some—he made a shrewd and careful assessment of its manning requirements. "In estimating the number of her crew," he wrote Welles, "I allowed 15 men and a quarter gunner for the two guns, 11 men for the powder division, and 1 for the wheel, which I deem ample for the efficient working of her guns in action. That would leave 12 men (including those available in the engineering department) to supply deficiencies at the guns, caused by sickness or casualties."

This was modern thinking. Worden saw his engineers' primary function as tending machinery, and only a distant second one to stand in as fighting sailors. And there would be a lot of engineers. On a sailing ship with auxiliary steam, the total number of them ranged from 10 to 20 percent of the ship's company. On the *Monitor*, the figure was closer to 40 percent.

Captain Worden turned out to be fortunate in his chief engineer, who had arrived in New York more than a month earlier. He bore the reassuring name of Isaac Newton and had won Stimers's strong approval while serving with him aboard the *Roanoke.* Newton had been watching the *Monitor* under construction, and he liked everything he'd seen. He shared Ericsson's conviction that

a steam plant on a sailing vessel—which described half the significant fighting ships in the Navy—was an archaism. "In all vessels
now being built for the navy," he wrote, "speed under steam is the
sine qua non; the hallucination of *auxiliary steam power* has been
exploded." For him, masts and sails were auxiliary to steam, rather
than the other way around, and at best should be done away with
altogether. Even so, Newton encountered drawbacks on his new,
entirely rigging-free ship. "As there are no sails and ropes on the
Monitor, the spare time this deficiency gives the first Lieut. causes
me very great annoyance."

WORDEN HAD TO FIND A crew. Welles, fearing this might
prove time-consuming and difficult, wrote that if volunteers were
not forthcoming, he would draft enough men. He needn't have
worried. The ship of the line *North Carolina* and the frigate *Sabine*
were in New York Harbor (the former was never going anywhere
else; launched in 1820, she had been immobile for more than
twenty years, a receiving ship housing sailors pending assignment).
Worden went aboard both and spoke about the *Monitor* to their
assembled crews in forthright terms: "I won't draft any of you
for service on that thing. I can't promise to get you to Hampton
Roads, but if I ever do, I think she will do good service." Not the
tenor of Shakespeare's King Harry encouraging his soldiers before
Agincourt, but it worked: more men stepped forward to volunteer
than Worden had room for.

A very different crowd from the largely homogenous crew of
the *Merrimack*, the *Monitor*'s men were a microcosm of the dispa-
rate elements alloyed into the Northern war effort.

More than a third came from the tides of immigration that
had flowed into the country in recent years: three from Germany,
among them Master's Mate George Frederickson (Keeler thought
him "a good honest Dutchman"), one from Alaska, another from
Quebec, four from England, one from Austria, a Scott named
Fenwick, three Swedes, and many whose families had been driven

from Ireland by the potato famine of little more than a decade earlier: Garety (or Garetty, Garrety, or Garity), Hannan, Connelly, Joice, Malone, Mooney, Egan, Driscoll, Quinn . . . Others were from earlier arrivals that had settled in Baltimore, Boston, Philadelphia, Portland, Syracuse; five enlisted from New York City, three from the *Monitor*'s natal Brooklyn.

Some were black. During the *Monitor*'s life a tenth of her crew were African-American; that's a close reflection of their percentage in the national population, and it is remarkable. The US Navy seems to have been one of the more advanced social forces in the country during the early 1860s. Years would pass before black soldiers were permitted to join Union forces in the field, but the Navy recruited them from the start. In part this speaks to tradition—a quarter of Oliver Hazard Perry's crew at the Battle of Lake Erie in 1813 were African-American—and part is pragmatism: on land only the ability to shoulder a musket mattered at the outset; sea service demanded more specific skills. Mere utility, though, doesn't account for a Navy man, Robert Blake, becoming the first African-American to win the Medal of Honor. He worked a gun that drove the Confederates away from their shore battery during a hard-fought battle on Christmas Day 1863.

This is not to say that the Navy was the Peaceable Kingdom. Aboard the USS *Brazileira* some of the white complement mounted a skit called "Nigger Serenade" and augmented the hilarity with "Nigger in a Daguerreotype Gallery." The septic little theatrical so poisoned the shipboard atmosphere that the captain had to transfer his African-American sailors to another vessel to avoid violence.

But such incitements were the exception. The black and white crewmen of the *Monitor* lived together with no record of any friction; Worden never had to cope with internal ructions on his ship. After the war he said of his crew, "A better one no naval commander ever had the honor to command."

CHAPTER 19

Like a Duck

The *Monitor* slides into the East River on January 30, 1862;
in fact, she did not yet have her turret.

That crew's ship was still standing on Brooklyn soil while they
assembled. When Lewis N. Stodder, one of the two acting
masters, was studying the *Monitor* at Rowland's yard, a fellow on-
looker remarked, "You had better take a good look at her now, as
you won't see her after she strikes the water. She's bound to go to
the bottom of the East River and stick there, sure."

Although he'd built her, Thomas Rowland shared the man's
doubts. Probably at his own expense, he had a large watertight
wooden cradle constructed beneath the *Monitor*'s stern to help
buoy her as she slid down the ways into her new element.

That was just about to happen. With Rowland's flotation device
in place, his part was over.

Thursday, January 30, 1862, was, according to Smith's exacting calculations, eighteen days after the deadline he'd set had expired. However those working days might be tallied, they had witnessed a prodigious feat of engineering. The *Monitor* was ready to be launched.

No public announcement had been made of the event, but rumor's busy telegraph summoned a substantial crowd to Rowland's works that morning. Some came warm with patriotism; others were there to lay bets that the ship would behave just the way Stodder's bystander had predicted.

John Ericsson, as always, was confident. No small, fidgety corporal's guard stood on the *Monitor*'s deck as at the *Merrimack*'s launching. Ericsson had posted himself twenty feet in from the stern, with Captain Worden and Lieutenant Greene at attention beside him.

A little before ten o'clock, workmen lifted sledgehammers and knocked away chocks and braces. The low dark hull shuddered, inched forward, picked up speed. The yardmen jumped back as the sharp bow shoveled up several hundred gallons of East River brine and, rising, shrugged it away. Sliding out from Rowland's cautious carpentry, the stern dipped and lifted and steadied. A correspondent from the *New York World* wrote that it "was very evident even to the dullest observer that the battery hadn't the least intention of sinking." The battery was drawing even less water than its creator had predicted, her 660-odd tons (the turret would add some 120 more) bringing her bottom down just eleven feet and four inches below the surface, and leaving only eighteen inches of freeboard. The boast Ericsson had made to the Ironclad Board three months earlier turned out to be justified: the *Monitor* rode in the river like a duck.

As the ship calmly accustomed itself to the gentle swell, steam whistles on harbor craft began to blurt and shrill, and everyone— even those who had lost their bets—cheered. The oarsmen in a rowboat that had prudently been standing by to retrieve Ericsson and the officers from the river pulled back to the shore, while line handlers drew the ship alongside its dock. Ericsson climbed down from the deck and went to speak to reporters. They asked him about the *Merrimack*. With what for him was becoming humility, he said he *thought* the *Monitor* could sink her in a few minutes. No matter what, he added, his ship could stand hours of cannon fire from any earthly source.

GUSTAVUS FOX WIRED ERICSSON, "I congratulate you and trust she will be a success. Ready her for sea, as the *Merrimack* is nearly ready at Norfolk and we wish to send her there."

She wouldn't have done much good there in her present state, despite her triumphant buoyancy. The turret was still missing, and so were the guns.

But for all Ericsson's frustrations, things were moving swiftly now. Six hours after the *Monitor* didn't sink, the components of the turret had been piled on her deck. And that same day, Ericsson learned that he would be getting his guns.

They had already caused him considerable vexation. He'd long known he couldn't get the fifteen-inch ones he deemed ideal and had planned for twelve-inch Dahlgrens. Now it was looking as if he would have to settle for eleven-inch. No matter what their bore, he wanted the muzzles cut back eighteen inches so the cannon could more easily be handled inside the turret. Like so much else, this alarmed Commodore Smith. He believed the barrels could be shortened only at the expense of accuracy, and he suspected Ericsson of asking for the modification because he'd made the turret too small. "My object and my pride," Smith wrote, "is fixed in these XI inch guns. I cannot agree to shorten them and would not like to ask Dahlgren's consent to do so, knowing he would object to it."

Stimers backed Ericsson. The whole point of this ship, he argued, was that cannon fire couldn't harm it. It had been designed for close fighting, so "the greater accuracy at long ranges, secured by the greater length, would very seldom be available, whereas, the convenience and consequent rapidity of loading the shorter length, would add to the effectiveness of the vessel at every discharge of the guns."

Ericsson lost that fight, and Dahlgren himself raised another complication that would have greater ramifications than barrel length. The specter of the *Princeton* explosion still hovered over the service all these years later. Although Dahlgren had designed his eleven-inch cannon to take a thirty-pound powder charge, he asked—and the Navy ordered—that no more than fifteen pounds be loaded into the guns.

At least those guns were finally on the way. The USS *Dacotah*, doubtless to her captain's dismay, was deprived of two eleven-inch Dahlgrens, good pieces cast just two years earlier.

The turret that would house them was still a week and a half away from completion when, the day after the launching, Worden fired the boilers for the first time. That went satisfactorily. Steam was the life of the ship; steam not only powered the vessel and its turret, but also kept it dry—with big Worthington and Adams pumps—and warm.

On February 13 Keeler wrote Anna, "Yesterday I saw my iron home for the first time" and "you may rest assured that your *better half* will be in no more danger from rebel compliments than if he was seated with you at home."

Two days later the yard turned Keeler's iron home over to the Navy for trials. On the seventeenth the completed turret was tested and performed nobly. The single engineer at his controls put in the clutch, and twenty-five pounds of steam pressure rotated 120 tons of turret at a sure if stately pace of one revolution every twenty-two and a half seconds.

The first modest sea trial did not go so well. On February 19, Captain Worden ordered the anchor raised and headed out into the East River. Ericsson said the *Monitor* would steam at nine knots; she made three.

After a disconsolate return to the dock, Stimers found that the controversy about when to cut off steam to a cylinder that had long ago embroiled Isherwood was still pertinent. The superintendent of DeLamater Iron Works, the trusted company that had built the engines, had set the cutoff valves so that they stopped the flow of steam when the pistons were only halfway through their stroke. Half the stroke meant half the power. Ericsson was only half surprised; he had been disappointed in his hope that the DeLamater superintendent was "too stupid to make a mistake."

Back from the brief, bad cruise, Worden was further frustrated to receive an order from Welles telling him to "proceed with the USS *Monitor*, under your command, to Hampton Roads, Virginia." His ship was in no condition to proceed as far as Coney Island. The problem, however, turned out to have been one of inept implementation rather than of bad design, requiring only some readjustment of the valves. Stimers and Ericsson quickly corrected it.

On the twenty-fourth Ericsson impatiently wrote Gustavus Fox, "We fully expected that the vessel would have been put in commission today but Captain Worden, whose health and energy are not equal to the occasion, does not think his arrangements sufficiently advanced. Mr. Blunt, whom Captain Worden employs to regulate the compass, appears to me altogether too slow. Commodore Paulding has given peremptory orders to hasten everything, yet the nice system of doing work in the yard is not calculated to forward matters."

The next day, with the *Monitor*'s machinery presumably in good order, the Navy took full possession of her. At least on paper: the final 25 percent of the payment had been withheld by the contractual mandate that the ship prove itself under enemy fire, and the backers had received a fraction of the reimbursement already promised them. Nonetheless, on February 25, 1862, Ericsson's battery was commissioned as the third-rate (a reflection of its size, not governmental contempt) steamer USS *Monitor.*

She steamed over to the Brooklyn Navy Yard and began to take aboard her crew.

"Well here I am, dear Anna," Keeler wrote that same day, "on ship board at last in my little cubby hole of a state room, Small but nicely furnished. My boy has made my bed but it has a full wheelbarrow load of books, blanks, paper, bundles, boxes, bottles of ink, &c, &c, deposited on top which has got to be removed to their proper plans before I can turn in, for there is no place to lay them outside till morning. I am full of *write* but unfortunately the time is wanting as we are to start tomorrow morning."

They didn't.

On the twenty-eighth Keeler told Anna, "When I last wrote you everything was hurry and confusion on board expecting to start immediately. Powder, shot, shell, grape & canister were taken on board in abundance [along with 80 tons of coal] & I had made, as I supposed, my last visit ashore as we were under sailing orders & were to leave the same day, but our preparations were so numerous we were delayed till the next morning (yesterday) when our hawsers were cast loose & we were on our way to Hampton Roads."

Everything went wrong, including the weather, which served up a blinding snowstorm. Through it, Keeler reported, "We ran first to the New York side then to Brooklyn & so back and forth across the river, first to one side and then to the other." This was not a result of Worden's testing his ship's agility. The *Monitor* staggered about "like a drunken man on a side walk, till we brought up against the gas works [on the Brooklyn shore] with a shock that nearly took us from our feet." The ship "would not answer her helm at all"—Keeler had picked up proper nautical language in no time—"so we took a tow back to the Yard & we are now waiting for alterations in her steering apparatus. . . . All are getting impatient & want to get alongside the *Merrimac*—still I should not be surprised if we met with further delays & eventually were obliged to have a new rudder."

That's what Commodore Paulding wanted. He proposed to haul the ship out of the water and hang a better one. Later Ericsson wrote, "I was all but ordered by the government officials to *change the rudder.* Knowing the perfect proportions of it I got so angry at being thus importuned that I told them I would be damned before I did." At the time he merely barked, "The *Monitor* is mine, and I say it shall not be done! They would waste a month in doing that; I will make her steer as easily in three days."

February gave way to March as Ericsson and Stimers rigged pulleys between the tiller and the steering-wheel drum. They said they'd solved the problem, that now the ship could turn handily.

Worden asked the Navy Department to send a commission to be on hand during the ship's next trial. It is a rare captain who wants a commission on his deck, and naturally it angered Ericsson, but one can sympathize with Worden's caution. Accordingly, Flag Officer Gregory, Chief Engineer Garvin, and Naval Constructor Hartt were on hand when, on the afternoon of March 3, as Stodder recorded in the log, "2:15 with 30 lbs steam making 50 Revolutions turned with helm hard a starboard turned in 4 min 15 sec within a compass 3 times her length & proceeded towards the yard against a strong ebb tide vessel going at the maximum speed of 6 & ¼ knots an hour."

The steering worked, but now the guns made trouble. Parked under the loom of the Jersey Palisades—the *Monitor* had made it to the Hudson River—the gunners loaded and fired for the first time. Ericsson's tireless chief draftsman, Charles MacCord, who knew the *Monitor* nearly as well as its creator did, explained, "The friction for taking up [that is, damping] the recoil was produced by means of two levers, actuated by a screw, with a handwheel at the side of the gun carriages. Since there were two guns, pointing in the same direction, with very little space between them, the handwheels were, of course, placed on the outer side of the gun carriages."

This arrangement naturally suggested "that the whole mechanism was right-handed for one and left-handed for the other." That is, the trainers of the two guns must turn their handles in opposite directions. "But this was not so; in order to save time, it was made the same for each."

Still testy about that initial firing many years later, MacCord continued, "Chief Engineer Stimers, by whom the first trial was conducted, would seem not to have made himself acquainted under the construction here adopted. Grasping the handwheel on gun No. 1, he turned it *to the right* [MacCord's indignation smolders in those italics] until the resistance in his judgment indicated a proper degree of compression, and gave the order to fire."

MacCord's description of what followed is full of levers and supporting brackets and such, but the result was that "the great weapon gave a sullen roar, and, being entirely free, flew back until it was stopped by the cascabel [a melodic old word for the knob on the end of a cannon] striking against the interior of the turret."

MacCord's pique seems justified by what happened next. "One would imagine the experience sufficient to inspire caution; but, curiously enough, Engineer Stimers seems to have concluded that what was thus proved wrong for one was exactly the correct thing for the other. And so, without looking under the gun to see what was there and make sure of what he was really doing, he at once proceeded to experiment with gun No. 2 in the same manner, and with precisely the same results." Stimers had, in minutes, disabled both (which is to say, all) the *Monitor*'s guns.

Stimers here displayed the cocky certitude that annoyed so many who served with him. But the engineer's arrogance stood on a firm foundation; a few days later he would save the *Monitor* and all aboard her.

The turret crew reseated the guns, Stimers figured out the perversities of those handwheels, and they tried again. This time Master's Mate George Frederickson was able to report, "First of firing blank cartridges, second a stand of grape [walnut-size balls blasted as from a giant shotgun], canister [a bucketful of musket bullets] with a full charge of powder." The guns remained on their carriages, their cascabels clear of the turret wall.

By day's end, the hastily convened commission pronounced the ship, although a knot or two slower than promised, "in all respects satisfactory."

It did not satisfy two sailors named John Atkins and Norman McPherson: that night they stole the ship's boat that the *Monitor*

kept on her deck and, according to the log, "left for parts unknown."
Most of the crew, though, believed the *Monitor* had done well. The
officers held a celebratory banquet, which turned out to be about
as successful as that first, veering trip down the East River.

Keeler reported to Anna, "Commodore Gregory & other
notables from the Yard were with us & arrangements were made
on board to give them a dinner suited to the occasion. The pre-
liminaries were all right, but unfortunately we found upon seating
ourselves at the table that 'the wisest plans of mice & men gang
aft aglee' (I don't know as the quotation is right, you may correct
it if it isn't) for to sum it up in one short sentence, the Steward,
upon whom it all depended was drunk. I suppose he had been testing the brandy & Champaine before putting it on the table." The
steward, Daniel Moore, committed such enormities as serving the
fish "before we had finished the soup, & Champaine glasses were
furnished us to drink our brandy from & vice versa."

The succession of mishaps—during the trials, not the dinner—
gave the *Monitor*'s men time to get acquainted with their novel surroundings. The officers' quarters, though comfortably outfitted,
were minute, and—for the first time since artillery went to sea—
at the bow rather than the stern. The space behind staterooms
and wardroom, all sixteen by twenty-five feet of it, was home to
forty-nine of the crew. They slung their hammocks from overhead
hooks, although only about half the hammocks contained sleepers
at any given time; the rest of the men were up and about on watch.

Light was scarce. Alvah Hunter, who served aboard the *Nahant*,
a second-generation monitor, described the eerie glow cast by the
"deadlights" in the deck. They "were made of circular plates of
thick glass enclosed in metal frames, which were hinged on one
side and secured in place by a stout thumb-screw at the opposite
side. There was a beveled edge around the metal frame of the light,
which shut against and into a rubber gasket set into the deadlight
frame, and this gasket was supposed to make the deadlight watertight. . . . The water flowing across the deck when we were at
sea, and waves flowing over, caused very curious and interesting

lighting effects in the rooms beneath. The water twisted about and boiled in the deadlight-cavity, and, being more or less charged with air bubbles, the constantly changing shades of green light were a pleasure to study." The feeble light, which would be extinguished entirely by iron disks when battle approached, needed help. "Whenever I write," said Keeler, "day or night in my state room, I have to use a candle, it is so dark. My little deck light lets in light enough for all purposes except reading and writing."

Along with getting used to living in aqueous twilight, everyone aboard had to master the intricacies of flushing the heads. When the ship's surgeon got the valve sequence wrong, water pressure threw him off his seat while blasting the contents of the bowl up into his face.

Floating in its bath of limitless winter chill, the iron ship was debilitatingly cold. To Anna's question about what seafaring life was like, Keeler replied, "I have made the discovery that there are some things about it not very romantic, such as getting up as we did this morning & eating breakfast with the Ther.[mometer] in the ward room at 35°, shivering so that one can hardly find the way to his mouth. My first night on board was spent between a pair of linen sheets—if I have an enemy I wish him no greater ill than to be similarly situated with the surrounding temperature at freezing. . . . As you may suppose, the next night I discarded bed *linen* & substituted *cotton* & piled on top every movable thing in my room except the iron safe."

Soon radiators would be installed, and Keeler's nights improve, but at first officers and crew alike moved close to the furnaces whenever they could.

George Geer, a fireman recently transferred from the *North Carolina*, wrote his wife, "It is so cold we almost freese nights and I am most frose writing this Lettor."

The twenty-five-year-old Geer had just signed up for a three-year hitch with the Navy. He and his wife, Martha, lived on Pitt Street, a tenement block just off Delancey on Manhattan's Lower East Side. Although determined to do his duty, Geer was tantalized by the sight of his home, clearly visible to him behind the mesh of harbor-craft rigging whenever he could emerge from this new belowdecks life. "I tride very hard to get on shore today but could not."

Instead, Martha came to him, for the novel weapon was open to anyone who cared to visit Brooklyn. She brought her husband a bag of clothing. He gave her a month's pay, which was welcome, as they'd seen precious little money in the years since he'd abandoned his father's stove foundry back in Troy, New York.

Geer complained about the coldness of his quarters (though he liked the quarters themselves: "Our ship is much more comfortable than the old *North Carolina*") on March 2. All that week Captain Worden received orders to get moving. "Weather permitting," Flag Officer Paulding appended, and weather at last did so on the morning of March 6. A storm had blown itself out the night before; at about eleven o'clock Worden gave the order to up anchor and get under way.

By then, the *Monitor* had already acquired a nickname: "cheesebox on a raft." The tag still clings to it decades after the cheesebox has disappeared from the American visual lexicon. The name was humorous, but its suggestion of gimcrack ineffectuality contains a pinch of anxiety. John Dahlgren spoke with no amusement at all when he first saw the ship afloat and thought it "a mere speck, a hat upon the water."

The Navy was nervous enough about the *Monitor* to put consorts around her lest she suddenly founder. As she made her way downstream, Worden passed a four-hundred-foot towline to the tug *Seth Low*. Two gunboats, the *Currituck* and the *Sachem*, joined the little flotilla.

Whatever comfort they offered was blighted by the ship's send-off. John Driscoll, one of the *Monitor*'s Irishmen, wrote, "It was customary at that time when a craft was going on the blockade for the crew of the receiving ship *North Carolina* to man the netting and give the departing vessel three cheers, as she passed down the Bay, also for the ferry boats and other steam craft to toot there [*sic*] whistles a parting salute. No[t] so when the *Monitor* started out. As we passed the *North Carolina* not a head was seen above the rail not a whistle sounded to cheer us as we went out. Those we passed seemed to think it would be better to have played the funeral dirge than to have given us the customary cheer."

The *Monitor*, quite literally cheerless, plugged along past Sandy Hook and out into the Atlantic as light drained from the brief day. The Navy hadn't designed her; the Navy hadn't built her; the Navy hadn't paid for her: she still belonged to a Swedish engineer and a couple of Connecticut businessmen. But she was on her way to fight the Navy's war.

CHAPTER 20

A Visit to Lincoln

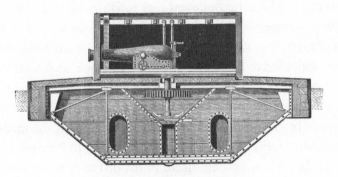

A midship cross section of the *Monitor*.
Lincoln had more faith in the turret and its two guns
than did his most trusted naval aide, Gustavus Fox.

Early the next morning Gustavus Fox took his Treasury friend Lucius Chittenden along with him to see Lincoln. The President greatly enjoyed the assistant secretary and always welcomed him. Lincoln could relax in Fox's presence and often came to his home at odd hours to chat and drape his long frame over the furniture. Virginia, Fox's wife, wrote of one such visit, "He distorts his features terribly & throws himself around promiscuously." Before she and her sister Minna entered the room to serve tea that day, "Gus said he had been full length on the sofa!"

This Friday morning, though, the visit had been arranged beforehand. "No one else was present at our interview with the President," Chittenden wrote, "and I cannot now undertake to give the precise words used, but the substance of the conversation I shall probably never forget." After that cautionary remark, he goes on to quote Lincoln at great length.

Chittenden reconstructed the conversation years later, and yet what he reports the President as saying has an unmistakable Lincolnesque tenor.

The talk was all of Hampton Roads. "Captain Fox was an officer of infinite coolness and self-command," said Chittenden, yet that day he was visibly troubled. He "observed that, from his latest information, which he believed was reliable, he did not expect that the *Merrimac* would make her appearance before Sunday, the 9th of March. She might, however, come out at any time, for her engines appeared to be working well at the dock, and, so far as his agent could discover, her armor was completed, and the work still going on was not connected with her motive-power or with her batteries. He said that he wanted to be there when she made her attack." After telling Lincoln he planned to go to Newport News the next day, "Captain Fox, quite in his ordinary tone, observed that he supposed that the President was prepared for very disastrous results from the expected encounter."

"No, why should I be?" asked Lincoln. "We have three of our most effective war-vessels in Hampton Roads, and any number of small craft that will hang on to the stern of the *Merrimac* like small dogs on the haunches of a bear. They may not be able to tear her down, but they will interfere with the comfort of her voyage. Her trial-trip will not be a pleasure-trip, I am certain."

Fox said the President wasn't taking "into account all the possibilities of the *Merrimac*. True, she may break down, she may accomplish nothing, she may not be shot-proof, but she will be commanded by a skilled naval officer. The engineers who have had charge of her construction are as competent as any in their profession. If they risk her in action, you may be sure she will do good work."

Now, on the eve of the ship's new career, the two men recapitulated all the worries and hopes of the North.

"Suppose she does," said Lincoln. "Have we not three good ships against her?"

True, said Fox. "But if she proves invulnerable? Suppose our heaviest shot and shell rebound from her armor harmless as rubber balls? Suppose she strikes our ships, one after the other, with her ram, and opens a hole in them as large as a barn door or a turnpike gate? Suppose they are powerless to resist her, and she sinks them all in a half-hour?"

Chittenden remembered Lincoln smiling then. "You are looking for great disasters, captain. We have had a big share of bad luck already, but I do not believe the future has any such misfortunes in store for us as you anticipate."

That irked Fox. "I anticipate nothing which may not happen from the coming encounter, nor have I mentioned the worst possibilities. If the *Merrimac* proves invulnerable, if she meets the expectations of her officers, although she may not be able to go outside the capes, she can do an immense damage without going to sea. If she sinks our ships, who is to prevent her dropping her anchor in the Potomac, where that steamer lies"—Fox pointed to a ship moored in plain sight in the river—"and throwing her hundred-pound shells into this room, or battering down the walls of the Capitol?"

Chittenden said the President replied, "The Almighty." Lincoln almost never voiced the complacent certainty that God was his ally, but the rest of his answer sounds more like him: "I expect setbacks, defeats; we have had them and shall have them. They are common to all wars. But I have not the slightest fear of any result which shall fatally impair our military and naval strength."

Fox felt he had to say, "I do most sincerely hope you are right, Mr. President," before immediately adding, "But it is my duty, as one of your officers, to use to the best advantage my own judgment as well as the materials which the country places in our hands. The iron-clad is a new element in naval warfare. . . . Frankly, we cannot even guess what the *Merrimac* will do."

"Speaking of iron-clads," said Lincoln, "you do not seem to take our little *Monitor* into the account. I believe in the *Monitor*, and her commander. If captain Worden does not give a good account of the *Monitor* and himself, I shall have made a mistake in following

my judgment for the first time since I have been here, captain."
This last, if Lincoln actually said anything like it, would have been
humorous self-mockery; no man of his stature ever more readily
admitted to having made mistakes.

Fox held firm. "It is not prudent to place any reliance on the
Monitor. She is an experiment, wholly untried. She may be already
at the bottom of the ocean. . . . We know nothing about her. She
may not have stood heavy weather at all, and we have had strong
gales since she sailed. She is very liable to break down; she went
to sea without one thorough trial-trip, when she should have had
several. We ought not to be disappointed if she does not reach the
mouth of the James. If she arrives, she may break down with the
firing of her first gun, or be sunk or disabled by the first gun from
the enemy. The clear dictate of prudence is to place no reliance
on her."

For the first time in the discussion Lincoln replied with some
asperity. "No, no, captain. I respect your judgment, as you have
good reason to know, but this time you are all wrong. The *Monitor* was one of my inspirations; I believed in her firmly when that
energetic contractor first showed me Ericsson's plans. Captain Ericsson's plain but rather enthusiastic demonstration made my conversion permanent. It was called a floating battery then; I called it
a raft. I caught some of the inventor's enthusiasm, and it has been
growing upon me. I thought then, and I am confident now, it is just
what we want. I am sure that the *Monitor* is still afloat, and that
she will yet give a good account of herself."

Lincoln paused and then came up with a biblical reference, the
first to be applied to the ship since Captain Davis of the Ironclad Board disparaged it with his lines from Exodus. "Sometimes
I think she may be the veritable sling with a stone that shall yet
smite the *Merrimac* Philistine in the forehead."

Fox and Chittenden then "took our leave, and walked to the
west entrance of the Treasury slowly and in silence." At that moment, Fox was closer to the mark than was Lincoln. As the two
friends walked through the streets of morning Washington, the

Monitor hadn't quite sunk, but she was in dire trouble somewhere off Delaware.

When the two reached the Treasury, the intransigent Fox, soon to depart for Hampton Roads, told Chittenden that Lincoln had swayed him a little. "I have avoided reliance upon the *Monitor*," he said. "Perhaps she may yet prove the good angel who will take us out of the Slough of Despond."

"We separated," Chittenden wrote, "I to the labors of forty-eight slow and anxious hours, he to witness the battle which changed all the conditions of naval warfare."

CHAPTER 21

March 8: Iron Against Wood

The *Cumberland*'s men defiantly—and hopelessly—battle the *Merrimack*.

The US Navy lost 1,084 men killed in action during the Civil War. Even though a third of them suffered about the worst death imaginable, flayed by steam bursting from shattered boilers, the toll, when set beside, say, Antietam, where 2,108 Union soldiers died in a single day, seems modest.

The soldiers, however, had no reason to envy their maritime peers. The sea battles were far fewer than land ones, and each was fought by far fewer men. But the grim calculus of war revealed that when the big ground forces met one another, and the smaller naval ones did, soldiers and sailors faced exactly the same odds of getting killed: one in sixty-five. Your chances were no better behind a naval gun than on the murderous slopes of Fredericksburg.

This implacable ratio was demonstrated most starkly beneath the high, clear skies of Hampton Roads on Saturday, March 8, 1862, before a vast audience.

No other naval engagement in history has been witnessed by so many who did not take part in it. A distant corollary might be John Paul Jones's battle with HMS *Serapis* in the American Revolution, fought so close to the British shore that townsfolk gathered on Flamborough Head to watch. That famous contest may have drawn a few dozen spectators; the immense amphitheater of Hampton Roads held thousands.

There was no aerial watcher on March 8, but seven months earlier a Union observation balloon had jolted gently up through thick, motionless early-August air. The occupant in his wicker basket, peering through a telescope from his two-thousand-foot-high perch, took in a view previously granted only to the gods.

To the north he saw the Union forces, still building batteries along the shore. Beyond them the Roads—three miles wide, eight long—glinted between the Federals and the Confederates, who were also strengthening their positions. On the Rebel left, the James River made a broad thoroughfare to Richmond, but one barred by Union warships. South of the James, the smaller Elizabeth River ran past Norfolk into the Roads.

Newport News lay beneath the basket, and east of it an arc of Union shore curved in and then out again, running seven miles to peaceably named Old Point Comfort. There Fortress Monroe commanded the approaches to the Chesapeake and the Atlantic beyond. The largest masonry fortification ever built in the United States, Monroe was the headquarters of General Wool's Union Department of Virginia, and the only bastion in the state still held by the North. At the mouth of the Elizabeth a fingernail of lighter water showed the Middle Ground, a reef that rose close to the surface.

So the situation remained in March, although many more soldiers and guns had arrived, and some of the ships on station were different. Near Fortress Monroe the *St. Lawrence* and the *Roanoke* rode at anchor. The former, a sailing frigate mounting eight eight-inch shell guns and forty-two 32-pounders, had just arrived two days earlier from blockade duty along the Carolina coast; the latter was one of the 1854 steam frigates, heavily armed with forty-three Dahlgrens, a sister ship of the *Merrimack*'s in her preconversion days. So was the *Minnesota*, Goldsborough's flagship; she was at anchor to the south, and farther south still, at Newport News, lay the *Congress* and the *Cumberland*. The fourth ship to bear her name, the frigate *Congress* was twenty years old; she mounted four eight-inch guns and forty-eight 32-pounders. Like the *Cumberland*, she had no steam plant and had to depend on her sails to bring her into action or, should the wind fail, on the unreliable efforts of steam tugs. However game these little boats might be, they were, compared with the warships, fragile as eggshells.

Although engineless, the *Cumberland* was a strong fighting ship, armed with twenty-two nine-inch Dahlgrens, one ten-inch, and an especially powerful cannon, a 70-pounder rifle mounted at her stern that could pivot through a wide arc to command 180 degrees of sea. With the ceaseless rumors of the *Merrimack*'s imminence, this piece had come to be seen as the *Cumberland*'s most valuable weapon, and its crew had been put through the paces of loading and firing until they were sick of the sight of their wonderful gun.

The man responsible for that training was the *Cumberland*'s gunnery officer, Lieutenant Thomas Selfridge Jr.

He loved his ship as much as he did her rifle. The *Cumberland* had been at Hampton Roads since the beginning of the war, and so had Selfridge. In fact, he had helped ensure that the *Cumberland* was afloat and flying the Stars and Stripes, and not just another grove of charred sticks on the bottom of the Elizabeth.

Selfridge's father was a Navy man too, then in command of the steam frigate *Mississippi* in the Gulf Squadron. He had joined the service in 1818 and would stay with it until his retirement a year after the war ended. When he died at ninety-eight in 1902, the Royal Navy ordered all its ships to fly their flags at half-mast in honor of the world's oldest admiral.

Thomas Jr. wrote, "My own naval education may be said to have begun soon after emerging from the cradle." He entered Annapolis in 1851 and after graduation shipped aboard the USS

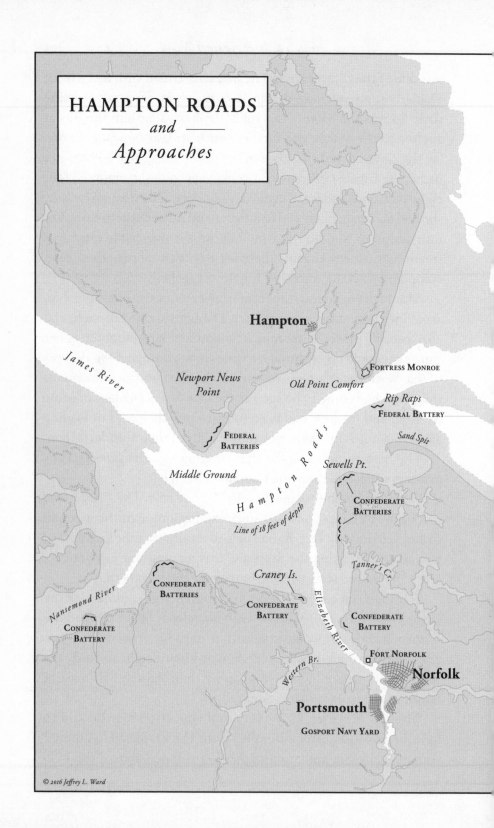

HAMPTON ROADS
— *and* —
Approaches

James River

Hampton

Newport News
Point

FORTRESS MONROE

Old Point Comfort

Rip Raps
FEDERAL BATTERY

FEDERAL
BATTERIES

Sand Spit

Middle Ground

Sewells Pt.

Hampton Roads

CONFEDERATE
BATTERIES

Line of 18 feet of depth

Tanner's Cr.

Nansemond River

CONFEDERATE
BATTERIES

Craney Is.

CONFEDERATE
BATTERY

CONFEDERATE
BATTERY

Elizabeth River

CONFEDERATE
BATTERY

CONFEDERATE
BATTERY

FORT NORFOLK

Norfolk

Western Br.

Portsmouth

GOSPORT NAVY YARD

© 2016 Jeffrey L. Ward

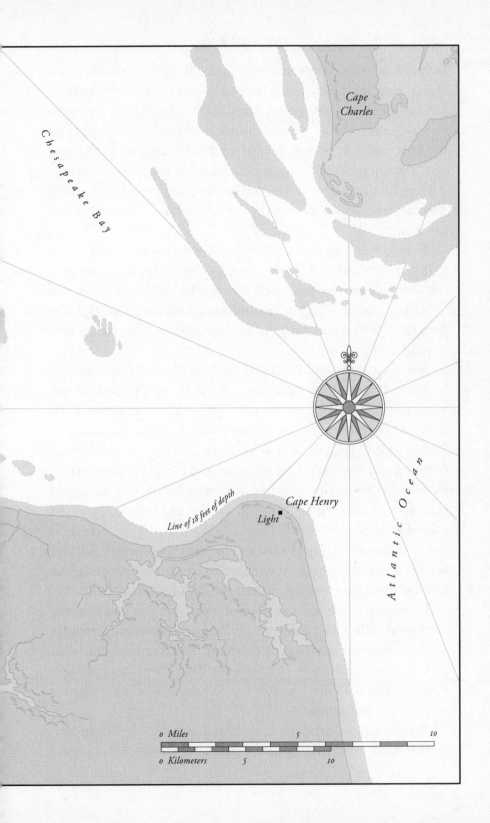

Cape
Charles

Chesapeake Bay

Atlantic Ocean

Cape Henry

Line of 18 feet of depth   Light ■

o Miles   5   10

o Kilometers   5   10

Independence (the Navy's first ship of the line, in commission for ninety-nine years until being burned in 1915 to recover her metal fittings for their scrap value). He sailed to the Pacific, where he learned gunnery under Captain Josiah Tattnall, who would one day command the converted *Merrimack*. Tattnall, said Selfridge, was "a gunnery 'sharp,'" and he took a shine to the midshipman, putting him in charge of the *Independence*'s quarterdeck battery. The early responsibility gave the young man a lifelong enthusiasm for artillery.

In 1860 Selfridge got promoted to lieutenant and was ordered to the *Cumberland*—"this fine frigate"—and sent to Veracruz until the shock of secession brought his ship to Hampton Roads the following March. The *Cumberland* went into the Norfolk Navy Yard for refitting, and, he said, "the next four months were a very anxious time."

Just as Isherwood had, Selfridge found himself increasingly frustrated, and by the same man. "At first the *Cumberland* was anchored off the Naval Hospital, where she commanded the approaches to the city, but within a few days, on the advice of Commodore McCauley's pro-Southern officers, she was moved to a berth off the Navy Yard higher up the river." When Selfridge got word that the move had been made to allow the sinking of obstructions that would keep the *Cumberland* from escaping, "I volunteered to take the brig-of-war *Dolphin*, then lying at the yard out of commission, [and] with a crew from the *Cumberland*, tow her with the ship's boat to Craney Island [at the mouth of the Elizabeth] and prevent the further sinking of obstructions."

His plan was ignored, but the *Cumberland* fared better than the *Merrimack*. When McCauley ordered the yard destroyed, Selfridge wrote, "I was sent ashore to do this work. It seemed an impossible task with my small force of only a few boat crews, and we were compelled to limit the work to the spiking of a number of guns and other minor measures."

While his hundred men were pecking away at Norfolk's sprawl-ing infrastructure, Selfridge got word that "a steamer was to come from Richmond carrying a large number of soldiers to board and take the *Cumberland* by surprise."

Cumberland crewmen hung netting over the ship's sides to entangle boarders. "At about 8 P.M. the same day that the *Merrimac* had been scuttled, the drums unexpectedly beat to quarters, and I rushed to my 10-inch pivot gun on the forecastle."

A big steamer took shape in the dusk, heading toward them.

"I had laid the pivot gun towards her and taken the lock string myself, for fear that the gun captain might misfire from excitement."

The *Cumberland* hailed the stranger. No answer. More hails. Silence.

Selfridge called to his captain, "Shall I fire, sir?"

"No, we will hail her one more time."

A wise decision. This time the newcomer answered and revealed herself as the sloop of war *Pawnee*, "down from Washington with Commodore Paulding and a number of officers, with orders to evacuate and destroy the Navy Yard immediately, after taking out certain ships of special value."

Selfridge never forgot that stretch of anxious waiting with the lanyard in his hand: "A moment more, and a ten-inch shell would have swept decks crowded with soldiers."

Nor did he forget, as he wrote years later, his conviction that "the Yard could have been held by the *Cumberland* and the *Pawnee*."

Nevertheless, at least the *Cumberland* lived to fight another day and brought out three thousand small arms amid the "magnificent, if melancholy and depressing spectacle" of "one fourth of the whole Federal Navy . . . and its largest naval base" in flames.

After refitting in Boston, the *Cumberland* returned to the mouth of the James to guard against Rebel privateers believed to be in Richmond. "Here we lay all winter, having a rather monotonous though strenuous time, with constant drills calculated to meet every contingency in a possible combat with the *Merrimack*."

All Selfridge and his men knew about their opponent was that she would be armored, so they took aboard extra nine-inch solid shot, which hit harder than shell, filled their cartridges with thirteen pounds of powder rather than the regulation ten, and doubled the ropes on the guns to stand the increased recoil. "But our greatest advantage," said Selfridge, "lay in the exceptional quality of a model crew, that has never been excelled and perhaps rarely equaled. It had been recruited principally from Boston and vicinity, and few changes beyond those incident to expiration of enlistment had occurred since 1860; notwithstanding many inducements to desert, held out to them by Confederate sympathizers during the trying days at Norfolk. Those splendid men were proud of their ship, they felt the mutual dependence upon each other arising from long association, and they had been subject to a discipline which gave them great faith in themselves and in the power of their ship." Selfridge ended his tribute with a touch of bitterness: "They really believed themselves invincible, and, indeed, could they have had a fair fight, would have shown themselves to be such."

Although those four hundred men, like all the Union sailors in the Roads, had been expecting the resurrected *Merrimack* for weeks, the squadron was little better prepared for its enemy's arrival than another American fleet would be on December 7, 1941.

The captain of the *Cumberland*, William Radford, wasn't aboard her, having been called over to the *Roanoke* to sit on a court of inquiry whose purpose has long been forgotten. A more senior officer was absent too. For a month, Flag Officer Louis Goldsborough had been overseeing naval operations off Hatteras Inlet. This sounds like honorable work, but Gideon Welles didn't think so. Despite Goldsborough's stated confidence that his Hampton Roads ships could take care of the *Merrimack*, the secretary of the navy believed he'd gone south to escape her: "I have never been satisfied with the conduct of the Flag officer in those days, who was absent in North Carolina—purposely and unnecessarily absent, in my apprehension, through fear of the *Merrimac* which he knew was completed, and ready to come out. . . . He had wordy pretensions, some capacity, but not hard courage."

While Goldsborough was away, Captain John Marston, of the *Roanoke*, had charge of all the Federal vessels in Hampton Roads, and with Radford off on the *Roanoke* the *Cumberland* command had devolved upon her executive officer, George Morris. Selfridge, second to Morris, was officer of the deck, enjoying a brief but real rise in responsibility if not in rank, and a prematurely pleasant spring noon. "The 8th of March, 1862, came and a finer morning I never saw in the southern latitude," wrote his shipmate Seaman William Reblen. "The sun came up smiling in all its splendor. It was 'up hammocks' that morning and then 'holystone' and wash decks as usual. After breakfast (it being Saturday) it was 'up all bags,' and every old tar went through his bag, mending and getting ready for Sunday's muster 'round the capstan." A Boston newspaperman who was there wrote, "Never has a brighter day smiled upon Old Virginia. . . . The hours crept lazily along, the sea and shore in this region saw nothing to vary the monotony of the scene. Now and then . . . a sailor might be noted, on shipboard, telling how much he hoped the Merrimac would show herself, and how certainly she would be sunk by our war vessels."

It was washday, and clothing had been hung in the rigging to dry. The workaday pennants maintained a trace of shipshape order: white garments flapped on the starboard side, blue to port.

This state of nautical undress was peculiar, for there had been warnings.

A Massachusetts man named Joseph McDonald had been in the Navy since July. Arriving at Hampton Roads, he'd nearly been picked for service on the *Congress*, but instead was sent aboard the *Minnesota*. Having a modern turn of mind, McDonald said he "was glad they left me for the steam frigate, for I preferred the latter to a sailing vessel, as I might get a position as a fireman and better pay, and would not have to climb the rigging." Besides, "I wanted to be where there was machinery."

He soon left the *Minnesota*, "for there was a call for a fireman on the *Dragon*, a small steamer which was intended for use as a dispatch and picket boat." He spent his nights by Sewells Point, as near as they could get to the Rebel ironclad. "We all knew that the Confederates were fitting up the old *Merrimac* into some kind of a battery. Everyone was guessing as to when she would come out."

The *Dragon*'s crew got an unusual chance to make an accurate guess. Civilians could still pass through the lines without great difficulty, and "there were many folks wanting to go North (Union folks), and the Confederate truce-boat used to notify us of this by coming out with a white flag up to a certain line beyond which it was not safe to go. When we saw this we would meet them, and bring the people to Fortress Monroe. Well, when the boats were made fast and the officers were busy with their very formal and dignified manners," the ordinary seamen, Union and Confederate, "were trading newspapers, tobacco, etc., *all on the quiet.*"

They also exchanged good-humored taunts, and most of all, they liked to gossip. Sometime around the first of March, the *Dragon*'s engineer, "with a wink and a nod toward the Navy-yard," asked his counterpart, "How about this old *Merrimac*?"

The Confederate engineer said, "Oh, she's all right." Then, pride overcoming discretion, he added, "You look out. She may be out in about a week."

The *Dragon*'s engineer didn't believe it. "Oh no, she draws too much water, too heavy."

"Never mind," the Confederate shot back. "She's all right."

Whether or not the gist of this conversation had made its way higher up the ladder of authority than the *Dragon*'s captain, no increased precautions had been taken. Laundry day remained inviolate, and the jerseys and trousers cast skipping shadows about Selfridge's feet.

Despite the benignity of the scene, there were signs of something out of the ordinary. Two visiting French warships had for days been anchored near the *Merrimack*. They maintained a scrupulous neutrality, their crews giving no word of any doings they might have seen on the ironclad. Today, at the break of dawn, the signal officer at Fortress Monroe saw that both ships had steam up and were preparing to get under way. Normally they would have notified the fort if they planned on leaving to allow for the usual exchange of salutes. If they weren't leaving, why were they shifting their anchorage so early? Hours later, smudges of smoke revealed the presence of small steamers.

Two of them were the *Beaufort* and the *Raleigh*; the others, miles away, the *Patrick Henry*, the *Jamestown*, and the *Teaser*. Those three had long been present up the James, kept there by the Union ships, but now they had moved much closer to Newport News, although still well out of range of the *Cumberland* and *Congress* batteries. Mirages shimmering on the water made Selfridge unsure, but he thought he also saw the thicker smoke of a larger ship.

On the *Dragon*, Joseph McDonald, watching with the other sailors, "saw black smoke coming down the river from the Navy-yard and knew something unusual was happening. Pretty soon that great black thing, different from any vessel ever seen before, poked her nose around Sewell's Point . . . followed by . . . two or three other small gunboats, just like an old duck with her brood.

"My, didn't orders ring out sharp, and men jump lively!"

The first Federal vessel to act was not one of the big warships but an Albany-built Hudson River tugboat, the *Zouave*, recently equipped with a 30-pound rifle and a 24-pound howitzer, and drafted into service with all her crew. No surviving record tells how that crew might have felt about their wholesale transplantation from Nyack or Hastings-Upon-Hudson to the middle of a naval war, but they were about to put in a better day's work than Goldsborough. By night the *Zouave* poked about the Roads as a sentry, and during the days she tended to the *Congress* and the *Cumberland*. Her master, Henry Reaney, wrote, "On the 8th of March, after coming in from picket duty on the James River, we went to Fort Monroe for the mail and fresh provisions, which we got on the arrival of the mail-boat from Baltimore."

Hundreds of the addressees would never read their letters.

"A little after dinner [it would be years before that word entirely ceased to mean "lunch"], about 12:30, the quartermaster on watch called my attention to black smoke in the Elizabeth River, close to Craney Island. We let go from the wharf and ran alongside the *Cumberland*."

Selfridge leaned over the rail and "ordered us to run down toward Pig Point and find out what was coming down from Norfolk. It did not take us long to find out, for we had not gone over two miles when we saw what to all appearances looked like the roof of a very big barn belching forth smoke as though from a chimney on fire."

Nobody on the *Zouave* had any idea what it was. This seems strange, as everyone near Hampton Roads, along with most Americans who read newspapers, knew about the looming threat of the Confederate ram. Today the *Merrimack*'s profile, like that of its Northern opponent, is as familiar as the face on the dollar bill; in the early spring of 1862 only the workers and citizens of Norfolk had ever seen anything like it. Almost every contemporary account of the ship's first sortie imbues it with a near-supernatural strangeness.

Even so, the initial puzzlement didn't last long on the *Zouave*. Reaney wrote, "The boatswain's mate was the first to make out the Confederate flag, and then we all guessed it was the *Merrimac* come out at last."

The mystery solved, the little tug steamed right in to give battle. "When we were satisfied it was the enemy, we went to quarters and fired our 30-pounder Parrott [rifle], which was not answered. We fired again, taking deliberate aim, and were rather surprised that it was unnoticed; we fired, I think, about six shots when our recall signal was hoisted on the *Cumberland*."

The *Cumberland* wasn't interested—at least not primarily interested—in saving the *Zouave* from certain annihilation. On that windless noontide, the big warship would need the tug to help move her into a position where her guns would bear on the *Merrimack*. The *Zouave* was beginning an extraordinarily busy day, but her skipper was always proudest that his boat "fired the first shot at the *Merrimack*."

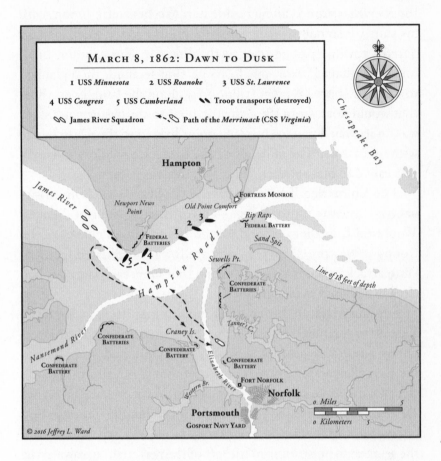

OF COURSE THE *MERRIMACK* HAD seen the *Zouave*, but Buchanan was not after tugboats. He stood on top of the casemate, occasionally looking down through the grating at the silent gun crews gathered about the weapons they had never fired, warmed by the heat rising from the engine room, where the temperature already was on its way to 120 degrees.

The engines were, for once, behaving. Not so the steering. Lieutenant Wood said, "From the start . . . we saw that she was slow, not over five knots. She steered so badly that, with her great length, it took from thirty to forty minutes to turn. . . . She was as unmanageable as a waterlogged vessel."

The *Merrimack*'s two small squadron-mates, the *Beaufort* and the *Raleigh*, steamed along beside her. At a little after noon, with his ship's deep hull straying close to shallow water, Buchanan ordered a towline passed over to the *Beaufort*. Her captain, Lieutenant William Parker, saw to its getting secured, then glanced toward the shore. "A great stillness lay along the land. Everything that would float, from the army tug-boat to the oysterman's skiff, was on its way down to the same point loaded to the water's edge with spectators." For miles along the banks US soldiers and civilians called to one another, "The *Merrimack* is coming!"

The Union fleet knew it now too. Picket vessels hoisted signal 551—"Enemy approaching"—and in Fortress Monroe General Wool told Brigadier General Joseph Mansfield, in charge of the troops at Newport News, to prepare for a coordinated Confederate attack, of course not knowing that General Magruder had already declined to launch one.

Captain Marston, his court of inquiry forgotten, ordered the *Roanoke* to get under way. Soon the ship had steam up, but this was purely a reflexive gesture: a broken crank pin had immobilized the propeller, and her engine was useful only as ballast. Marston signaled the *Minnesota* to get moving too and fixed his glass on the *Merrimack*. If she passed to the right of the Middle Ground she'd be coming for the *Roanoke*, the *Minnesota*, and the *St. Lawrence*. But she seemed to be heading to the left of the reef, making toward the *Congress* and the *Cumberland*. Captain Radford had himself rowed to the shore; he wanted to be with his own ship and figured a horse could get him there faster than the crippled *Roanoke*.

The *Minnesota*'s engines were in good shape, but nobody was paying them much heed. The engineers were deep in a game of chess. When an excited midshipman appeared spilling the news that the *Merrimack* was on the way, one of the players looked up briefly from the board and, thinking it a prank, "complimented him on his command of countenance" and told him to leave them alone. They'd heard this particular alarm over and over during the torpid preceding weeks, "but refused to be sold again, and went on with our game." The next word came from Gresham Van Brunt, the captain. "This looked like work." Eight minutes later the *Minnesota* was under way.

Miles off, aboard the *Congress*, the captain, Joseph B. Smith, was in his cabin discussing some needed repairs with a gunner. Smith was a popular officer, affable and, secure in his competence, generally easygoing. Like so many in the fleet, he came from a naval family: his father was John Ericsson's frequent correspondent Commodore Joseph Smith of the Ironclad Board. The repair problem got dropped as soon as the ship's quartermaster offered his telescope to the surgeon, Edward Shippen: "I wish you would take the glass and have a look over there, sir. I believe *that thing* is a-comin' down at last."

On the neighboring *Cumberland*, Selfridge had already squinted through the mirages to determine he really was seeing the long-heralded threat. He told Morris, who ordered the ship cleared for action. Down came the laundry, and the gun crews cast loose their pieces while other sailors went about the ancient, ominous routine of sprinkling sand along the decks so footing could be maintained when the blood began to flow.

By one o'clock the *Merrimack* was clearly visible to everyone on the *Cumberland*, and looking to Acting Master's Mate Charles O'Neill, as it had to Reaney of the *Zouave*, "like the roof of a house with one smokestack."

Fleeting white pillars of roiled water announced that the Union shore batteries had opened fire, but no Confederate gun answered until Captain Parker of the *Beaufort*, perhaps irked by what he called his men's "careless *insouciance*" about what was soon to happen, and without waiting for orders, fired his single 32-pound rifle at the *Congress*.

On the *Merrimack*, Eugenius Jack was "down in the fire-room twenty feet under water, with no little anxiety, I confess, as to what the issue would be to this experiment of naval warfare . . . and not a little weak-kneed too." He knew he was as safe as anyone could be aboard the ship: his post "was the bomb proof of bomb proofs, but I assure you that I would have taken the station of the junior 3rd

Asst. on the fighting deck and the risk of shot and shell rather than be so far away from what was going on." Jack was one of the first to experience the protective claustrophobia of mechanized warfare.

"The suspense was awful, but it was relieved occasionally by some information through an ash-chute." Craning his neck to put an ear to it, Jack got word from "my comrade White what was going on so far as his observations extended, I knew when the battle was begun by the dull reports of the enemies artillery."

Ashton Ramsay, Jack's superior, had come topside to join Captain Buchanan. He thought his plant was performing far better than Wood did. "'How fast is she going, do you think?' I asked one of the pilots.

"'Eight or nine knots an hour,' he replied, making a rapid calculation from objects ashore. The *Merrimac* as an ironclad was faster under steam than she had ever been before with her top hamper of masts and sails."

This may have been something of an exaggeration (one of the crewmen below remarked, "If this is all the speed we can make, we better get out and walk"), but "I presented myself to the commodore. 'The machinery is all right, sir,' I assured him."

Out of the channel with plenty of water under his keel, Buchanan ordered Parker to cast off the towline. Earlier he had said to Ramsay, "I am going to ram the *Cumberland*. I am told she has the new rifled guns, the only ones in their whole fleet, we have cause to fear. The moment we are out in the Roads, I'm going to make right for her and ram her."

Here he was in the Roads and it was time for Ramsay to go below. "I remember him telling me," wrote the engineer, "in case of my feeling a collision, not to wait for the signal to reverse, but to do so with all the power of the machinery, as in the excitement of the moment he might forget to give the signal, or be incapacitated from doing so."

Down on the shadowy gun deck, a powder boy approached Midshipman Henry Marmaduke, captain of No. 2 gun. "Mr. Marmaduke, I'm likely to be killed in this fight." He held out his purse.

"If I am, will you send my money to my father?" Marmaduke said he would.

Lieutenant Eggleston, responsible for guns 4 and 5, which were to fire hot shot, was concerned about the cannonballs heating on the trivets in the furnace a few yards below him.

At the bow, Lieutenant Charles Simms trained his seven-inch Brooke rifle, the *Merrimack*'s answer to the rifled guns Buchanan believed the *Cumberland* mounted. She only had the one, but Buchanan was right to be wary of it.

He held his fire until he had closed to fifteen hundred yards. The *Cumberland* was dead ahead, and, in that fine day, looking fully worthy of the celebratory portraits the printmakers Currier & Ives had struck off in her honor: tall (the word *skyscraper* was a nautical term before buildings usurped it), and handsome with her black hull and the wide white horizontal stripe above it making the gunports even more minatory. To Selfridge, she was "an inspiring sight; a splendid type of an old-time frigate: towering masts, long yards, neat and trim man-of-war-appearance." Basking at the pinnacle of centuries of naval evolution, she was the equal of her British rivals, of the best products of the age of fighting sail. But Selfridge's calling her an "old-time frigate" is the most telling phrase in his fond description. In the next few hours, every sailing frigate was to become a picturesque antique.

"Fire!"

The Brooke rifle sent its missile into the *Cumberland*'s starboard rail. A cannonball can turn any piece of a wooden ship's elegant architecture into shrapnel. The flying fragments of bowsprit or hull or railing were known as *splinters*, today a denatured word for something slightly more annoying than a paper cut. Then, it meant a whirling airborne sawblade that could cut down a dozen men.

"That first shot," wrote Selfridge, "passed through the starboard hammock netting, killing and wounding nine marines. . . . These men, the first to fall, were promptly carried below, and their groans were something new to us and served as an introduction to a scene of carnage unparalleled in the war."

His forward gun crew fired. The shot went wide, and by then Simms on the *Merrimack* had reloaded and fired, scoring another direct hit. "The shell," said Selfridge, "burst among the crew as they were running the gun out, after loading for a second shot [and] literally destroyed the whole crew except the powder boy, and disabled the gun for the remainder of the action. The captain of the gun, a splendid seaman named Kirker . . . had both arms taken off at the shoulder as he was holding his handspike and guiding the gun. He passed me when being carried below, but not a groan escaped him."

Buchanan's first target was the *Cumberland*, but his ship passed the *Congress* on the way. Aboard Captain Smith's frigate, a crewman remembered, "the *Merrimack* was steaming slowly towards us, and every eye in the vessel was on her. Not a word was spoken, and the silence that prevailed was awful. The time seemed hours before she reached us."

When she did, Eggleston saw the *Congress* slide into the three-by-four-foot window of his gunport and was briefly taken back to the days of peace, when he'd spent three years aboard her: "Little did I think then that I should ever lift a hand for her destruction." The moment of nostalgia passed; the glowing shot rolled down the gun barrels, and Eggleston looked on "the *Congress* only about a hundred yards distant. But for an instant she was visible, for suddenly there leaped from her sides the flash of thirty-five guns."

Unlike the shot from the *Cumberland*'s bow gun, the shells from that broadside went home. Iron blasted into iron made what one of the Brooke rifle's crew called "a terrible noise." He said that the sailors at the gun (and this must be an understatement) "gave a start." Simms called out, "Be quiet, men, I have received as heavy a fire in open air."

That calmed the gun crew, but probably not as much as the result of the broadside. Ramsay said, "We were met by a veritable storm of shells which must have sunk any ship then afloat—except the *Merrimac.* They struck our sloping sides, were deflected upward to burst harmlessly in the air, or rolled down and fell hissing into the water, dashing the spray up into our ports."

Buchanan was intent on destroying the *Cumberland*, but even the passing slap he gave the *Congress* all but disabled the ship. The *Merrimack*'s four-gun broadside, said a *Congress* officer, "dismounted an eight-inch gun and either killed or wounded every one of the gun's crew, while the slaughter at the other guns was fearful. There were comparatively few wounded, the fragments of the huge shells she threw killing outright as a general thing. Our clean and handsome deck was in an instant changed into a slaughter-pen, with lopped off legs and arms and bleeding, blackened bodies scattered about by the shells. . . . One poor fellow had his chest transfixed by a splinter of oak as thick as the wrist, but the shell wounds were even worse." Moreover, Eggleston's hot shots both started fires, one close to the forward magazine.

That devastating broadside, and the return fire that, said Selfridge, watching from the *Cumberland*, "merely rattled from the sloping armor like hail upon a roof . . . caused us neither surprise nor shaken confidence in our powers, since the *Congress* armament could fire nothing to compare with the solid shot of 80 pounds which we could deliver."

But the *Cumberland* couldn't deliver a lot of it because "we had much difficulty in bringing any guns to bear." Earlier the ship had rigged "springs"—cables lashed to the anchor chains that, hauled in or let out, could pivot the ship "to meet the maneuvers of a mobile enemy." These "now proved useless from the fact of the turn of the tide having swung the *Cumberland* athwart the channel; thus bringing the springs in line with her keel" where they could give no traction. Three times the gun crews ran from rail to rail as small twitches of motion suggested that first one flank, then the other, might offer a clear shot. But just a few of the forward nine-inch guns, jimmied around to "extreme train," were able to reply.

Those that could bear struck the *Merrimack*, only, as A. B. Smith, the *Cumberland*'s pilot said, to bounce "upon her mailed side like India-rubber."

Selfridge remembered that the *Merrimack* "lay about 300 yards sharp on the starboard bow, raking the *Cumberland* with every gun from her broadsides," but most witnesses reported that Buchanan went straight in to ram. "Now she nears the *Cumberland*...," wrote a Northern correspondent, "silent and still, weird and mysterious, like some devilish and superhuman monster, or the horrible creation of a nightmare. Now but a biscuit toss from the ship, and from the sides of both pour out a living tide of fire and smoke, of solid shot and heavy shell." Smith, the pilot, wrote, "As she came plowing through the water right onward to our port bow, she looked like a huge half-submerged crocodile.... At her prow I could see the iron ram projecting, straight forward, somewhat above the water's edge, and apparently a mass of iron." The protean creature reminded the *New York Times* correspondent of a different animal: "Slowly she moves and horribly upon the doomed vessel. Like a rhinoceros she sinks down her head and frightful horn."

The *Cumberland* had hung its sides with logs as a protection against the floating mines the Confederates were deploying. The *Merrimack*'s ram went through them as decisively as a butcher's knife might part the straws of a broom and, with thirty-two hundred tons behind it, broached the *Cumberland*'s hull. "With a dead, soul rendering crunch," the *Times* reporter said, "she pierces her in the starboard bow, lifting her up as a man does a toy."

Eggleston, with no forward view through his gunport, thought the *Merrimack* had run aground. Jack, in his dark cocoon of furnace fires and hot metal, had apparently ceased getting bulletins from the ash chute because he was taken by surprise when "there came a tremor throughout the ship and I was nearly thrown from the coal bucket on which I was sitting."

The *Merrimack* had stabbed a hole in the *Cumberland*'s side "wide enough," said Wood, "to drive in a horse and cart." Jubilant hyperbole: the gash was about seven feet across. Nonetheless, it was a mortal wound.

And one that nearly killed the *Merrimack* too.

The Union ship went down by the bow, bringing her seventeen hundred tons to bear on the ram that still impaled her. "As the *Cumberland* began to sink," wrote Selfridge, "the *Merrimac* was also carried down until her forward deck was under water." Jack felt it at once: "There was at first a settling motion to our vessel that aroused suspicions that our own ship had been injured too, and was sinking." Half a century later Selfridge continued to regret the wasted seconds when the *Cumberland*'s starboard anchor hung above her assassin's bow. If it "had been let go it would have fallen on the *Merrimack*'s deck and probably have held the two ships together, thus sinking the *Merrimac* with the *Cumberland*."

For Ramsay, "the crux of what followed was down in the engine-room. Two gongs, the signal to stop, were quickly followed by three, the signal to reverse. There was an ominous pause, then a crash, shaking us all off our feet. The engines labored. The vessel was shaken in every fiber. Our bow was visibly depressed. We seemed to be bearing down with a weight on our prow. Thud, thud, thud, came the rain of shot on our shield from the double-decked battery of the *Congress*."

A boiler burst, or so Ramsay thought; but "no, it was the explosion of a shell in our stack. Was any one hit? No, thank God! The firemen had been warned to keep away from the up-take, so the fragments of shell fell harmlessly on the iron floor-plates." The reprieve seemed over almost as soon as it began. "For a moment the whole weight of [the *Cumberland*] hung on our prow and threatened to carry us down with her, the return wave of the collision curling up into our bow port."

The long-ago haste of a yard worker may have saved the *Merrimack*. The imperfectly fastened ram broke off. "We had left our cast-iron beak in the side of the *Cumberland*. Like a wasp we could sting but once, leaving the sting in the wound."

As the *Merrimack* backed free, the ebb tide that had kept Selfridge from using his full battery brought the ironclad "up broadside to us . . . finally giving the *Cumberland* her first fair opportunity to fight back. That it was quickly and fully exploited regardless of our sinking condition, and not withstanding the carnage that surrounded us is sufficient justification for the emphasis which I have placed upon the qualities of that peerless crew. Three solid broadsides in quick succession were poured into the *Merrimac* at a distance of not more than one hundred yards."

Even sinking, the *Cumberland* gave the *Merrimack* a bad half hour. A shot sheared off the muzzle of Midshipman Marmaduke's gun, killing one of its crew and opening Marmaduke's arm. As he lay on the deck, the powder boy who had entrusted his purse to him ran over. "Oh, Mr. Marmaduke, you're going to die. Give me back my money."

Whatever the fate of the purse, Marmaduke didn't die, but got up and kept working his broken gun. Ramsay wrote, " 'The muzzle of our gun has been shot away,' cried one of the gunners.

" 'No matter, keep on loading and firing—do the best you can with it,' replied lieutenant Jones."

The wadding from the Union cartridges set the *Merrimack*'s basting of grease afire. To Midshipman Littlepage, commanding gun No. 4, "It seemed that she was literally frying from one end to the other." A heavy odor of cooking bacon blew in through the gunports to blend with the sulfurous reek of powder smoke.

"Don't this smell like hell?" one of Littlepage's gunners called out, and another replied with mordant bravado, "It certainly does, and I think we'll all be there in a few minutes."

Unprecedented fighting techniques had to be mastered on the spot. "Don't lean against the shield," an order never before heard at sea, was issued because the men who did got knocked to the deck and, stunned, were carried below with blood leaking from their ears. Every now and then, these brand-new directives were interrupted by ones that went back to the earliest days of gunpowder at sea: "Put out that pipe and don't light it again on peril of your life!"

"The men were fighting like demons," said Ramsay, "there was no thought or time for the wounded or dying as they tugged away at their guns, training and sighting their pieces while the orders rang out: 'Sponge, load, fire.'"

On the Union ship, Acting Master's Mate Charles O'Neill wrote, "The shot and shell from the *Merrimack* crashed through the wooden sides of the *Cumberland* as if they had been made of paper, carrying huge splinters with them and dealing death and destruction on every hand. Several shot and shell entered on one side and passed out through the other carrying everything before them." The valuable rifle was wrecked before it could fire a shot.

Selfridge did not exaggerate the tenacity with which his men fought. One gunner, both legs shot away, struggled back to his Dahlgren on his elbows and yanked off a final round before dying; another, who had lost his arms, died exhorting his comrades to "Give 'em fits!"

The dead were dragged over to the unengaged side of the ship, the wounded carried below. "No one flinched," wrote Selfridge, "but everyone went on rapidly loading and firing; the places of the killed and wounded being taken promptly by others. . . . The carnage was frightful. Great splinters torn from the ship's side and decks caused more casualties than the enemy's shell. Every first and second captain of the guns of the first division was killed or wounded, and with a box of cannon primers in my pocket, I went from gun to gun firing them as fast as the decimated crews could load."

As the bow lowered, water reached the forward magazine; sailors carried topside all the gunpowder they could save. "The once clean and beautiful deck," said O'Neill, "was slippery with blood, blackened with powder and looked like a slaughter house." A newspaper correspondent reported seeing blood running from the *Cumberland*'s scuppers, although it is difficult to imagine how, as both ships were encased in a soiled cumulus of smoke so thick that some on the nearby *Congress* thought the *Merrimack* had sunk.

But it wasn't the Confederate ship that was going down. The men at the *Cumberland*'s forward guns fired until the water closed steaming and spitting over the hot muzzles. Selfridge heard from the berth deck below, "which by this time was filled with the badly wounded, heart-rending cries . . . from the poor fellows as they realized their helplessness to escape slow death from drowning."

He remembered it was about then that a hail came from the *Merrimack* asking if the *Cumberland* would surrender. Lieutenant Morris, who'd had command of her only since Captain Radford had gone off that morning, shouted back, "Never! We'll sink alongside!"

"Whereupon," said Selfridge, "the enemy resumed her old raking position on our starboard bow and again opened upon the doomed ship." He "gathered together the remnants of the first division, some thirty men, and took them forward, with the object of transporting No. 1 gun to the bridle port, in a position where it would bear upon the *Merrimac*. The tackles had been scarcely hooked, when a shell, passing through the starboard bow, burst among them, killing and maiming the greater number."

Selfridge tried to keep working the cannon still above water, but "not a gun's crew could be mustered from the six crews of brave fellows who had gone into action so confident in their ship only three quarters of an hour before."

Men had been sent to the pumps, but the water was quickly gaining on them. The *Merrimack*'s fire kept slamming in. Selfridge looked about the gun deck. "It was covered with the dead and wounded and slippery with blood. Some guns were left run in from their last shot; rammers and sponges, broken and powder blackened, lay in every direction. The large galley was demolished and its scattered contents added to the general blood-spattered confusion."

A few guns at the stern were still firing, but that could not last much longer. The more water that gushed into the *Cumberland*, the more quickly she settled. A violent lurch tore loose a starboard gun from its moorings and it caromed down across the canted deck, crushing a sailor. Below the din of the cannon came the hollow, sibilant booming of air expelled by the rising water in the berth deck, where the wounded were drowning.

Morris gave the order to abandon ship.

"The survivors rushed aft," wrote Selfridge, "some up ladders from the berth and gun decks, others along the spar deck. Fortunately, all the boats had been lowered before the action commenced, and two of the largest were uninjured. Some of the survivors jumped into these boats moored astern, some climbed the rigging, and still others saved themselves on gratings and wooden material from the deck."

While those who could swim began to pull for the shore, the *Cumberland* fired a final, defiant shot. Selfridge believed "that this act of heroism was performed by Coxswain Matthew C. Tierney, who had been mortally wounded and who perished in the ship."

Selfridge was among the last to leave, but not before a moment of farce. "Turning to the wardroom hatch ladder, almost perpendicular from the ship having a heavy list to port, I found it blocked by our fat drummer, Joselyn, struggling up with his drum."

Thus checked, Selfridge pulled off his coat, threw away his sword, and "squeezed through a gunport. In doing so, however, the heel of my boot became jammed against the port sill by the gun. . . . For a few precious moments it seemed as though I must be carried down by the rapidly sinking ship; but with much difficulty, from a bent position I finally succeeded in wrenching off the boot-heel and thus freeing my foot. Then jumping into the icy water, encumbered with boots and clothing, I swam to the launch astern and was picked up exhausted."

The drummer also got away safely, floating on his instrument until one of the several small boats that had put out from the Union shore took him aboard.

When the *Cumberland* came to rest on the shallow bottom, her masts stood above the water, one of them still flying the American flag, with 121 dead below it.

As the smoke began to lift, the men aboard the *Congress* saw the *Merrimack* steaming away. Perhaps their gunfire and that of their stricken sister had done the Rebel rhinoceros some harm after all. Those who weren't fighting the flames the hot shot had started, or answering the fire from the *Beaufort* and the *Raleigh*, left their guns to cheer.

But Buchanan wasn't through. "Having sunk the *Cumberland*, I turned our attention to the *Congress*." He couldn't do that as quickly as he would have liked, for his ship's every movement came at the cost of slow, ponderous work. "We were constantly busy with the operation of the condensing engines," Jack wrote. "The four boilers had to be fired and the linkgear of the engines was hard to operate. To reverse, after ramming, two men had to force the reversing gear to activate. . . . We also constantly worked the pumps to relieve the ship of bilge."

Also, that deep hull had to be kept away from the bottom. "We were some time in getting our proper position," said Buchanan, "in consequence of the shoalness of the water and the great difficulty of managing the ship when in or near mud. To succeed in my object I was obliged to run the ship a short distance above the [Union] batteries in the James River. . . . During all the time her keel was in the mud; of course she moved slowly."

She moved even more slowly now. The fragments of the *Cumberland*'s shell that had burst in her stack had pierced it in a score of places, starving the draft that nourished the fires, filling the engine room with smoke, and shaving several knots off her speed.

The *Merrimack*'s sluggishness and her immense turning radius did not keep her from doing a lot of damage on her detour. The *Times* correspondent who had worried about the danger she might pose to troop transports had his prescience validated when the ironclad passed along the Federal shore. "A large transport steamer along side of the wharf was blown up," Buchanan reported, "one schooner sunk, and another captured and sent to Norfolk."

By now Buchanan had his whole fleet. The *Merrimack* had freed the Confederate gunboats in the James River, and Commander Tucker's *Patrick Henry*, along with the *Teaser* and the *Jamestown* took up station beside her. "At this time," wrote Parker, "I observed the James river squadron coming gallantly into action; they were under a very heavy fire while passing the Newport News batteries, but got by without receiving much damage. All of our vessels now directed their fire upon the *Congress*. . . . The fire on this unfortunate ship was perfectly terrific."

Parker would ever after be nettled by what he saw as the stingy attention history paid the *Merrimack*'s consorts. Just as his Yankee counterpart Captain Reaney in the *Zouave* had fired the first Union shot in the battle, so had Parker's *Beaufort* got off the first Confederate one. All the Rebel gunboats were closely engaged that day, and yet, Parker wrote, "If they are alluded to at all it is in a light way; and the gunboats are frequently denominated tugs." Not that they were all that formidable: "It is difficult to make anyone at the present day understand what absurd and ridiculous men-of-war our gunboats really were. The magazine and boiler being above the waterline, and the hull of one-fourth inch iron, or one inch planking, a man serving in one of them stood a chance of death in four forms: he could be killed by the enemy's shot, (this was the legitimate form); he could be drowned by his vessel being sunk, (this might also be called a legitimate form); he could be blown up by a shot exploding the magazine, or he could be scalded to death by a shot passing through the boiler—the last two methods I always considered unlawful." Years later, Parker proudly quoted Gideon Welles himself on the showing those gunboats made: "One of the smaller steamers poured in a constant fire on her [the *Congress*'s] starboard quarter. Two other steamers of the enemy also approached from James river firing upon the unfortunate frigate with precision and severe effect."

The gunboats were faster than the *Merrimack*, but she was steadily returning to the battle. All the while Buchanan traded fire with shore batteries, none of which inconvenienced his ship as it headed back toward the *Congress*, where, he wrote, the "men who had left their guns and gave three cheers . . . were soon sadly undeceived." For the second time, the frigate's crew had to watch the slow approach of disaster.

When Captain Smith saw the swift destruction of his neighbor, he ordered the *Zouave* over. Reaney, who had been doing his best for the dying *Cumberland*, said, "It seemed cruel to me to leave her." Cruel, perhaps, but necessary, because the *Congress* was still afloat and armed.

"We were in a rather tight place," Reaney wrote, "being between the fire of the gunboats and our own batteries on the shore, the shot from which was falling all around us. However, we kept loading and firing as fast as we were able, until, seeing the *Congress* had loosed her foretopsail and made signal for us to come alongside, we ran down on her, leaving the *Cumberland* just as the *Merrimac* was crossing her bow." Smith ordered Reaney to tow the frigate to the shore and ground her. This was a decision any captain hated to make, but it would transform the *Congress* into an unsinkable battery.

"There was hardly a breath of wind," wrote Reaney, "so that her topsail and jib were of no account in moving her. It took some time to get our lines fast, owing to the horrible condition of affairs on the gun-deck, which was on fire. The cries of the wounded were terrible. The men were not all regular men-of-war's men — I think some were soldiers; but, anyhow, the tug's crew had to get on board to make our lines fast. When everything was ready, Lieut. Smith ordered me to go ahead, with our helm hard-a-starboard so as to get her into shoal water."

The *Congress* crept into the shallows where the *Merrimack* couldn't follow. Nonetheless, the *Merrimack* was close enough. Buchanan put his ship two hundred yards off his enemy's stern and joined the *Beaufort* and *Raleigh* in picking her apart with, Reaney said, "broadside after broadside, that raked her fore and aft, overthrowing several of the guns and killing a number of the crew."

The *Congress* surgeon, Dr. Shippen, had been appalled by the work of that first broadside: all around him were "lopped off arms and legs and bleeding, blackened bodies scattered by the shells, while blood and brains actually dripped from the beams." Now, four hours into the awful afternoon, things were much worse. "In the wardroom and steerage the bulkheads were all knocked down by shell and axe-men making way for the hose, forming a scene of perfect ruin and desolation. Clothing, books, glass, china, photographs, chairs, bedding, and table were all mixed in one confused heap."

Somewhere in the midst of all that jumping wreckage, the *Congress* paymaster was supervising a scratched-together party handing powder to the guns. A shell, said Shippen, "ranged through the stern-frame lower down, passed through the ward-room pantry, on the starboard side, through the ward-room and steerage, and out upon the berth-deck, killing or mortally wounding, in its passage, every one of the 'full-boxes'—that is, the cooks and ward-room boys, who were powder passers from the after magazine." The unhurt paymaster in charge of them, McKean Buchanan, was Captain Buchanan's brother.

"The blood," wrote Reaney (and there's no doubt he truly *did* see this), "was running from the *Congress* scuppers on to our deck like water on a wash-deck morning." The *Zouave* also came in for punishment. "The tallow-cup on top of our cylinder, and the pilot-house and billet-head on the stem were shattered by shot. . . . Our *Zouave* figure-head, which was a fixture on the pilot-house, carried away by a shot on its way over the bows, disabled the crew of the rifle."

Still the *Zouave* stood by, and still Captain Smith continued to fight his ship until, at about four thirty, a shell fragment took off his head. That left Lieutenant Austin Pendergrast in command. He didn't hold it long. Many of his crew were dead or down, none of his guns could bear, and any further resistance would only extinguish lives whose possessors could not possibly affect the outcome.

Pendergrast hoisted a white flag.

Reaney, his *Zouave* lashed to the *Congress*, "told Lieut. Pendergrast that if he did not want me any more, I'd leave and try to escape. He told me to take care of myself, as they had surrendered. We cut our lines and backed astern."

A second white flag joined the first. On the *Merrimack*, someone shouted, "The *Congress* has surrendered. Look out of the port. See, she has run up white flags. The officers are waving their handkerchiefs." Buchanan ordered his men to cease firing, and officers hurried up onto the deck. Lieutenant Jones, who, Ramsay said, "seemed to be in a dozen places at once," sent them back below: "Stand by your guns, and, lieutenants, be ready to resume firing on the word. See that your guns are well supplied with ammunition during the lull. Dr. Garrett, see how those poor fellows yonder"— pointing to the wounded—"are coming on. Mr. Littlepage, tell Paymaster Semple to have a care of the berth-deck and use every precaution against fire." Jones went on to order the ship's boat to send men to take the surrender and told the carpenter to "sound the well, examine the forehold" and make sure water wasn't rising in it. Ramsay's admiration shines through the quiet sentence: "Such was Catesby Ap. R. Jones, the executive officer of the *Merrimac.*"

Without being told to do so, the *Beaufort*'s Captain Parker, who was much closer to the wrecked and burning frigate than was the *Merrimack*, sent Midshipman Charles Mallory in a boat to claim the *Congress* and bring her captain to the *Beaufort.* Once on the ravaged deck, Mallory announced that he was now in charge, and then, Surgeon Shippen remembered, he proceeded to "gaze about a little, and pick up one or two carbines and cutlasses, I presume as trophies." He found Captain Smith's sword lying beside his corpse and took it too.

While Mallory was gathering his souvenirs, Buchanan ordered Parker to "go alongside the *Congress*, to take the officers and wounded men prisoners, to permit the others to escape to the shore, and then to burn the ship." When the *Beaufort* arrived, Mallory came across to her and handed the sword to Parker, who saw "Jos. B. Smith" engraved on the blade. Smith and Parker had had been together in Buchanan's academy; they were old friends. Parker took the sword and eventually it got back to Smith's father, the commodore.

Parker sent a midshipman, Virginius Newton, aboard the *Congress* to fetch the Yankee captain. Newton was subdued by what he found: "Confusion, death, and pitiable suffering reigned supreme, and the horrors of war quenched the passion of months."

Pendergrast came across to the *Beaufort*. Parker, expecting the traditional formalities of surrender, asked for his sword. Instead, Pendergrast handed him a standard-issue ship's cutlass; the old naval courtesies were eroding as quickly as the dominance of the wooden warship. Irritated, Parker told his captive he had orders to burn the ship. It was already smoldering from several fires, and Pendergrast replied that setting it further aflame would kill the wounded. Parker said orders were orders, but he began to have casualties evacuated to the *Beaufort*. Nor was he quite so mercilessly determined as he acted; a Union prisoner heard him say to himself, "My God, this is terrible. I wish this war was over."

While the two officers were arguing, rifle fire lashed across the deck of the *Beaufort*, killing, Parker said, everyone there save himself, Pendergrast, and another Northern officer. "Four bullets passed through my clothing; one of which carried off my cap cover and eye glass and another slightly wounded me in the left knee."

Watching from the shore, General Mansfield said, "I know the damned ship has surrendered, but we haven't." He ordered men of the Twentieth Indiana and the First New York Mounted Rifles to fire on the *Beaufort* and the *Raleigh*, which had joined it alongside the *Congress*. Backed up by two rifled cannon and a Dahlgren howitzer, with one of the guns worked by fourteen vengeful *Cumberland* survivors, they were all shooting from the shore, less than a half mile away.

"I now blew the steam-whistle," wrote Parker, "and my men came tumbling on board. The fire of the enemy still continuing from the shore, I cast off from the *Congress* and steamed ahead so that I could bring my bow gun to bear. I had no idea of being fired at any longer without returning it, and we had several deaths to avenge. We opened fire but could make little impression with our single gun upon the large number of men firing from intrechments on shore. The sides and masts of the *Beaufort* looked like the top of a pepper-box from the bullets, which went in one side and out at the other."

Deciding no good could come from this particular skirmish,

Parker took the *Beaufort* to Craney Island and handed the Union wounded over to French Forrest. Parker did not bother to report to Buchanan first, which was too bad, because it left his superior to draw his own conclusions about what was happening on the *Congress*. With the heavy smoke, and metal swarming overhead, that wasn't easily discerned. Buchanan thought—not unreasonably—that after running up the white flag, the *Congress* had begun firing again. This was among the most egregious violations of the rules of war, and it enraged the easily infuriated Buchanan. It also began a controversy that would fester for fifty years. A Union seaman remembered that just as Captain Pendergrast gave the order to cease, "I pulled the lanyard and fired what proved to be the last shot ever fired on the fated *Congress*." That would have been long before Parker came alongside. When Captain Reaney cut the *Zouave* loose, his ship had been badly beaten up, but was still full of fight. Years later Reaney wrote, "As soon as we got clear, [we] commenced firing, which, I think, gave rise to the charge of the *Congress* firing after she had struck her colors."

On the *Merrimack*, all they saw was what Lieutenant Robert Minor called "a dastardly, cowardly act." Buchanan muttered, "That ship must be burned."

The entire shore was now ringed with fire; a Union infantry officer wrote, "Clouds of white smoke rose in spiral columns to the skies, illuminated by the evening sunlight, while land and water seemed to tremble under the thunder of the cannonade." For Buchanan, this miles-wide action had narrowed to a furious desire to chastise the *Congress*. "Destroy that damned ship," he ordered, and grabbed a musket from the *Merrimack*'s small-arms locker. He carried it to the top of the casemate and began, one of his men said, "firing his rifle at the enemy's officers whenever he could get a chance." That was reckless self-indulgence for the man entrusted with his nation's most effective weapon, and Buchanan paid for it. A trooper of the New York Mounted Rifles remembered, "Whenever a man came up on top of the Merrimack we shot at him all together." A bullet struck Buchanan's left thigh high up near his groin, nicked but did not sever the femoral artery, and knocked him to the grating with a deep, painful wound.

"I was disabled," he wrote, "and transferred the command of the ship to that gallant intelligent officer, Lieutenant Jones, with orders to fight her as long as the men could stand to their guns."

He was more specific and harsher than that: he wanted that damned ship destroyed and told Jones, "Plug hot shot into her and don't leave her until she's afire. They must look after their own wounded, since they won't let us." "Dearly did they pay for their unparalleled treachery," said Eggleston. The *Merrimack*, invulnerable to any annoyance the shore could make, "raked her fore and aft with hot shot and shell till out of pity we stopped without waiting for orders."

Adding to Buchanan's conviction of general Yankee scurrility, Pendergrast, having surrendered to Parker, escaped to the Union shore. But what else could he have done? After receiving the unwelcome cutlass, Parker had allowed his captive to return to the *Congress* from the *Beaufort* to help with the wounded, then drew off to quarrel with Mansfield's infantry. As Pendergrast saw it, he'd been left with two choices: die for no good reason in the steady fire clawing through a helpless ship flying two flags of surrender, or leave. Parker (who later defended Pendergrast's action) kept the cutlass, but lost the man.

Catesby Jones, with the command he had wished for suddenly in his hands, wanted to destroy the *Minnesota*. Captain Van Brunt had got his frigate moving well before the fighting began and was about a mile away when his keel scraped the Middle Ground. Van Brunt thought the bottom "soft and mushy" enough to drive right over it and tried, but only mired his ship. By then the *St. Lawrence* and the *Roanoke* had also gone aground, been pulled off, and having no hope of joining the fight on time (and perhaps little desire to) sent the tugs that had freed them to help the *Minnesota*. Reaney too was going to her aid. "We headed for her, keeping as close to the beach on our side as possible, when about half-way, after passing all the enemy's vessels, we were struck by a shot which carried away our rudder-post and one of the blades of our propeller. . . . Being then unable to use our rudder, and heading directly for the enemy, we stopped and backed so as to get her head right, which we did, and with our large hawser out over our port quarter, we kept her going in the right direction, until the gun-boat *Whitehall* came to our assistance." The other tugs reached the *Minnesota*, but they couldn't do anything for her. The tide had been going out for hours, and the frigate was planted firmly as a county courthouse.

That same tide was running against the *Merrimack*. Much as Catesby Jones might have hoped to grapple with the stranded warship, his pilots—all three of them—were justifiably worried about the ship's deep draft and said they could not take her into close range. The *Patrick Henry* and the *Jamestown*, however, had the frigate under a hot fire. Thomas Rae, an engineer on the *Minnesota*, marveled at his calmness under the pounding. "I appreciated the danger, and was much cooler than I have been thinking it over since, but it did not seem more exciting than a game of snowballing. They carried men past me down to the cockpit to the surgeon, and a solid shot tore through the hammock netting within a few yards of me, killing two men and strewing the brains, even the head of one, all over the deck, yet it seemed all in place."

The ebbing tide spared Rae further tests of his mettle. The Middle Ground could trap the *Merrimack* as surely as it had the *Minnesota*. "We fought," Jones said, "until it was so dark that we could not see to point the guns with accuracy." Why risk his ship in the dark on an uncertain bottom, when he could reap an easy victory in the morning? The *Minnesota* wasn't going anywhere. Jones headed the *Merrimack* back to the protection of the Confederate guns at Sewells Point and called it a day.

Quite a day; the US Navy had never had a worse one. Long afterward, Captain Parker, thinking back on March 8, 1862, tallied the human cost: "The loss in killed and drowned on board the *Cumberland*, as reported by her commander, was 121, and the surgeon reports 14 wounded." That is a shocking disparity: the wounded in any battle usually far outnumber the dead. ". . . Lieutenant Pendergrast's report . . . gives the total number of killed and missing as 136; he then deducts 26 wounded, taken on shore, which leaves 110. If there were 60 wounded men when I went alongside, as he said (and this number was certainly not exaggerated), if he sent 26 on shore, these, with the 5 I had, would account for 31; which leaves 29 unaccounted for, or still on board"—here Parker begins to speak with some heat—"and there is reason to fear that some wounded men were left on board to be consumed by the flames, who would have been taken off by the *Beaufort* and *Raleigh*, under the flag of truce, had they not been fired upon by the troops on shore. . . . The *Minnesota* lost three killed and 16 wounded, and there were some casualties reported among the other vessels. From what I can gather, I think the loss in the Federal fleet in killed, drowned, wounded and missing amounted to nearly 400 men.

"On our side the *Merrimac* lost 21 in killed and wounded; the *Patrick Henry*, 14; the *Beaufort*, 8; the *Raleigh* had Lieutenant Tayloe and Midshipman Hutter killed, how many men I do not know. . . . Our total loss, however, did not exceed 60." It was in fact less than half that; two dead and eight wounded on the *Merrimack*, and in the entire Confederate fleet, just twenty-seven killed and wounded.

As darkness fell, nobody on either side had any idea of these figures, but all knew the Union had suffered a terrible defeat. Small boats were taking off *Cumberland* survivors who had sought safety in the ship's rigging when she went down. The still-calm waters of the Roads winked with little red crescents of reflected fire from the blazing *Congress*, where, working fast, the survivors saved as many of the wounded as they could, lowering them with a line rigged to the foreyard into ship's boats that had survived the fight. The officers wanted to bring away their captain, but knew the men on the burning vessel, well aware of the fires eating toward tons of gunpowder, would bridle at risking their lives for a corpse. They covered Smith with a blanket, tied him to a cot, and smuggled him to land.

Before that, Shippen said, he "took from his body his watch and chain . . . and saw that they got back to Commodore Smith." Later, the watch was stolen, a crime with an affecting outcome. "The newspapers," said Shippen, "in reporting the robbery, dwelt on the distress occasioned to the admiral by the loss of the memento. Soon after, to the surprise of the family, they received the watch by express, with a letter from the burglars, declaring that if they had known the history of the watch they had taken, nothing would have induced them to touch it."

WHEN THOMAS SELFRIDGE HAD REACHED the shore, "furious over the loss of the ship in which I had taken such pride, shivering with cold from soaking wet and scanty clothing, the reaction from the long endured, frightful, experiences of battle impelled me to tears, and I sobbed like a child."

He pulled himself together, helped prepare for the expected Confederate attack by land, and at some point during that forlorn evening met up with his captain. Radford had tried hard to get in the battle: Selfridge said that after Radford got ashore at Old Point Comfort, he "rode overland at such a pace, that, on dismounting at Newport News, the horse dropped dead. He was on time only to see his ship sinking."

Selfridge probably went with Captain Radford to help the wounded in the hospital, a slower and perhaps sadder recapitulation of the *Cumberland*'s gun deck: tourniquets, amputations, screaming.

Selfridge believed he had one more duty to perform. "The flag of the *Cumberland* was still flying above water at her gaff. . . . Seeing an opportunity to get this flag while the *Merrimack* was up the river, I called for volunteers and pulling off to the ship in a small skiff, took down the flag and returned safely to shore."

There, he was "met by kind friends in a New York Zouave regiment, who took us to the headquarters of Brigadier General Phelps, where, after hiding the flag in a corner underneath a sofa, an outfit of dry clothing, comprising Zouave boots, trousers, and blue shirts, with overcoat made me comfortable."

Selfridge "spent the night in the headquarters building, sleeping very soundly after the exhausting day's work." He had one more loss to suffer: "In the morning great was my regret to discover that the *Cumberland*'s flag had been taken from its hiding place." Unlike Captain Smith's watch, it was never returned.

Few other Union men got much sleep that night. Engineer Rae found his *Minnesota* infected with a hopeless gaiety: "We enjoyed ourselves, for none cared to look forward to the morrow, as there was but one termination possible."

Captain Van Brunt thought so too. A few days earlier, he had been eager to meet this new foe: "The Merrimack is still invisible to us, but report says she is ready to come out. I sincerely wish she would; I am quite tired of hearing of her. . . . The sooner she gives us the opportunity to test her strength, the better."

Having tested her strength, the captain spent a wakeful night weighing what to do while the tugs tried to move his ship. The most expedient course was to blow up the *Minnesota* to keep it from falling into Rebel hands. But that was a terrible option, one to be taken only in a final crisis. He could send many of his men ashore, leaving only enough volunteers to serve the guns, but he would be condemning them—and himself—to death or captivity. So he brooded on his quarterdeck, every once in a while looking over to the dim shape of the equally helpless *Zouave*, which the tug had turned over to the doubtful safety of the *Minnesota*'s battery.

On the shore, survivors of the *Cumberland* and the *Congress*, still shocked and half-deafened from their afternoon's labors, wandered between the ghostly white files of Union tents trying to find one another.

Some made their way to Fortress Monroe, where the mood was no better than aboard the *Minnesota*. An officer there wrote, "The whole aspect at headquarters was gloomy," and the thick, moated walls he stood behind offered no reassurance. Even Monroe's largest guns, he said, would be "as useless as musket balls against the ironclad," which "had the ability to shell and destroy the vast stores in and about the fort without the least power on our part to resist her."

To General Wool, commanding Monroe, fell the unhappy duty of telling Washington what had happened. He was able to do it because the telegraph line between his headquarters and the capital had fortuitously begun operation that very day: the *Cumberland* is sunk and the *Congress* surrendered, Wool wired Secretary of War Edwin Stanton; the *Minnesota* and the *St. Lawrence* "probably will be taken."

A *Congress* orphan said, "It was a long and dreary night for us. We all expected to be taken prisoners the next day." For a reporter in the fort, "The night was not half so heavy as our hearts, nor so dark as our prospects." A Northern newspaperman expanded on the universal dread:

> The most alarming crisis of the Civil War was at hand. As the sun went down that night over Hampton Roads every Union heart in the fleet and in the fortress throbbed with despair. There was no gleam of hope. The *Merrimac* was impervious to balls, and could go where she pleased. In the morning it would be easy work for her to destroy our whole fleet. She could then shell Newport News and Fortress Monroe at her leisure, setting everything combustible in flames, and driving every man from the guns. As the news of the terrible disaster was flashed over the country by the telegraph wires all faces wore an expression of consternation. The writer was in Washington at the time. Congress was in session. The panic cannot be described. There was absolutely nothing to prevent the *Merrimac* from ascending the Potomac and laying the capital in ashes. Baltimore, Philadelphia, New York, Boston and Portland were in a state of terror. . . . The *Merrimac* could laugh at forts.

THE *FORT-TAUNTER* DROPPED ANCHOR—A single anchor, the other having been shot away, its flailing chain causing several casualties—at about eight o'clock. The *Merrimack* was sound, but shaken, demanding attention before the galley fires could be lit, at ten, and the tired crew could settle down to dinner.

Tired, but exultant. Although seriously wounded, Lieutenant Minor happily summed up the day: "THE IRON and the HEAVY GUNS did the work. It was a great victory."

Before he ate, Catesby Jones went over the ship, noting the hollows the Union gunfire had pocked in the casemate. The new captain couldn't have kept track of them all: the *Merrimack* had been hit ninety-seven times. But no shot had broken through the shield. He discovered that "the prow was twisted and the armor somewhat damaged; the anchors and all flag staffs shot away and the smokestack and steampipe were riddled." He seems not to have noticed the prow was not only bent, but shorn of its ram.

Jones went to the captain's cabin, where the officers from the gunboats had congregated and were going over the triumphant afternoon. Amid the flow of high spirits, the recumbent Buchanan was suffering, and grim. Along with all his anger at the Yankees, he had a good deal to spare for Captain Parker, who had usurped his privilege of opening the battle and had then failed to destroy the *Congress*. Beneath his pique lay a more intimate concern. He had scant reason to think McKean had survived the afternoon, and he broke up the convivial gathering by telling the solicitous officers around him, "My brother, Paymaster Buchanan, was on board the *Congress*."

Many of the crew went topside to watch what E. A. Jack called "the revel of the flames" on the *Congress*. Not Jack, who, "too tired to stay on the deck with my shipmates . . . sought my state room and there on the floor were two of the men who had been killed in that day's action. I did not care much for such room mates, it was too suggestive, so I waited until they were removed to shore, then sought my berth and was soon oblivious of what I had passed through or of what was to come."

The engineer's last waking thoughts were about the doubts cast on his captain's dedication to the Confederate cause. Catesby

Jones suspected that Buchanan's determination to hammer the *Congress* long after it had lost any power to resist came in part from his wanting to give no hint of staying his hand to spare his brother. If so, the commodore would have been pleased to know what occurred to Jack on the verge of sleep: "The days fight was directed in its most eventful part by Capt. Buchanan and we all felt now that the impeachments upon his loyalty to the South, or his bravery were groundless."

Ashton Ramsay, too wrought up to turn in, stayed on top of the casemate to watch the end of the *Congress* and never forgot it: "All the evening we stood on deck watching the brilliant display of the burning ship. Every part of her was on fire at the same time, the red-tongued flames running up shrouds, masts, and stays, and extending out to the yard-arms. She stood in bold relief against the black background, lighting up the Roads." As the flames reached cannon that had been abandoned after loading, the guns eerily fired themselves, and "a shell would hiss at random through the darkness. About midnight came the grand finale. The magazines exploded, shooting up a huge column of firebrands hundreds of feet in the air, and then the burning hulk burst asunder and melted into the waters."

Pieces of the ship rattled down on Fortress Monroe, seven miles away. The soldiers there knew these embers were the first gusts of a gale whose full force would break on them in the morning.

CHAPTER 22

Frightful News

Secretary of War Edwin Stanton. When word of the *Merrimack*'s
first day's work reached Washington, Gideon Welles said Stanton's
"wailings and woeful predictions" were "inexpressibly ludicrous."

John Dahlgren was at the Navy Yard early the next day. He was
going through papers and feeling mildly guilty about skipping
Sunday church services when the President came in. Lincoln
was a frequent visitor, but not at such an hour.

"Frightful news," he said, and told what the *Merrimack* had done
the day before. Dahlgren's first thought was to block the Potomac.

He and Lincoln drove in the President's carriage to the White
House, where a small crowd had already gathered: Secretary of
War Stanton; Secretary of State William Seward; Montgomery
Meigs, the quartermaster general; Salmon Chase, secretary of the

treasury; George McClellan, general-in-chief of the Union Army; Lincoln's secretaries John Nicolay and John Hay; and Gideon Welles. With a professional Navy man's jaundiced view of civilian thoughts on military matters, Dahlgren said, "There was a hasty and very promiscuous emission of opinion without much regard to rank." None of it came from Meigs, who sat glum and silent. Stanton was the most vocal.

Gideon Welles once wrote that the necessity of cooperation between the secretary of the navy and the secretary of war had brought the two men "into harmonious action, but with no cordial intimacy." This shows a restraint not always evident in their dealings, for Welles loathed Edwin Stanton, which should be kept in mind when reading his account—the best we have—of that distraught cabinet meeting.

Like Dahlgren, Welles had been up early. He'd just arrived at the Navy Department when the assistant secretary of war entered, holding Wool's telegram to Stanton. "I called at once on the President," said Welles. "Several members of the Cabinet soon gathered and there was general excitement and alarm. . . . But the most frightened man on that gloomy day was the Secretary of War. He was at times almost frantic."

Stanton gave voice to all the worst fears: "The Merrimac he said would destroy every vessel in the service,—could lay every city on the coast under contribution [that is, hold them for ransom]. . . . Likely the first movement would be to come up the Potomac and disperse congress, destroy the capitol and public buildings, or she might go to New York and Boston and destroy those cities."

During this litany of disaster, Welles said, Stanton "walked the room with his eyes fixed on me, [and] I saw well the estimation in which he held me." Stanton concluded by asking "what vessel or means we had to resist or prevent the Merrimac to do whatever she pleased."

Welles gave a reply nicely calculated to needle his questioner: the Union warships "were not as great or as extensive as I wished," but—and one can imagine how much Stanton liked hearing this—

"it was certain she could not come to Washington and go to New York at the same time." Welles added that the *Monitor* was on hand to check her. In fact, he had no idea where this spark of hope might have blown, only that it had recently set out from New York.

Stanton asked in a "sneering" manner, "What is the size and strength of this 'Monitor,' how many guns does she carry?"

"When I mentioned she had two guns, his mingled look of incredulity and contempt cannot be described; and the tone of his voice as he asked if my reliance was on this craft with her two guns is equally indescribable." Welles does a creditable job of trying, though: "There was censure, bitterness and a breaking out of pent-up hatred that I could not misunderstand ... [as] he attempted to exercise toward me that rude and offensive insolence for which he became notorious in the discharge of his official duties."

Welles was a little smug about the coolness with which he met Stanton's hectoring: "The President always gave me credit for being the most calm and self possessed of any member of the government," and "in all that painful time my composure was not disturbed." He nonetheless admitted, "That day and its incidents were the most uncomfortable of my life."

Something close to panic does seem to have crackled in the room that morning. General McClellan, who rarely underestimated a threat, left the meeting and told General Wool, "The performances of the Merrimac place a new aspect on everything, & may very probably change my whole plan of campaign" to move up the Peninsula and take Richmond. Welles thought Dahlgren no help at all and wrote, "The President himself was so deeply interested and excited, that he could not deliberate or be satisfied with the opinions of non-professional men, but ordered his carriage and drove furiously to the Navy Yard to see and consult with Admiral Dahlgren and other naval officers who might be there. Dahlgren had, to a great extent, his regard and confidence; but in this instance D. who knew not of the preparation or purposes of the [Navy] department could give the president no advice[,] which seemed to increase the panic."

Seward, "who had been desponding, contrary to his usual cus-
tom and temperament," deferred to the gloomy Meigs. "Both
Dahlgren and Meigs were intelligent officers . . . but neither of
them had the fighting qualities of Farragut or Sherman and in that
time of general alarm were not the men to allay panic."

Welles was disgusted by Stanton's "wailings and woeful predictions," which drove Lincoln "repeatedly to the window and [he]
looked down the Potomac—the view being uninterrupted for
miles—to see if the Merrimac was not coming in sight."

The Navy secretary told the President, "Our information of
the Merrimac, for we had every few days report of her condition
was, that she could not venture out side, and was to be used in
Hampton Roads, the Chesapeake & the river."

This cheered up Lincoln—who was also "delighted" that "my
assistant Fox was absent at Hampton Roads in anticipation of the
arrival of the Monitor"—but not the war secretary: "There was
throughout the whole day, something inexpressibly ludicrous in
the wild, frantic talk, action and rage of Stanton as he ran from
room to room—sat down and jumped up after writing a few
words—swung his arms, scolded and raved."

John Hay agreed with Welles about Stanton's behavior. He
was, Lincoln's secretary said, "fearfully stampeded. He said they
would capture our fleet, take Ft. Monroe, be in Washington before
night."

Right in the heart of Washington too: looking once again down
the Potomac for a baleful smear of coal smoke, Stanton said, "Not
unlikely we shall have a shell or cannonball from her guns in the
White House before we leave this room." Then he went off and,
Welles reported, "telegraphed to the Governors of the Northern
states and the Mayors of some of the cities, warning them of the
danger and advising, as I was told, that rafts of timber and other
obstructions should be placed in the mouths of the harbors."

While the mayor of Bangor, Maine, presumably was deciding
what to do about the Penobscot River, Dahlgren went off to secure
the Potomac.

Welles left on an errand that he dreaded. It was still before noon, and he knew that Commodore Smith would be at the services in St. John's Church. Welles went to the door and sent in an usher to summon the commodore. When Smith joined him on the church steps, Welles told him of the loss of his son's ship.

Smith thought it over. "The *Congress* sunk. Then Joe is dead."

Welles assured him there was no reason to believe that: there had been no reports of casualties, and the battle had been fought close to shore. Surely there were many survivors.

Smith shook his head. "You don't know Joe as well as I do. He would not survive his ship."

IN THE MEETING, JOHN DAHLGREN had spoken about his plan to sink ships to block the Potomac. Welles was against it, saying that would only be doing the Rebels' work for them. Anything that could keep the *Merrimack* out would also bottle up every Union vessel.

Late in the day, Dahlgren took Stanton and Seward out on a steamer to tour the river, scouting places where the *Merrimack* might appear. Stanton put Dahlgren in emergency command of the Army batteries along the shore and told him to sink his obstacles.

Dahlgren began assembling a gaggle of sixty canal barges, and he did it quickly. By dusk he reported to Lincoln and Welles that the work was well under way.

This was the first Welles had heard the project was going forward. "I received during the evening a telegram from Dahlgren at the Navy Yard, stating he had secured a large number of boats and had a large force loading them with stone and gravel and asking if he was acting in conformity with my wishes. I answered no."

Welles ordered the preparations stopped. The cabinet met again, and "Stanton with affected calmness but his voice trembling with emotion, enquired if I had given orders to prevent the boats which he had provided from being prepared and loaded."

Welles replied that this was Navy business, not Stanton's, and he had approved no such undertaking.

"Stanton said he had given the order to Meigs and Dahlgren, and done it with the approval of the President."

Stanton turned to Lincoln, who allowed that was true. After all, "no harm would come from it, if it did no good."

Welles remembered saying he "was very sorry to hear it." He was infuriated to hear it. "For five of six months we had labored with Genl McClellan and the War Department to get this avenue open to unrestricted navigation . . . [and] we were now about to shut ourselves off."

The angry Welles was far from the mild, vaporous figure some reporters had seen. He finished his protest with a pro forma "as the President had authorized the proceeding, I had no more to say except to express my dissent." Glowering, he told Dahlgren to go ahead.

Lincoln, impressed enough by Welles's wrath to strike a compromise, told Dahlgren he should get the boats ready, but not sink them until the President himself gave the order.

Welles said of the argument "the passages were sharp and pungent," but that afterward Stanton always treated him "with courtesy and consideration."

That emollient Stanton only appeared later. During those frantic meetings, Welles displayed a courage as steady as that of any hard-pressed battlefield commander. He was gambling everything from his reputation to the safety of the Union on the newborn ship he had come to trust.

CHAPTER 23

The Short, Bad Voyage

The *Monitor* under tow in heavy weather on her way to do battle.

Despite its paltry send-off, the *Monitor*'s voyage south began well. If there had been no time to exercise the guns, at least officers and crew were getting used to one another in their tight quarters. "As far as I know my fellow officers," Paymaster Keeler had written Anna, "I am very well pleased with them & hope everything will pass pleasantly while we are shut up together." (A few days later he amended this: "Some of the officers as I get acquainted with them I like better, others not so well.") They were also getting acquainted with their circumstances. Something was truly dreamlike about them, as dreams so often meld fantasy with the particularities of the waking world. Shipboard routine was basically the same as it would have been on any frigate when the sailors of 1812 were in their prime; but the iron surroundings where it took place were a disorienting change from an airy world of standing rigging, planking underfoot, and snowy parabolas of canvas overhead.

In time, life aboard would settle into the familiar, and then the monotonous. But that lay beyond a harrowing voyage.

Captain Worden had been apprehensive from the start: "Never was a vessel launched that so much needed trial-trips to test her machinery and get her crew acquainted to their novel duties. We went to sea practically without them."

All was serene, however, for the first few hours. Keeler wrote Anna, "4 o'clock P.M. We have just parted with our pilot & may consider ourselves at sea. We have a fine westerly wind, a smooth sea & as fair a sky as we could expect in the month of March.

"We are in tow of the tug *Seth Low* & convoyed by the U.S. Steam Gun Boats *Currituck* & *Sachem*, who are ordered to accompany us the whole distance. Our boat proves to be much more buoyant than we expected & no water of consequence has yet found its way on deck. Our hatchways are covered with glass hatches & the only means of access to the deck is up through the top of the tower & then down to the deck."

Five hours later: "I have just returned from the top of the turret. The moon is shining bright, the water smooth & everything seems favourable. The green lights of the gun boats are on our lee beam but a short distance off & the tug is pulling lustily at our big hawser, about 400 feet ahead. A number of sail are visible in different directions, their white sails glistening in the moon light. Not a sea has yet passed over our deck, it is as dry as when we left port." Alban Stimers wrote Ericsson, "I never saw a vessel more buoyant or less shocked. . . . There has not been sufficient movement to disturb a wine glass sitting on the table."

That night at supper—bread and butter, beef, cheese, coffee—"we had a merry company . . . the Captain telling some of his experiences as a Midshipman."

Things were less merry twelve hours later when, on awakening, Keeler "found much more motion to the vessel & could see the green water through my deck light as the waves rolled across the deck."

Worden felt that increased motion right away, and he took it hard. He and the ship's surgeon, Daniel Logue, became seasick and sought the only thing that helped the condition, fresh air. They climbed on top of the turret to shiver there under the awning, rigged across a circle of posts around the rim, which did little to impede the driving scud. Seasickness is more debilitating than anyone who hasn't experienced it can imagine, but much worse was to come.

Ericsson had designed his turret to seat securely on the magnificently machined bronze ring, its weight making the seal against the soft but firm metal watertight. He had been omnipresent during every phase of the ship's construction, but he wasn't at the Brooklyn Navy Yard when, just before the *Monitor* set off, well-meaning mechanics decided to add a safety measure by laying a coil of hemp rope between the turret and the ring to ensure the ship stayed dry. How well the rope would do that became evident as soon as the seas began to rise at daybreak on March 7. Keeler wrote, "The water had worked under the tower during the night & drowned out the sailors whose hammocks were hung on the berth deck immediately below. The water was coming down this morning from under the tower and from the hatches & deck lights & various other openings, and making it very wet and disagreeable below." By noon, with the waves running ten feet high, the sea was flowing in through the impromptu gasket "like a waterfall," said Lieutenant Greene. "It would strike the pilot-house and go over the turret in beautiful curves, and it came through the narrow eyelets in the pilot-house with such force as to knock the helmsman completely round from the wheel."

Keeler wrote, "Now the top of every sea that breaks against our side rolls unobstructed over the deck dashing & foaming at a terrible rate. . . . Now we scoop up a huge volume of water on one side &, as it rolls to the other with the motion of the vessel, is met by a sea coming from the opposite direction, the accumulative weight seeming sufficient to bury us forever." More and more men joined the captain and the surgeon on the turret.

Keeler, squinting through the stinging murk, was slightly reassured to see the gunboats, with their higher freeboard, "roll the muzzles of their guns under & as far as motion was concerned they were much more uncomfortable than ourselves."

That didn't last. "The wind continued to increase after dinner with a heavier sea pouring across our deck with an almost resistless force, every now & then breaking against our smoke pipes, which are only about Six feet high, adding a torrent of water down on our fires."

That John Ericsson was so often right about engineering matters is a good thing, because he was just as unshakably adamant when he was wrong. He'd wanted only the *Monitor*'s turret to rise above her deck, but had nonetheless designed a pair of removable funnels against just such an eventuality as this mounting storm. Worden thought them too short; Ericsson bridled at that (his annoyance showing in those peevish complaints about the captain's supposed lassitude while the ship was being fitted out), until Worden, with a fatalistic shrug, told him, "You build your vessel and I will sail her."

He also beat down Stimers on an even more crucial matter. Just aft of the stacks were two more openings in the deck. They stood above the blowers, big fans that fed air to the entire ship, supplying the draft that kept the boiler fires burning and the oxygen that kept the crew alive.

To keep seawater out of these vital lungs, Ericsson designed two intake pipes that Stimers, acolyte though he was, declared too low. He protested and got the usual Ericsson response to criticism: the inventor "was very obstinate," Stimers said, "and insisted four feet was high enough."

Like Worden, Stimers eventually gave in. But he never recanted, writing later of those "air pipes," if "Captain Ericsson had made them as high as I wanted them (the same height as the turret) we would have suffered little inconvenience."

The inconvenience they did suffer nearly killed them all.

As seawater piled along the deck, Ericsson's stumpy pipes sucked it in, and the blower fans beat it into a soaking spray. Belts of industrial leather turned the fans; the material is strong (after all, it holds a cow together), but once drenched it stretched, became slack, loosened its hold. The fans stuttered and slowed. The belts lost traction; one of them broke. The blowers stopped.

The boiler fires, starved of their oxygen and rained on through the stacks, died down. Steam pressure dropped, and all the ship's mechanisms, the pumps included, grew sluggish, then still.

Stimers and Newton struggled with the belting in an orderly, well-thought-out space that had become as dangerous as any battlefield. Stimers wrote, "The fires burned with a sickly blaze, converting all the air in the engine and firerooms into carbonic-acid-gas a few inhalations of which are sufficient to destroy animal life."

This was the subtle killer we know today as carbon monoxide, and before it destroys animal life, it clouds the animal brain. In the blighted orange firelight, with drunken, failing perceptions, the lurching deck flinging them against a hundred barely learned pipes and valves, working in conditions never before experienced by any human being, Stimers and Newton fumbled at the belts' lacings while behind them the propeller slowed to a halt.

Fireman First Class John Driscoll, one of the ship's Irishmen, had abandoned his wife and children in county Cork to come to America, and he might well have regretted that decision when he went into the mephitic engine room where men were already lying unconscious on the deck. He didn't abandon them, though. The shaky orthography of his account conveys a sense of the situation's urgency.

Coming off watch at four in the afternoon, Driscoll

retired to a loft under the turret where the hammocks were stowed. . . . I had scarcley gotten asleep when the belt on the port side blower flew off. . . . By this time the fan box was full of water. . . . While attempting to get the port blower started the star-board belt . . . blew off and since all draft was cut off the gas soon filled the engine room, suffocating all who was in there at that time The other firemen on the berth deck smelling the gas, rushed in a body to the engine room . . . and dragged out those who were overcome The last man to be carried out was Chief Engineer Newton.

The ladder leading to the turret was very close to where I was asleep and when Newton . . . was being carried up the noise awakened me. So I rushed like the others to the engine room The only means of reaching the engine room was by a narrow passage leading from the berth deck and passing between the boilers and the coal bunkers. As the pressure of gas was so strong I was forced to retreat but by tyeing a silk handkerchief over my mouth and nose and keeping so close to the floor as possible, I succeeded in reaching the engine room and it was thick with gas Like the others I tried to start one of the blowers but the belt flew off. . . . Rushing into the store room I procured a hammer and chisel and knocked a hole through the sheet box While I was working the water from the tower was rushing over me but it helped to expell the gas from about me When the water was all out there was nothing to prevent the fan from starting 5 minutes had not elapsed since the time I had entered the engine room until I got the blower started. . . . At this time the crew were all up . . . on top of the turrett I had scarcley gotten one blower started when two seman came into the engine room They had wet cloths over their mouth They informed that they had been sent by Captain Worden to find me and bring me up on the turret supposing that like the others I had been overcome by the gas and was over-looked. . . . I had informed Capt. Worden of what I had done and the condittion of things in the engine room and requested that I get some help from among the seamen and then I received a glass of brandy which relieved me of my troubles a great deal.

Driscoll got his well-earned drink from Keeler, who wrote, "Turning to go down from the turret I met one of our engineers coming up the steps, pale, blackened, wet & staggering along gasping for breath. He asked me for brandy & I turned to go down & get him some & I met the sailors dragging up the firemen & other engineers apparent[ly] lifeless."

Faced with what he thought was a fresh-made corpse, Keeler did not merely fetch the brandy, but went on down to "the engine room, the door of which was open." The paymaster realized it was letting the lethal gas into the rest of the ship. "As I went to shut it one of our Sailors said he believed that one of the engineers was still in there—no time was to be lost, though by this time I had almost suffocated myself I ran in over heaps of coal and ashes and fortunately found the man lying insensible. One of the Sailors who had followed me helped pull him out & close the door. We got him to the top of the tower, but he was nearly gone."

He didn't die. Nobody did that night. But when one hears of the "highest traditions" of the US Navy, it would be well to remember, along with the battles, how the men of the *Monitor*, thinking their fellows were expiring all about them, again and again returned to that engine room.

Alban Stimers perhaps spent the most time there. Whenever he became, as he said, "weak in the knees," he would stagger out into the storm until his head cleared, then go back. But the blower Driscoll had fixed failed again, and Stimers could not coax either of them into life.

Finally he pulled himself up to the turret, where he found "three engineers and several firemen senseless," and lay down choking beside them.

Newton, who had also been out for a while, "recovered sufficiently," said Stimers, "to feel that he was responsible for doing all in his power, though not enough to use his best judgment, and away he went to the fire room and put a hose in the nozzle for wetting down the fires, but before he could do much, had to leave, arriving at the berth deck just before he gave out entirely. One of the firemen happened to look in there to see if there was anyone left and brought him out. They got him to the top of the turret and after some anxious work on the part of the surgeon"—Logue had overcome his seasickness—"he began to revive, but his case looked doubtful for several hours."

Lieutenant Greene began organizing parties of sailors, leading them into the lethal chamber to fight briefly with the belting, then back out again before they lost consciousness. After a while he found breathing easier, but only because the fires had burned themselves too low to generate poison gas. Greene said, "The water continued to pour down the smoke-stacks and blower-pipes in such quantities that there was imminent danger the ship would founder."

He set the men to the hand pumps, but these had to push water up through seventeen feet of hose to squirt it from the turret, and they proved too weak for the job. Greene put together a bucket brigade. He knew this was like trying to bail a swiftly filling bathtub with so many thimbles, but at least it gave the men little time to imagine what would happen when the water overtook their efforts.

Up on the turret—"It was a sorry looking company," said Keeler, "which crowded the only *habitable* part of our vessel"—Worden ordered the American flag lowered, restrung, and run back up with the field of stars at the bottom, the old signal flown by a ship in its last extremity. The gunboats were themselves in too much trouble to help, but the rugged little *Seth Low*—a forgotten hero of the saga—saw and acted. The wind was blowing seaward from the land; the water must be calmer closer to shore. Her side-wheels threshing as gray hummocks of ocean mounded over the paddle boxes that housed them, the tug dragged her heavy charge into the teeth of the storm. For five hours the *Seth Low* churned landward, the gunboats struggling after. As the weary flotilla neared Fenwick Island, Delaware, the seas relaxed, and the wind began to drop.

By eight o'clock the blower pipes were inhaling again. Coal carefully sprinkled into the furnaces took and burned. Steam pressure rose, and the propeller began to turn; the work was no longer all the *Seth Low*'s to do. The pumps came back to life; the fans blew the last of the deadly fumes away.

THE CREW WENT TO A late supper, a Spartan one of crackers and cheese washed down with water, but welcome enough to men who knew they were going to survive the night.

With the engineering crew worn and shaken, Keeler remembered his days as proprietor of the La Salle Iron Works, and "my mechanical genius came into play, as I took charge of the engines till morning when the engineers were sufficiently recovered to take care of their duties."

Greene told Worden he'd take the eight to midnight watch; the captain, still seasick, accepted with thanks. As the storm blew itself out around him, the executive officer stood on the turret while the *Monitor* steamed ahead as blithely as its designer had promised it would. Speaking of her with the fond irritation of a new-made veteran, Greene wrote, "Smooth sea, clear sky, the moon out and the old tank going along five or six knots very nicely."

When he was relieved, in the first minutes of March 8, he gratefully fell into a deep sleep. It lasted about an hour before the old tank emitted "the most infernal noise I've ever heard in my life."

It "resembled the death groans of 20 men" and came from the bow; Greene and Worden were there in seconds. The fickle moon had vanished, the storm was back, coming head-on now, pushing the waves into the anchor well and then—blasting the trumpeting air before them—up into the hawsepipe through which the anchor chain ran. Behind the noise came the water in "a perfect stream," Greene said, jetting with fire-hose velocity to scour the long wardroom table and volley into the berth deck beyond.

Amid the myriad duties of setting out, Greene had neglected to plug the hawsehole ("a gross oversight on the part of the executive officer," Ericsson later complained, lest he be blamed). Working waist deep in water, the captain and his exec stopped most of the influx, but by now the *Monitor* was again in the same weather that had drowned the blower pipes, and again the blowers started to jitter and skid.

The two men went back up on the turret to hail the *Seth Low* and found their ship was directly downwind of its tug, which could hear no voices calling for help, nor, in the storm, notice any signal. "We then commenced to think the *Monitor* would never see daylight," Greene said. "We watched carefully every drop of water that went down the blowers and sent continually to ask the fireman how the blowers were going. His only answer was 'slowly—but could not be going much longer.'"

Then the wheel ropes jumped off their track and scrambled themselves into an incoherent tangle. That meant the helm no longer had any control over the rudder; the ship slewed around broadside to wind and waves, a maritime condition only a few good shoves away from eternity.

With their tons of floundering iron jerking viciously at the towline, Greene and Worden expected it to part, and that would be that. But the hawser was new and good, and the *Seth Low* slogged along obliviously with its thrashing burden.

Stimers was in the wheelhouse, and his efforts alone got the tiller lines rerigged after a mad half hour. The motion of the ship eased as the rudder bit, but the continual queries sent to the engine room always returned the same dismal message: "Blowers going slowly but can't last much longer."

Greene was back on watch at four o'clock, aching for the dawn to bring enough light to see by. Already feeling he had "lived ten good years" since leaving New York, he now endured "the longest hour and a half I ever spent. I certainly thought old Sol had stopped in China and never intended to pay another visit."

The sun confirmed its reliability first with a lessening of the darkness rather than a coming of light, but at around five thirty the *Monitor* made visual contact with the *Seth Low.* By eight the tug had it back into quiet waters. The blowers and pumps were ticking over nicely, the hawsehole had long since ceased to keen its death song, and crewmen were cheerily comparing the first lavender blossomings of pie-size bruises whose genesis they could not remember. Captain Worden was over his seasickness.

"Breakfast tasted good I assure you," said Keeler.

OUT OF THE FRYING PAN, the *Monitor* steamed on toward the fire.

Steamed through a fine, fair day. By noon the ship, drying out under a cordial sun, was a dozen miles away from Chesapeake

Bay, with Cape Charles off to the west. An hour or two later, the doughty towrope gave up and snapped, "but fortunately," Greene said, "it was quite smooth and we secured it without difficulty." Four o'clock: Cape Henry had risen off to port, with Hampton Roads open beyond it.

Now the crew began to hear a steady, distant grumble of cannon fire.

Worden ordered the ship cleared for action.

The *Seth Low* slipped its tow, and as their friend in need fell away astern, the *Monitor* sailors struck down the stacks and the awning that had given such scant comfort during the past forty-eight hours.

The turret was "keyed up"—lifted on its spindle to rotate for the first time at sea—and rose clear of the remnants of its foolish rope packing.

So far, so good; and that was as far as the good went. During the journey down from Brooklyn the raw new metal within the ship had so thirstily received the invading seawater that the machinery powering the fighting tools had grown an orange coating of fresh rust thick enough to freeze the turret in place.

So the exhausted crew became the first to undertake what would forever after be the most hated job on any metal fighting ship. The big screw and wedge that lifted the turret had to be chiseled free of rust, and so did the donkey engine that turned it. Even the gun carriages had seized up.

While crewmen chipped away, light began to leave the day.

"As we neared the land," Keeler wrote, "clouds of smoke could be seen hanging over it in the direction of the Fortress & as we approached still nearer little black spots could occasionally be seen suddenly springing into the air, remaining stationary for a moment or two & then gradually expanding into a large white cloud—these were shells & tended to increase the excitement. As the darkness increased, the flashes of guns lit up the distant horizon & bursting shells flashed in the air."

A pilot came out to meet them. He would have been surprised for the first time in his life to climb from his boat *down* onto the deck of a warship. The news he brought surprised the men of the *Monitor* at least as much: one Union frigate sunk, another dying, both done in by a single adversary in a single afternoon, the massacre interrupted only by ebbing tide and nightfall, and certain to be resumed in the morning. A lot to take in.

Despite their dreadful voyage, and what they'd just learned, the *Monitor* crew only wanted to hurry to the scene of the calamity. "Our hearts were very full," wrote Greene, "and we vowed vengeance on the *Merrimac*." A few hours earlier they'd all been listening with desperate hope for the reassuring sound of their engines. Now that noise was merely a frustration. "How slow we seemed to move," said Keeler, "—the moments were hours. Oh, how we longed to be there—but our iron hull crept slowly on & the monotonous clank, clank, of the engine betokened no increase in our speed. No supper was eaten that night as you may suppose.

"As we neared the harbor the firing slackened & only an occasional gun lit up the darkness." They steamed by ships that wanted nothing more to do with Hampton Roads. "Vessels were leaving like a covey of frightened quails & their lights danced over the water in all directions."

The *Monitor* clanked forward past them and came first to Captain Marston's undamaged *Roanoke*. Worden and Stimers went aboard and learned of an order from Washington that, had it been received, would have changed the course of the war.

After much internal second-guessing about having sent the *Monitor* to Hampton Roads, Gideon Welles decided that his unique asset would be better deployed in defense of the capital. On the morning of the sixth he telegraphed Commander Paulding at the Brooklyn Navy Yard, directing him to tell Worden to forget the Roads and instead take his ship to an anchorage in the Potomac "below Alexandria," there to await an attempt on the city. Paulding moved at once to alert Worden, but the *Monitor* had already cast off. The courier sent after it ran into the same vile weather that nearly did in the ironclad and turned back with the message undelivered.

The order had reached Marston by the time he received Worden and Stimers in his cabin, but during the hours that had passed since Welles changed his mind, the naval world too had changed. The two captains agreed that the *Monitor* must stay right there and try to save the *Minnesota*. Worden returned to his ship and scrawled a hurried note to his wife: "I arrived here an hour since and am going immediately to the assistance of the *Minnesota* near Newport News. The *Merrimack* has made sad work among our vessels. God bless you and our little ones. Devotedly, Worden."

Before he could help the *Minnesota*, though, he had to get to her, and that turned out to be difficult. No pilot was willing to steer the ship through the shallows because, once arrived at the goal, he would be stuck during the fight that was sure to come either aboard this eccentric, virgin curiosity or the *Minnesota*. Neither prospect was appealing.

After two hours and twenty-four refusals, Worden turned up a Dublin man named Samuel Howard, acting master of the bark USS *Amanda*. Although the *Amanda* had arrived in Hampton Roads just in time to witness the afternoon's carnage, and Howard had $500 in the bank and a wife and four children he wanted to see again, he agreed not only to conn the *Monitor* to the frigate, but to stay with her during whatever the morrow might bring. Across waters lit by the flaming *Congress*, the ironclad nudged its way through clusters of wreckage and came alongside the *Minnesota* at about one in the morning.

Worden sent Greene aboard to announce his presence, and, said Captain Van Brunt, "All on board felt that we had a friend that would stand by us in our hour of trial."

ALL ON BOARD FELT NOTHING of the sort. Van Brunt wrote about how relieved he'd been only after twenty-four eventful hours had revised his initial response to the *Monitor*'s arrival. At the time he stared down from his quarterdeck with incredulous dismay.

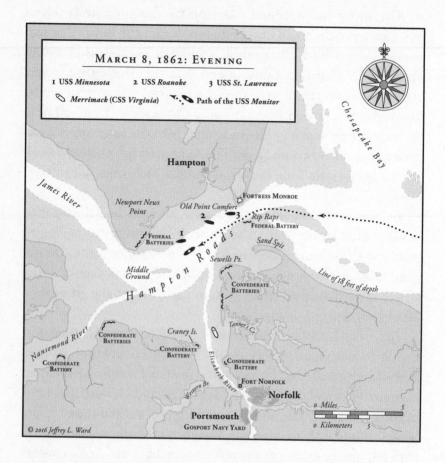

MARCH 8, 1862: EVENING

1 USS *Minnesota*   2 USS *Roanoke*   3 USS *St. Lawrence*

⬧ Merrimack (CSS *Virginia*)   ⬧ᐧᐧᐧ Path of the USS *Monitor*

Chesapeake Bay

Hampton

James River

Newport News
Point   Old Point Comfort

FORTRESS MONROE

2 3   *Rip Raps*
FEDERAL BATTERY

FEDERAL
BATTERIES   1

H a m p t o n   R o a d s

Sand Spit

*Middle
Ground*

Sewells Pt.

CONFEDERATE
BATTERIES

Line of 18 feet of depth

Nansemond River

CONFEDERATE
BATTERIES

Craney Is.

CONFEDERATE
BATTERY

Tanner's C.

CONFEDERATE
BATTERY

CONFEDERATE
BATTERY

Elizabeth River

Western Br.

CONFEDERATE
BATTERY

FORT NORFOLK

Norfolk

0 Miles   5

© 2016 Jeffrey L. Ward

Portsmouth
GOSPORT NAVY YARD

0 Kilometers   5

The captain saw not the means of his salvation, but a ludicrous novelty, whose turret, at twenty feet across, was less than a tenth the length of the ship it was supposed to protect and contained two guns to the *Minnesota*'s forty-four. Was this pathetic metal pie plate the famous Ericsson ram? Was this what the mighty industries of the North had so tardily sent to counter the titan that had cut its killing path through a Union fleet a few hours earlier? It was, and Van Brunt despaired.

One *Monitor* sailor would have understood, if not embraced, the captain's disgust. "How insignificant she looked," he wrote. "She was but a speck on the dark blue sea at night, almost a laughable object by day."

Still hoping to float his ship when the tide ran full in an hour, Van Brunt was mostly concerned that the *Monitor* would be in the way when the *Minnesota* got free. She seemed about to do so, and those *Monitor* men not coping with the rust infestation shifted the ironclad clear. The *Minnesota*, after a few indecisive trembles, settled back into the mud.

About then, Keeler witnessed another disturbing portent, which he saw with very different feelings from Ashton Ramsay's. The *Congress* "was wrapped in one sheet of flame, when suddenly a volcano seemed to open instantaneously, almost beneath our feet and a vast column of flame and fire shot forth till it seemed to pierce the skies. Pieces of burning timbers, exploding shells, huge fragments of the wreck, grenades and rockets filled the air and fell sparkling and hissing in all directions. It did not flash up and vanish in an instant, but seemed to remain for a moment or two, an immense column of fire, one end on the earth and the other in the heavens. It soon vanished and a dense thick cloud of smoke hid everything from view. We were about two miles from the wreck and the dull heavy explosion seemed almost to lift us out of the water."

Afterward, flurries of alarm kept the *Monitor*'s men awake. "Everything on board of us," Keeler wrote, "had been prepared for action as far as was possible as we came up the harbour & the report every little while through the night that the *Merrimac* was coming kept all hands to quarters through the night. No one slept."

No one slept aboard the *Dragon* either. After moving the *Roanoke*, McDonald's tug had been sent to the *Minnesota*—where the crew could not have been heartened by the sight of the battered *Zouave*—to help tow it off the bottom. All night the *Dragon* labored, the lines between the two ships as taut as they were useless. "The next morning," wrote McDonald, "was a fine one, clear and bright. There was the little *Monitor* flat on the water, like a turtle. We all commenced to comment on her and make fun. 'Pshaw! That thing? Why, we could lick her ourselves!'"

Keeler was on the turtle's turret when dawn broke. "The first rays of morning light saw the *Minnesota* surrounded by tugs into which were being tumbled the bags & hammocks of the men & barrels & bags of provisions, some of which went into the boats & some into the water, which was covered with barrels of rice, whiskey, flour, beans, sugar, which were thrown overboard to lighten the ship."

A tugboat butted through the jetsam bearing Gustavus Fox, just arrived from Washington. He had stopped at the *Roanoke* to annoy Marston by brusquely usurping his command of the theater (for Goldsborough was still, as Welles would have put it, hiding in North Carolina). Fox had learned that the *Monitor* had survived its maiden voyage to arrive, he said, "at the moment the novelist would have produced her."

But right then he was no more confident than Van Brunt that the novel would have a happy ending. He'd ordered Marston to send every Federal sailing ship away from the Roads immediately, and to have his steamers prepared "to move out at the moment."

Fox went aboard the *Minnesota* to consult with Van Brunt and was back on his tug when the lifting morning mist revealed the Confederate ships at Sewells Point raising steam. The dawn light also showed that the *Minnesota*'s side, high and impervious as a mountain range in the cosmetic darkness, had been cruelly hurt the day before.

Worden ordered his men to breakfast. Driscoll, back from helping dog down the protective covers over the glass deck lights, said, "We had corned beef hard tack and coffee." When they were finished eating, the captain addressed the ship's company. Driscoll's description of the talk shows Worden had stuck by his pledge that he would sail only with those who wanted to: "We had all volunentered to go with him[,] that now haveing seen what the *Merrimac* had done and from all appearances was now capable of doing and that the fate of the *Cumberland* may soon be ours that if any one regretted the step he had taken he would put him on the *Roanoke*."

Worden's audience had seen the broken blower belts and the

rust and the silent pumps and the dying engines; they'd seen the bobbing remnants of one strong man-of-war and watched another explode; their own ship had almost drowned them twice.

Driscoll said Captain Worden "was answered by every man jumping to his feet and giving three cheers."

ON THE UNION SHORE SOLDIERS and the sailors who had escaped from the *Cumberland* and the *Congress* came out into a mild dawn that promised another clement day. All of them knew what it would bring and were early ready for action. Daylight showed that another ship had replaced the two vanished frigates. The newcomer seemed a poor substitute to Surgeon Shippen, who had survived his ordeal on the *Congress*. "No one in our camp seemed to know what it was or how it came there," he wrote, "but at last it was conceded that it must be the strange new iron-clad which we heard was being built in New York by Ericsson." Strange, and hardly imposing: "She seemed so small and trifling that we feared she would only constitute additional prey for the leviathan."

Keeler had assured his wife throughout that his ship was a haven of perfect safety; now he felt a twinge of doubt. As the chain lifting the *Monitor*'s anchor rattled in the strident hawsepipe, he looked at the coronas of fresh white splinters around the holes in the *Minnesota*'s hull and wondered if the *Monitor* really could keep the *Merrimack* from finishing the job. "The idea of assistance or protection being offered to the huge thing by the little pigmy at her side seemed absolutely ridiculous."

Ridiculous or not, Worden was going to try. The *Minnesota* hoisted a signal ordering him to engage the *Merrimack*, which was perhaps officious of Van Brunt, and in any event unnecessary. "The signal was not seen by us," said Greene. "Other work was in hand, and Captain Worden required no signal." He was already under way, determined to follow Nelson's terse dictum about how to win sea battles: "Always go right at 'em."

In a final exchange, Worden had asked Captain Van Brunt what he planned to do.

"If I cannot lighten my ship off, I shall destroy her."

Worden said, "I will stand by to the last if I can help you."

As Keeler remembered it, Van Brunt said in farewell, "No, sir, you cannot help me."

CHAPTER 24

March 9: Iron Against Iron

The ships in close action: this lithograph by the marine artist J. O. Davidson shows the *Merrimack*'s pilot house, the conical peak toward her bow.

The crew of the *Merrimack* had passed a more restful night than the men of the *Monitor*, but not all that much more restful. They'd turned in still vibrating from a day of furious work rewarded by a victory as complete as any in naval history and were facing the certainty of more of the same in a few hours.

Nor did what sleep they got last long. The ship was astir before dawn. Surgeon Phillips, as tired as anyone aboard, had spent the night onshore tending to the wounded. He was back aboard the *Merrimack* in time for breakfast, which was the crew's favorite—ham, corn bread, and coffee—on this auspicious morning, followed with a particular treat. William Cline, the private who had been disappointed by the lack of ceremony when the ship was launched, happily reported, "We began the day with two jiggers of whiskey and a hearty breakfast."

After downing his whiskey, Phillips went to Buchanan's cabin. He found the captain in pain, but full of stubborn resolve. Phillips checked the wound and asked him to go ashore. Buchanan refused. He knew he couldn't take any active role in the fighting to come, but he wanted to be there. Phillips finally prevailed by saying his presence might interfere with the treatment of any future wounded.

Catesby Jones bade his captain farewell as the stretcher-bearers took him off the ship, then went about checking on the cannon, telling the crews of the two with their muzzles shot away the same thing he had said in the heat of the day before: *Never mind; fire them anyway; we won't need accuracy, just punch.*

Below, the boilers creaked with the expanding steam. The anchor was aweigh at six thirty, while the Confederate colors rose on the new staff that had replaced the several shot away the day before, always replanted under fire. Near the flagpole, black smoke drooled sluggishly along the deck. The stack had been so riddled by the *Cumberland* that, Phillips said, it "would have permitted a flock of crows to fly through it without inconvenience." Those wounds left the draft badly diminished; the *Merrimack* could make only half the speed she'd had when she met the *Cumberland*, but that was an irritant rather than a disaster: if your prey can't move, a slow pursuit doesn't matter.

The signal bell clanged in the engine room, and Ramsay opened his valves. The *Merrimack* turned her bow and steamed into Hampton Roads as the gunboats—*Patrick Henry, Teaser, Jamestown*—fell in beside her to advance, said Private Cline, into a day "as bright and beautiful as the day proceding [*sic*] it. The broad waters of Hampton Roads were as smooth as glass, not a ripple on its surface, an ideal day to go to Church."

One of the prayers the *Merrimack*'s men might have offered that Day of Rest was quickly answered. The lifting mist revealed that the *Minnesota* hadn't moved during the night. There she lay, stranded, right where the ironclad had left her. Some tugs were still in attendance—and the frigate had gained a new consort.

"We left our anchorage shortly before eight o'clock . . . ," wrote Ashton Ramsay, "and steamed across and up stream toward the *Minnesota*, thinking to make short work of her and soon return with her colors trailing under ours. We approached her slowly, feeling our way cautiously along the edge of the channel, when suddenly, to our astonishment, a black object that looked like the historic description, 'a barrel-head afloat with a cheese-box on top of it,' moved slowly out from under the *Minnesota*."

Jones apparently knew at once what the interloper was—"an iron battery," he said—but his officers seem to have been as baffled by it as the men of the *Zouave* had by its counterpart the day before. Some thought it "the Yankee water schooner," a cistern mounted on a low hull that attended to the Union ships' water supplies. Lieutenant Hunter Davidson, commanding guns 2 and 3, said "the *Minnesota*'s crew are leaving on a raft." Others believed the vessel was, at this most unlikely moment, taking a boiler to shore for repair.

John Eggleston, looking from his gunport, was completely stumped. "We could see nothing but the resemblance of a large cheese box," which was "the strangest looking craft we had ever seen."

The crew of the gunboat *Patrick Henry* spotted it at the same time. Lieutenant James Rochelle, the *Henry*'s executive officer, saw "no sails, no wheels, no smokestack, no guns. What could it be?" In the excited discussion that followed the sighting, "some thought it was a water tank . . . others were of the opinion that it was a floating magazine replenishing her [the *Minnesota*'s] exhausted stock of ammunition; a few visionary characters feebly intimated that it might be the *Monitor*, which the Northern papers had been boasting about for a long time."

On the *Merrimack*, Davidson figured it out and said to his gunners, "By George, it is the Ericsson battery, look out for hot work." Only Lieutenant Wood realized that "she could not have made her appearance at a more inopportune moment."

Whatever its nature, the floating anomaly looked inconsequential to Catesby Jones and had no part in his plans. His business was with the *Minnesota*, and he ordered Simms to get ready. As he had the day before, the bow gunner would open the battle with his Brooke rifle. Jones gave the word; Simms fired the first shot while the frigate was a mile and a half distant.

McDonald of the *Dragon*, watching from alongside Van Brunt's ship, said the *Merrimack* "came straight for us and commenced to fire. She came for the stern of the *Minnesota*, as of course only two guns could then bear on her, perhaps intending to rake the ship as she did the *Congress*. Her first shot struck the water and bounced toward us, but then fell short. The next went through the flag."

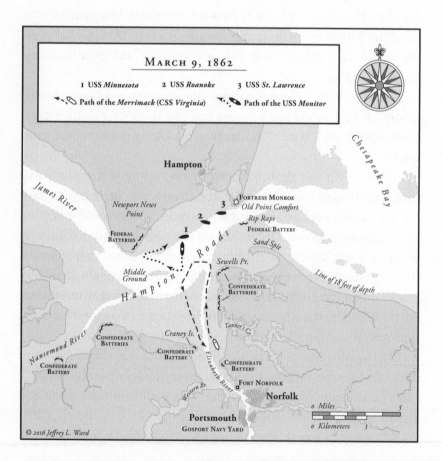

Just as McDonald realized that yesterday's miseries were again to be visited upon the Union ships, "the little *Monitor* sailed right out, around the *Minnesota*, right in between her and the *Merrimac*, and let go with her two guns as if to say, 'Hold *on*! Stop *a minute*!'"

PAYMASTER KEELER HAD BEEN MIFFED at the lack of enthusiasm shown by the men his ship was there to help. To assurances that the *Monitor* would do its best for them, "the replies came curt & crispy. As the *Merrimac* approached, we slowly steamed out of the shadow of our towering friend no ways daunted by her ungracious replies."

Most aboard missed the caustic good-byes, as they were already at their action stations. At the bow in the wheelhouse were Quartermaster Peter Williams, who would steer the *Monitor*, and the intrepid Howard, who had agreed to keep piloting it. Worden would join them shortly; when the fighting began these would be the only three on the hermetic vessel to get any real view of what was happening.

Engineer Newton was at the throttle, surrounded by the men who would be stoking the boilers, and those who'd tend the dozens of oil cups that bled lubricant into the moving parts and constantly had to be topped up lest friction weld the elaborate components into mere sculpture. The deck-light covers had been fastened down; the men in the hull could see only by the flare of the engine fires and the sallow shine of the battle lanterns.

Lieutenant Greene was in the turret, along with eighteen other men. Acting Master Louis Stodder had his hands on the controls that turned the turret, Stimers was there to keep his expert's eye on everything, and the sponges and the rammers the two eight-man gun crews held made a temporary palisade around the shoulder-high black bulbs of the Dahlgrens. A good supply of 168-pound shot, swung up from the locker, lay around the turret's inner wall.

"Every one on board of us was at his post," wrote Keeler, "except the doctor & myself who having no place assigned us in the immediate working of the ship were making the most of our time in taking a good look at our still distant but approaching foe. A puff of smoke arose from her side & a shell howled over our heads & crashed into the side of the *Minnesota*. Capt. Worden, who was on deck, came up & said more sternly than I ever heard him speak before, 'Gentlemen, that is the *Merrimac*, you had better go below.'"

Keeler and the surgeon—not waiting for "a second *invitation*"—scrambled up the ladder onto the turret and dropped down the hatchway, followed by Worden. As the captain descended to the passage that led to the pilothouse, he noticed the eleven-inch iron globe being hoisted into the throat of one of the guns, and told the crew, "Send them that with our compliments, my lads."

After that, silence, broken only by the scrape and clack of the ship's workings.

"A few straggling rays of light," wrote Keeler, "found their way from the top of the tower to the depths below, which was dimly lighted by lanterns. Every one was at his post, fixed like a Statue, the most profound silence reigned—if there had been a coward heart there its throb would have been audible, so *intense* was the stillness."

The paymaster wrote this to his wife at the end of the same day he'd begun waiting in clammy darkness to discover what the *Merrimack* could do to him. The experience was still so fresh as to be immediate when he told Anna he felt "a peculiar sensation, I do not think it was fear, but it was different from anything I ever knew before. We were enclosed in what we supposed to be an impenetrable armour—we knew that a powerful foe was about to meet us—ours was an untried experiment & our enemy's first fire might make it a coffin for us all."

Worden was also keenly aware of the novelty of the experiment he commanded, and his worries centered on more specific mechanical concerns that did his paymaster's.

He was not happy with the pilothouse: "It is built a little more than three feet above the deck, of bars of iron, ten by twelve inches square, built up like a log house, bolted with very large bolts at the corners where the bars interlock. The pilot stands upon a platform below, his head and shoulders in the pilot-house. The upper tier of bars is separated from the second by an open square of an inch, through which the pilot may look out at every point of the compass." All that was fine; but it is "a foursquare mass of iron provided with no means of deflecting a shell."

What troubled him more, though, was the most unusual fixture of his most unusual ship. "If a projectile struck the turret at an acute angle, it was expected to glance off without doing damage. But what would happen if it was fired on a straight line to the center of the turret, which in that case would receive the full force of the blow? It might break off the bolt-heads on the interior, which, flying across would kill the men at the guns; it might disarrange the revolving mechanism, and then we would be wholly disabled."

Worden's doubts did not make him timid about meeting the *Merrimack*. "We had come a very long way to fight her, and did not intend to waste our opportunity."

His audacity surprised Captain Van Brunt. The *Minnesota* had already opened fire—not likely to hurt a target a mile away that had easily shed the *Cumberland*'s shells when the guns were muzzle to muzzle, but what else could you do? Van Brunt watched the fall of his shot and kept a sour eye on his puny ally. He had expected the *Monitor* to stand off at a careful distance and try to hamper the Rebels' awful machine at the longest possible range. Instead, he wrote, Worden went straight for his opponent, the *Monitor* "completely covering my ship as far as was possible with her dimensions, and, much to my astonishment, laid herself alongside of the *Merrimack* and the contest was that of a pigmy to a giant."

GREENE WAITED FOR THE WORD to open fire. Ericsson had designed a "speaking trumpet" for the captain to communicate with the turret, but if it had ever worked, it didn't now, and Worden drafted the captain's clerk, who was his nephew, Daniel Toffey, and Keeler to carry his orders.

"Paymaster," Greene said, "ask the captain if I shall fire."

Keeler trotted forward. Worden said, "Tell Mr. Green [Keeler still hadn't fully learned his name] not to fire till I give the word, to be cool and deliberate, to take sure aim & not waste a shot."

At the next order, the engines slowed to a stop, and Stodder swung the turret around.

"Commence firing."

"I triced up the port," wrote Greene, "ran the gun out & fired the first gun and thus commenced the great battle between the *Monitor* and *Merrimac*."

"O what a relief it was" to Keeler "when, at the word, the gun over my head thundered out its challenge with a report which jarred our vessel, but it was music to us all."

The turret filled with powder smoke, which the blowers immediately distributed throughout the ship. Quartermaster Peter Truscott peered out of the sickle of space above the gun as the smoke cleared. "You can see surprise on a ship just as you can on a human being," he said, "and there was surprise all over the Merrimac."

THIRD ASSISTANT ENGINEER WHITE, IN charge of the *Merrimack*'s engine room gong and its perfectly functioning speaking tube, had "noticed a volume of smoke coming up from the opposite side of the *Minnesota* and there emerged the queerest looking craft afloat. Through our glasses we could see she was ironclad, sharp at both ends and appeared to be almost awash. Mounted amidships was a turret with ports and, as we looked, the turret began to revolve until her forward gun bore directly on us. . . .

"We didn't have long to wait before she fired. Her first shot fell a little short and sent up a geyser of water that fell on our top and rolled off. We fired our forward rifle and scored a direct hit on her turret."

This was exactly the blow Worden had feared. An enormous clang; the turret jerked and shuddered as a bulge popped out in its wall.

The frightened gunners looked to Greene, who looked to Stimers, who put a rhetorical question to the exec: "Did the shot come through?"

"No, sir, it didn't come through, but it made a big dent, just look a there, sir!"

"A big dent!" echoed Stimers, his exasperation laced with amusement. "Of course it made a big dent—that is just what we expected, but what do you care about that so long as it keeps out the shot?"

Greene saw that "a look of confidence passed over the men's faces." They turned back to their guns.

"Now mark the condition our men were in," Greene wrote his parents a few days later. "Since Friday morning 48 hours, they had no rest, and very little food. . . . As for myself I had not slept a wink for 51 hours and had been on my feet almost constantly. But after the first gun was fired we forgot all fatigue, hard work, and everything else & went to work fighting as hard as men ever fought."

AFTER THE *MERRIMACK* HAD STRUCK the turret, White said, "The *Monitor*'s next shot was better and caught us amidships with a resounding wham, but while the old boat shuddered, there seemed to be no appreciable damage. By this time we were getting pretty close, and both crafts were firing as fast as the guns could be served."

On the *Monitor*, that wasn't so fast, every six or seven minutes. Greene's saying he "triced up the port" makes the process sound brisk, but the stoppers proved so heavy that it took a whole gun crew to lift one free of the muzzle it shielded. Moreover, the rust made the turret difficult to manage. After wrestling with his controls for a while, Stodder turned them over to the stronger Stimers.

The ship's agility helped compensate for the awkwardness with its turret. "I had decided how I would fight her in advance," said Worden. "I would keep the *Monitor* moving on a circle just large enough to give time for loading the guns." This he did and his nimble vessel sailed rings around her lumbering opponent.

"When we came out for the second day's fight," wrote White, "thinking we would clean up the *Minnesota*, *Roanoke* and *St. Lawrence*, we were not entirely surprised to find the *Monitor*, for, while we did not know exactly what to expect we knew some craft had come in during the night. However we had no doubt we could handle her easily."

That wasn't happening. "We hovered about each other in spirals," wrote Ashton Ramsay, "gradually contacting the circuits until we were within point-blank range, but our shells glanced from the *Monitor*'s turret." That "shells" speaks to the *Merrimack*'s disadvantage. Prepared to meet only wooden opponents, she had armed herself almost solely with them. Engineer Jack wrote, "Our only hope to penetrate the *Monitor*'s shield was in the rifled cannon, but as the only projectiles for that were percussion shells, there was barely a chance that we might penetrate our adversary's defense by a lucky shot." Some of the shells simply disintegrated against the *Monitor*'s turret, and those that exploded rattled so harmlessly against it that a gunner on the Union ship cried, "The damned fools are firing canister at us." And they might as well have been.

The *Monitor* also had a problem with her guns. Worden had plenty of solid shot, but the stricture against putting more than fifteen pounds of powder behind each ball kept any from breaking through the *Merrimack*'s armor. The massive Dahlgrens proved themselves capable of standing more than twice the mandated charge; but that was later. Also, Worden had been restricted to the use of shot made of cast iron rather than heavier, denser wrought iron, which Dahlgren feared might damage the guns.

Nevertheless, the *Merrimack* took a hit that, Jack said, "broke the backers to the shield and sent a splinter into our engine room with about enough force to carry it halfway across the ship." The shield itself held.

The embattled ships stood for the most part between one and two hundred yards apart, occasionally coming so close together that their sides scraped (five times, according to Greene). Ramsay wrote, "On our gun-deck all was bustle, smoke, grimy figures, and stern commands, while down in the engine and boiler rooms the sixteen furnaces were belching out fire and smoke, and the firemen standing in front of them, like so many gladiators, tugged away with devil's claw and slice-bar, inducing by their exertions more and more combustion and heat. The noise of the crackling, roaring fires, escaping steam, and the loud and labored pulsations of the engines, together with the roar of battle above and the thud and vibrations of the huge masses of iron which were hurled against us produced a scene and sound to be compared only with the poet's picture of the lower regions."

The *Monitor*'s crew was in the same Dantean hell. "The men at the guns," said Keeler, "had stripped themselves to their waists & were covered with powder & smoke, the perspiration falling from them like rain."

A sailor on a second-generation monitor described the scene in his nearly identical turret during the Battle of Mobile Bay a year and a half later. "With the recoil of the gun a sudden tremor ran through the ship as though in collision followed an instant later by the roar of the explosion mingled with [the] deep voiced rushing note of the shot as it leaves the muzzle of the gun. The turret chamber . . . was instantly filled with blinding smoke mingled with particles of burning powder. . . .

"The sounds produced by the shot striking our turret were far different from what I anticipated. The scream of the shot would arrive at about the same time with the projectile . . . and then the air would be filled with that peculiar shrill singing sound of violently broken glass, or perhaps more like the noise made by flinging a nail violently through the air. The shock of discharge of our own guns was particularly especially hard on the ears of those in the turret. . . . But it was really a place of perfect safety."

So they were discovering on the *Monitor.* "Our tower was struck several times," wrote Greene, "and though the noise was pretty loud, it did not affect us any." Safe though the gunners might be, they had trouble with what a later naval generation would call fire control.

In an account he wrote years after the hasty letter to his

parents, Greene said, "Stimers was an active, muscular man, and did his utmost to control the motion of the turret; but in spite of his efforts, it was difficult, if not impossible, to secure accurate firing. . . . My only view of the world outside of the tower was over the muzzles of the guns, which cleared the port only by a few inches. When the guns were run in, the port-holes were covered by heavy iron pendulums, pierced with small holes to allow the rammer and sponge handlers to protrude while they were still in use. . . . The effect upon one shut up in a revolving drum is perplexing, and it is not a simple matter to keep the bearings. White marks had been placed upon the stationary deck immediately below the turret to indicate the direction of the starboard and port sides, and the bow and port sides, and bow and stern; but these marks were obliterated early in the action."

Greene also had to be careful not to kill his captain. When the guns were trained straight forward, the wheelhouse stood directly in front of them. "A careless or impatient hand, during the confusion arising from the whirligig motion of the tower, might let slip one of our big shot against the pilot-house. For this and other reasons I fired every gun while I remained in the turret."

Keeler and Toffey squeezed back and forth past one another as they ran the seventy-five feet between wheelhouse and turret, relaying orders and information, which Keeler remembered as:

"Tell Mr. Green that I am going to bring him on our starboard beam close along side."

"That was a good shot, went through her water line [actually, no such luck]."

"Don't let the men expose themselves, they are firing at us with rifles."

"That last shot brought the iron from her sides."

"She's too far off now, reserve your fire until you're sure."

Greene said, "Keller [he didn't get his colleague's name quite right either] and Toffey . . . performed their work with zeal and alacrity, but, both being landsmen, our technical communication sometimes miscarried."

With the white marks gone, and the turret fractious, and the shutters not getting any easier to lift, Greene decided to do away with the last altogether and had them triced up for good. Now he would fire at the *Merrimack* on the fly.

This desperate measure actually hurt morale on the *Merrimack*. Eggleston wrote that the "*Monitor*'s two eleven-inch guns, thoroughly protected, were really more formidable than our ten guns of from six to nine caliber. We never got sight of her guns except when they were about to fire at us. Then the turret slowly turned, presenting to us its solid side, and enabling the gunners to load without danger."

The *Merrimack* had been lucky so far. Ramsay knew that "the coal consumption of our two days' fight had lightened our prow until our unprotected submerged deck was almost awash. The armor on our sides below the water-line had been extended but about three feet, owing to our hasty departure before the work was finished. Lightened as we were, these exposed portions rendered us no longer an ironclad, and the *Monitor* might have pierced us between wind and water had she depressed her guns."

William Norris, the ship's master-at-arms, wrote, "Now, the enormous weight of her shield and battery, kept the *Virginia*, all the time, just hovering between floating and sinking. She was sluggish, sodden and entirely irresponsive to the breathing of the sea. In a very slight roughening of the waves, a sailor could tell in a moment, by the feel of her, under his feet that it was a touch and go matter whether she staid up, or went down." One well-aimed shot from "the splendid eleven-inch gun of the *Monitor*, and the *Virginia* would have gone to the bottom in five minutes."

Norris was scornful of what he believed was his enemy's carelessness. His peculiar, engaging verdict: "Not a shot appeared to have any 'motif.'"

No motif, but offering no good target either. Many of the Rebel shells passed right over the *Monitor*'s low deck. Captain Jones had ordered his men to fire at her gunports, but they proved too fleeting a target. So far, neither ship had done any serious damage to the other, and nobody had been wounded, although Stodder, having become cavalier about the turret's integrity, was leaning against its wall when a shot hit directly opposite and sent him cartwheeling to end up unconscious on the far side of both guns. (Was everybody tougher back then? Stodder was up and about within an hour.)

By ten o'clock the *Monitor* had fired every shot in her turret, and Greene said, "Worden hauled off for about fifteen minutes to replenish. The serving of the cartridges, weighing but fifteen pounds, was a matter of no difficulty; but the hoisting of the heavy shot was a slow and tedious operation, it being necessary that the turret should remain stationary, in order that the two scuttles, one in the deck and the other in the floor of the turret, should be in line."

The lull allowed Worden to satisfy himself about "what I believed to be the weakest point of the Monitor." He explained that "the deck is joined to the side of the hull by a right angle, or what sailors call a 'plank-shear.' If a projectile struck that angle what would happen? It would not be deflected; its whole force would be expended there. It might open a seam in the hull below the water-line . . . and sink us."

That angle had been hit, and more than once; Worden needed to know how it was holding. To the alarm of his officers, he went outside to see. "We had already learned that the *Merrimac* swarmed with sharpshooters, for their bullets were constantly spattering against our turret and our deck. If a man showed himself on deck he would draw their fire. But I did not much consider the sharpshooters. I ordered one of the pendulums to be hauled aside, and, crawling out of the port, walked to the side, lay down upon my chest, and examined it thoroughly. The hull was uninjured."

So was Worden. "I walked back and crawled into the turret— the bullets were falling on the iron deck about me as thick as hailstones in a storm. None struck me, I suppose because the vessel was moving. . . ."

Back inside the ship, "I told the men, what was true, that the

Merrimac could not sink us if we let her pound us for a month. The men cheered; the knowledge put new life into all." To further enliven that new life, he ordered the spirit room opened and gave everyone aboard a half gill of whiskey. Keeler, a teetotaler, grudgingly conceded, "If liquor ever does good to any one & is ever useful it must be on some such occasion."

CATESBY JONES DIDN'T WANT TO pound the *Monitor* for a month, or even for another five minutes. As soon as the Yankee was clear of his path, he made for the *Minnesota*. Half an hour earlier Hunter Davidson had been sure that "another shot or two from the *Monitor* . . . would have brought down the shield around our ears." Now, something almost as bad happened.

Just as the rearmed Union ship was returning to the fight, the *Merrimack* ran up on the Middle Ground shoal and stuck there. "Our situation was critical," said Ashton Ramsay. "The *Monitor* could, at her leisure, come close up to us and yet be out of our reach, owing to our inability to deflect our guns. In she came and began to sound every chink in our armor—every one but that which was actually vulnerable, had she known it."

That was the slice of underside the lightening ship had raised above the waterline. However haphazard the *Monitor*'s gunnery might be, she was bound to find it pretty soon. "We had to take all chances," said Ramsay. This meant somehow adding to the engines' power. Already they were backing with all their strength, the hull juddering as the propeller tried to claw it out into deep water.

"We lashed down the safety valves."

Safety valves are just that. They let the steam escape when the pressure has risen to the highest point the boiler can bear. More, and it will explode. Jones and Ramsay were risking the destruction of their ship. The stokers, said Ramsay, "heaped quick-burning combustibles into the already raging fires. . . . The propeller churned the mud and water furiously, but the ship did not stir."

Phillips, although a surgeon and not an engineer, knew very

well what was going on. Later, he heard that the pilot had run the *Merrimack* aground on purpose "through fear of passing through the *Minnesota*'s terrible broadside." If true, the man hadn't learned much during the past two hours, for the *Monitor* had already shown herself more dangerous than a dozen *Minnesota*s. Right now the palsied ship could do nothing against the *Monitor*; she was on them, Phillips said, "like a fierce dog," probing with her Dahlgrens for a mortal point. "Everyone was watching and waiting with an impatience which may well be imagined to be relieved of the horrible night-mare of inactivity."

As soon as the *Monitor* had fired its first shot, the Confederate gunboats had drawn off to a respectful distance, knowing it would be suicide to intervene in this unprecedented battle. Now Jones signaled them to come help. His flags took a long time unfurling in the gentle breeze, and when they did, the *Patrick Henry*'s signal officer read, "Disabled my propeller is."

Although the message sounded like an inept translation, the *Henry*'s captain knew what it meant, and the wooden ships reluctantly headed in to try to tow off the *Merrimack*.

Down in her engine room, said Ramsay, the black gang, running among the stuttering, stifled safety valves, "piled on oiled cotton waste, splints of wood, anything that would burn faster than coal. It seemed impossible that the boilers could stand the pressure we were crowding on them."

After an eternal quarter of an hour, "just as we were beginning to despair there was a perceptible movement, and the *Merrimac* slowly dragged herself off the shoal by main strength. We were saved."

So were the crews of the gunboats, which gratefully withdrew when they saw their flagship back afloat.

The two contestants grappled again. "The sounds of the conflict at this time were terrible," said Keeler. "The rapid firing of our own guns amid the clouds of smoke, the howling of the *Minnesota*'s shells, which was firing whole broadsides at a time just over our heads (two of her shot struck us), mingled with the crash of solid shot against our sides & the bursting of shells all around us."

With the *Merrimack*'s great manpower advantage in mind, Jones called for boarders. Wood issued hammers to a group of volunteers; if they clambered onto the *Monitor*'s deck, perhaps they could pound wedges under the turret's rim and freeze it into immobility. In the meantime an audacious seaman named John Hunt, one of Littlepage's gunners, pulled off his jacket and climbed into a port, saying he was going to jump aboard the "bloody little iron tub" and blind the pilothouse by throwing his coat over it. Littlepage talked him out of the foolhardy (but not wholly impossible) plan while the boarders prepared.

Worden was ready for them; he'd seen to it that grenades were at hand in the turret. "They're going to board us," he called to Keeler, "put in a round of canister."

Keeler alerted Greene, who told him, "Can't do it, both guns have solid shot."

"Give them to her, then," said the captain.

The men in the turret were confident. "Let 'em come," said a gunner. "We will amuse them some."

The ships passed close by one another, but too quickly for Wood's boarding party to leap across. Walking the gun deck, Jones was further frustrated to see that Eggleston's pieces were silent, their crews standing about cautiously peering out the ports. "Why are you not firing, Mr. Eggleston?"

The lieutenant replied, "Why, our powder is very precious, and after two hours' incessant firing I find that I can do her about as much damage by snapping my thumb at her every two minutes and a half."

A more thin-skinned skipper could have taken this as outright insubordination, but Jones had come to the same conclusion and merely said, "Never mind, we are getting ready to ram her."

To Wood, this "was a last resort. Seeing that our shots were ineffective, I was directed to convey to the engine room for orders for every man to be at his post." They had plenty of time to get there. "For an hour we maneuvered for position. Now go ahead! Now stop! Now astern! The Merrimac was as unwieldy as Noah's Ark."

On the *Monitor*, Worden told Keeler, "Look out now, they're going to run us down. Give them both guns."

Keeler rushed the message to Greene, feeling "this was the critical moment, one that I had feared from the beginning of the fight—if she could so easily pierce the heavy oak beams of the *Cumberland*, she surely could go through the 1/2 inch iron plates of our lower hull."

Although Jones apparently did not know his ship had left her ram in the *Cumberland*, he seems to have been more cautious than Buchanan had been the day before. Perhaps he remembered those moments when the impaled frigate nearly pulled his ship down with it. Ramsay said the captain "gave the signal to reverse the engines long before we reached the *Monitor*."

Worden had sheered off from his far heavier opponent by the time the collision came. "A moment of terrible suspense," Keeler wrote, "a heavy jar nearly throwing us from our feet—a rapid glance to detect the expected gush of water—she had failed to reach us below the water & we were safe."

John Driscoll, stationed at the foot of the turret ladder, said the "blow was a glancing one yet with such force as [to] jar the chimney off every lamp below and to slightley start one of the deck plates."

Ramsay "did not feel the slightest shock down in the engine-room, though we struck her fairly enough."

The attempt did more harm to the *Merrimack* than to her enemy. The *Monitor* came away with a few pale spikes of wood splayed under the bolt heads that had gouged them from the Southerner's hull. The *Merrimack* began taking in water at her bruised bow.

Ramsay wasn't worried. Jones twice called him up to report. The first time the engineer said, "It is impossible we can be making much water, for the skin of the vessel is plainly visible in the crank-pits." That is, even the lowest reaches of the machinery's housing were dry. On the second, Ramsay reported, "With the two large Worthington pumps, besides the bilge injections, we could keep her afloat for hours, even with a ten-inch shell in her hull."

Jones was still after the frigate. "We glided past the *Monitor* unscathed," Ramsay said, "but got between her and the *Minnesota*."

McDonald, watching from the *Dragon*, saw the *Merrimack* coming at him once again. "We were close to the side of the tall *Minnesota* . . . doing all we could to get her off the mud. . . . The upper guns of the frigate were roaring above us."

Someone yelled for him to get the tug clear. "We were in the way of the lower tier of guns. I sprang for one of the lines to cast it off. Just then I met my fate. One of the *Merrimac*'s shells went directly through our boiler. The explosion that followed drove a board with great force against my shoulder and head, partly stunning me, and throwing me toward the shell. A piece of that got to me, ripping up my left leg and splitting the thigh-bone. The air over me was so full of burning powder, steam, and smoke that in my half-stunned condition I thought I was suffocating in the water, and struck out as if to swim; but strong hands pulled me through a port-hole of the Minnesota and laid me out on the deck.

"The row of the battle continued, but my fighting was over. The long and the short of it is, that one of my burial-places is in Old Virginia, as I told a friend; — there is where I left my leg."

He didn't leave the rest of himself there because the *Monitor* was still keeping the *Merrimack* from finishing off the *Minnesota*.

Now it was Worden's turn to ram. He headed for the *Merrimack*'s fantail. William Norris said, "Our rudder and propeller were wholly unprotected, and a slight blow from her stern would have disabled both and ended the fight."

The *Merrimack*'s evasive maneuver, elephantine though it was, swung those vitals clear of the *Monitor*'s sharp bow. The Union ship, barely missing, passed very close. Jones, having given up on hitting its gunports, had ordered his gunners to fire at the pilot-house.

Writing long after, Ericsson described "the elongated sight-hole formed between the iron blocks" and said, somewhat defensively, that "it should be borne in mind that an opening of five-eights of an inch affords a vertical view 80 feet high at a distance of only 200 yards. More is not needed . . . [but] unfortunately the sight holes were subsequently altered, the iron blocks being raised and the opening between them increased." Worden was standing peering out through the widened slot as his ship passed the *Merrimack* and swam into the sights of her stern rifle. Wood tugged the lanyard and got off a clear shot—the single most telling of the battle—at a distance of no more than twenty yards.

"A heavy shell struck the pilot house," wrote Keeler. "I was standing near, waiting an order, heard the report which was un-usually heavy, a flash of light & a cloud of smoke filled the house. I noticed the Capt. stagger & put his hands to his eyes—I ran up to him & asked if he was hurt.

"'My eyes,' says he, 'I am blind.'"

Toffey caught his uncle as he stumbled backward through the spokes of sunshine the broken wheelhouse had let in. Greene wrote, "The flood of light rushing through the pilot-house, now partly open, caused Worden, blind as he was, to believe that the pilot-house was seriously injured, if not destroyed; he therefore gave orders to put the helm to starboard and 'sheer off.'"

Greene turned over the turret to Stimers, "went forward at once, and found [Worden] standing at the foot of the ladder lead-ing to the pilot-house.

"He was a ghastly sight, with his eyes closed and the blood ap-parently rushing from every pore in the upper part of his face. He told me that he was seriously wounded, and directed me to take command." While the twenty-three-year-old lieutenant absorbed this, he and Keeler and Surgeon Logue got Worden to the couch in his cabin. As Logue began with harried delicacy picking out grains of metal and paint and gunpowder from Worden's face, the captain gave his final order of the day: "Gentlemen, I leave it with you, do what you think best. I cannot see, but do not mind me. Save the *Minnesota* if you can."

Quartermaster Williams and Howard—both of whom had somehow escaped injury—followed the "sheer off" order and took the *Monitor* into the shallows. Greene left Worden and went to examine the wheelhouse. Wood's shell had split the nine-by-twelve bar on the second tier down from the iron roof, which had been kicked up and back, leaving an opening several inches wide. The damage was considerable, but Greene saw "the steering gear was still intact, and the pilot-house was not totally destroyed, as had been feared. . . . Exactly how much time elapsed from the moment that Worden was wounded until I reached the pilot-house and completed the examination of the injury at that point, and determined what course to pursue in the damaged condition of the vessel, it is impossible to state; but it could hardly have exceeded twenty minutes at the utmost."

However long or short the hiatus, it was enough to convince Catesby Jones and everyone else on the *Merrimack* that the *Monitor* was quitting. "The fight had continued for three hours," Jones said. "To us the *Monitor* appeared unharmed. We were therefore surprised to see her run off into shoal water where our great draft would not permit us to follow, and where our shells could not reach her." He once again started for the *Minnesota*.

Captain Van Brunt "then felt the fullest extent of my condition." He and his men were close to dropping with fatigue; his magazines were empty; and now the *Monitor* "stood down for Fortress Monroe, and we thought it probable that she had exhausted her supply of ammunition or sustained some injury." Van Brunt gave the order he'd been avoiding for a day and a night: *Prepare the ship for scuttling.*

On this, its third try at the *Minnesota*, the *Merrimack* started shooting from a long way off. The frigate, said Jones, was "out of range of the direct fire of our smooth-bore guns." Eggleston had to shoot his smoothbores "at ricochet—that is, with the gun level—so that the shot would skip along the surface like pebbles the boys 'skell' along a pond. But Davidson, with his rifle guns, just forward of me was actually 'plumping' the target with direct fire."

The rifle shots were hitting hard, but "it was at this juncture," wrote Ramsay, "that Lieutenant Jones had sent for me and said:

'The pilot will not place us near to the *Minnesota*, and we cannot afford the risk of getting aground again.'"

The captain went down to the gun deck and spoke with his officers. "The *Monitor* has given up the fight and run into shoal water, the pilots cannot take us any nearer to the *Minnesota*; this ship is leaking . . . ; the men are exhausted by being so long at their guns; the tide is ebbing, so, that we shall have to remain here all night unless we leave at once. I propose to return to Norfolk for repairs. What is your opinion?"

Unanimous agreement, save for Wood, whose blood was up: "I proposed to Jones to run down to Fortress Monroe and then clean up the Yankee ships there or run them out to sea."

Jones told Ramsay, "I'm going to haul off under the guns of Sewall's point and renew the action on the rise of the tide." To Ramsay, this was "as though a wet blanket had been thrown over me. His reasoning was doubtless good, but it ignored the moral effect of leaving the Roads without forcing the *Minnesota* to surrender."

Or the *Monitor.* On the Union ship, said Greene, "Having taken my station in the pilot-house and turning the vessel's head in the direction of the *Merrimac*, I saw that she was already in retreat."

In the first moments of his sudden command, he ordered the *Monitor* to steam out of the shallows toward the *Minnesota.* He fired at the *Merrimack* as he came, but he didn't pursue her. "I knew if another shot should strike our pilot house in the same place, our steering apparatus would be disabled and we should be at the mercy of the Batteries at Sewell's point. . . . We had strict orders to act on the defensive and protect the *Minnesota.* We had evidently finished the *Merrimac* as far as the *Minnesota* was concerned . . . and we had strict orders not to follow the *Merrimac* up; therefore, after the *Merrimac* had retreated, I went up to the *Minnesota* and remained by her."

Greene wrote this long after; if it carries a hint of anxious justification, that's because his decision not to keep after the Confederate ship clouded the rest of his too-short life.

Log of U.S. Steamer "Monitor" Lieut. J.L. Worden Comdg

Sunday March 9/62

Comes in fine weather & calm
At ½ past One piped all to quarters, hove up
Anchor, At 2 AM came to Anchor again

                Geo. Frederickson

4 to 8 P M fine weather & calm, at Sunrise saw
3 Steamers lying under Sewals Point, Made one
out to be the Rebel steamer Merrimac, At 8.20
got underweigh & stood towards her & piped all
hands to quarters,

                J. Unca

From 8 to Meridian fine clear weather, the Rebel
Steamers advancing & opened fire on the Minnesota
8.20 opened fire on the Merrimac, from that time
until 12, constantly engaged, with the Merrimac

                Louis Stodder

From Meridian to 4 P M. clear weather.
At 12,30 rifled shell struck the Pilot House severely
injuring Commander Worden. 1 P M the
Merrimac hauled off in a disabled condition,
Stood towards the "Minnesota" & received on board
Ass't Sec't of the Navy. 2 P M Capt Worden
left for Fort Monroe in charge of Surgeon Logue.

                Geo. Frederickson

4 to 6 P M fine weather. I came to Anchor
alongside the Minnesota.

                J. Unca

6 to 8 fine clear weather, and Lookout left,

                Louis Stodder

8 to 12 weather the same
10 P M. Lieut Edwin Flye joined the vessel
as Exte officer

                Geo. Frederickson

"8.20 opened fire on the Merrimac . . ." The *Monitor*'s log entry for March 8, 1862,
photographed on the fiftieth anniversary of the battle.

But not on this day. When the *Monitor* came alongside the *Minnesota*, which was still grounded even though lightened by the loss of seven eight-inch guns that had been pushed over the side and surrounded by a floating commissary of jettisoned barrels of rice and sugar, whiskey and flour and beans, the frigate's crew cheered and cheered.

No matter that the *Merrimack* was still afloat, it had gone away. Gustavus Fox, who had watched the battle from the *Minnesota*, wrote that when he'd gone aboard her, "she was about to be abandoned, before the engagement, because she was aground and no confidence was held in the little *Monitor* then standing out to meet the *Merrimack*."

Now he climbed down onto the deck of the ironclad, where Keeler was having a good time. "Our iron hatches were slid back & we sprang out on deck which was strewn with fragments of the fight." These were the concave iron remnants of the *Merrimack*'s shells; Keeler began to collect them to send to his son. While he was about this, Lieutenant Wood fired the final gun of the engagement from well over a mile away. Keeler ducked as the shot "shrieked just over our heads & exploded about 100 feet behind us." A few shards joined the others on the deck, and a cheerful seaman said, "Paymaster, here's some more pieces."

While Keeler was harvesting his souvenirs, Henry Wise, the Navy Department's assistant inspector of ordnance, arrived in a tug. Wise was the man who had long ago outfoxed the British spy sent to poach the secrets of the Dahlgren gun; and he had reluctantly held the torch to the *Merrimack* during the abandonment of Gosport. A close friend of Worden's—they'd roomed together at the Naval Academy—Wise at once went below with Fox to find the *Monitor*'s captain "with the surgeon sponging away the blood and powder from his closed eyes and blackened face."

Wise gave him a hug.

Worden asked, "Have I beat her off?"

"Jack! You've saved your country."

"Have I saved that fine ship, the *Minnesota*?"

"Yes, and whipped the *Merrimac* to boot."

"Then I don't care what happens to me."

Wise cared; he took his friend to shore and went with him to Washington. Worden wrote, "To his friendly care and attention in bringing me from Hampton Roads after my injuries in the *Monitor* and putting me in his own bed at his home in Washington, and the devoted care and attention given me there, for several weeks by himself and his wife, I am largely indebted for my recovery from the injuries I received, and their resulting complications."

Greene saw Worden off, then returned to his brand-new duties. He and his men were beginning to enjoy what would be a durable celebrity. "In a few minutes," Keeler said, "we were surrounded by small steamers & boats from Newport News, the Fortress, the various men of war, all eager to learn the extent of our injuries." There were none save Worden's.

Fox had Greene assemble the crew on deck. While the men smiled, teeth very white in their smoke-black faces, he told them how much the Navy Department appreciated their "great services."

After four hours of close action, the *Monitor* became a restaurant. "Our stewards went immediately to work," said Keeler, "& at our usual dinner hour the meal was on the table, much to the astonishment of visitors who came expecting to see a list of killed & wounded & a disabled vessel, instead of which was a merry party around the table enjoying some good beef steak, green peas &c."

Fox rose from his steak and peas to tell the officers, "Well, gentlemen, you don't look as though you were just through one of the greatest naval conflicts on record."

Greene answered with giddy savoir faire, "No, sir, we haven't done much fighting, merely drilling the men at the guns a little."

A few feet above the rejoicing table, crewmen walked about the deck, touching the fresh hollows in the turret and swapping happy ribaldries with sailors grinning down at them from the rail of the

Minnesota, where the carpenters were already at work patching the shot holes.

The smoke lifted off the water; the day gleamed about them. The sun stood overhead, barely past its zenith, shining down on the hundreds of men who now knew that they would be alive to see it set.

CHAPTER 25

Victors

A postcard from the early 1900s celebrates both combatants.

The Battle of Hampton Roads is unique in several ways. It was the first fight between metal warships, and the first between steam-driven ones. It was unique in what Fox called the novelist's timing of the *Monitor*'s arrival; and in the immense technological effort that put its two contestants hull to hull. And, if not unique, highly unusual in that even before their guns had cooled, each side believed it had won.

This conviction was not the result of any propaganda effort, or the natural desire to cast the best possible light on a contest that had been witnessed by thousands, and upon whose outcome much depended. The men of the *Monitor* and the men of the *Merrimack* really did think they'd beaten one another.

A significant exception was Catesby Jones, who, speaking confidentially, told Major Norris of the Signal Bureau that "the battle was a drawn one," and "the destruction of those wooden vessels was a matter of course especially so, being at anchor, but in not capturing that ironclad, I feel as if we had done nothing." He paused, then said, of the *Monitor*, "And yet, give me that vessel and I will sink this one in a matter of minutes."

Ashton Ramsay also hadn't been so sure of victory when Jones gave him the wet-blanket news that they were leaving the Roads while the *Minnesota* was still above water, but as his ship headed into the Elizabeth River, he was surprised to find that "she received a tremendous ovation from the crowds that lined the shores, while hundreds of small boats, gay with flags and bunting, converted our course into a triumphal procession."

One of the *Merrimack*'s crewmen thought the same thing: "No conqueror of ancient Rome ever enjoyed a prouder triumph than that which greeted us."

Captain Parker, who had been in such deep travail the day before, took the *Beaufort* into Norfolk Sunday night to find "the whole city was alive with joy and excitement. Nothing was talked of but the *Merrimac* and what she had accomplished. As to what she could do in the future, no limit was set on her powers. The papers indulged in the wildest speculations, and everybody went mad, as usual. At the North, the same fever prevailed. No battle that was ever fought caused as great a sensation throughout the civilized world. The moral effect at the North was most marvelous; and even now I can scarcely realize it."

The moral effect was certainly marvelous in Newport News. When Keeler, refreshed by "the first sleep for three nights," went ashore the next morning, he found himself "devoured." His ship was "on every one's tongue & the expressions of gratitude and joy embarrassed us as they are so numerous."

One citizen asked if he was from the *Monitor* and, when Keeler said yes, grabbed his hand: "My insurance is worth two thousand dollars. You can draw on me for that amount and it shall be honored."

Stared at as if "I was some strange being," he went into a grocery store to buy fresh vegetables for the crew. The proprietor urged him, "Tell your wardroom officers to come and see me whenever they come ashore. I have first-rate quarters and they are always welcome without expense. The safety of all I have is due to them."

News of the battle took a little while to reach the North. The telegraph at Fortress Monroe, which had been perfectly robust when it relayed Saturday's disaster to Washington, had fallen into maddening silence by the time the *Monitor* steamed out from the lee of the *Minnesota*. It didn't get fixed until six forty-five Sunday evening, when Fox telegraphed Welles:

"The *Monitor* arrived at 10 PM last night and went immediately to the protection of the *Minnesota*, lying aground just below Newport News.

"7 AM to-day the *Merrimack*, accompanied by two wooden steamers and several tugs, stood out toward the *Minnesota* and opened fire.

"The *Monitor* met them at once and opened her fire, when all the enemy's vessels retired, excepting the *Merrimack*. These two ironclad vessels fought part of the time touching each other, from 8 AM to noon, when the *Merrimack* retired. Whether she is injured or not it is impossible to say. Lieutenant J. L. Worden, who commanded the *Monitor*, handled her with great skill, assisted by Chief Engineer Stimers. Lieutenant Worden was injured by the cement from the pilot house being driven into his eyes, but I trust not seriously. The *Minnesota* kept up a continuous fire and is herself somewhat injured.

"She was moved considerably to-day, and will probably be off to-night. The *Monitor* is uninjured and ready at any moment to repel another attack."

Welles, with the greatest satisfaction, immediately demanded that Stanton cease preparations to sink his gravel barges. (A few weeks later, out for a sail with Stanton on an unvexed Potomac,

Lincoln teased his secretary of war. As they passed the barges, still marshaled along the bank, the President told the guests, "That is Stanton's navy," and went on, "It is as useless as the paps of a man to a sucking child. There may be some show to amuse the child, but they are good for nothing for service.")

Early Monday morning, Wise, having seen that Worden was comfortable, attended a meeting of Lincoln and his cabinet. The ordnance officer told his rapt audience about the fight, and Worden's wounding.

When he was done, the President asked where Worden was.

"At my house, sir."

Lincoln picked up his hat. "I don't know what you gentlemen are going to do, but for my part I am going to pay my respects to the young man who fought that battle."

The President accompanied Wise to his house, where his wife warned her tall visitor to mind the low ceilings. Lincoln smiled. "Yes, Mrs. Wise, it is just like my little home in Springfield." The two men went upstairs to the room where Worden lay, red eyes sightless in his blackened face.

Lincoln walked to the bed and put his hand on the captain's shoulder.

"Jack," said Wise, "here is the President, who has come to see you."

"You do me great honor, Mr. President, and I am only sorry that I can't see you."

"You need no man to do you honor, Lieutenant," said Lincoln, "for you have done great honor to yourself and to your country."

However much Worden valued the presidential praise, he was equally gratified, a while later, to get this letter:

TO OUR DEAR AND HONORED CAPTAIN.
DEAR SIR:

These few lines is from your own crew of the *Monitor*, with their kindest Love to you their Honored Captain, hoping to

God that they will have the pleasure of welcoming you back to us again soon, for we are all ready able and willing to meet Death or anything else, only give us back our Captain again. . . .

We all join with our kindest love to you, hoping that God will restore you to us again and hoping that your suffering is at an end. . . .

We remain until Death your Affectionate Crew.

THE MONITOR BOYS.

They got half their wish. Worden did not come back to the *Monitor*, but his sight returned. When Stanton heard the captain had lost the use of one eye, he exclaimed with rather grisly exuberance, "Then we will fill it with diamonds."

The rest of the nation shared the Monitor Boys' feelings. When the news broke, on Monday morning, the staid *New York Times* exulted, "If the battery had not arrived in time! One trembles to look along the line of this contingency. Suffice it to say that it *did* arrive in time and that the national cause has had an escape and a triumph whose romantic form stirs the mind with mingled wonder and joy."

CHAPTER 26

Echoes

An American cartoon shows Uncle Sam in *Monitor* guise giving
some sharp naval lessons to cowed European heads of state.

The wonder and joy swiftly spilled into that infallible barom-
eter of public enthusiasm, commerce. El Monitor cigars appeared, and Monitor hats, Monitor daguerreotype cases, Monitor
household flour, and the first of scores of commemorative Monitor coins and medallions (an early one showed the ship under the
affectionate legend OUR LITTLE MONITOR).

The entire North tried to stake a claim on the ship. The *Woon-
socket Patriot*, discovering that Greene was a Rhode Islander,
boasted that "Little Rhody has a finger in nearly every pie of this
war"; "Connecticut is always around," the *Hartford Evening Press*

said of Cornelius Bushnell, while the state promptly elected him
to its legislature; Rensselaer Iron Works sent a four-hundred-man
torchlight parade to Griswold's house. Little Rhody was especially
vocal: Howard, the pilot, was hailed in his hometown of Newport,
and the state even went so far as to claim Ericsson for a native
son because his namesake Leif was believed to have touched its
truncated shoreline a millennium earlier.

New York, which had a firmer claim on the inventor, played
a part in presenting him with a model of the *Monitor* cast out of
pure gold at a cost of $7,000, perhaps $170,000 in today's money.

Before that fourteen-pound keepsake came Ericsson's way, the
Navy Department released, just five days after the battle, the final
$68,750 owing him. His share of the *Monitor* profits was a substan-
tial $20,000.

Along with the hats and the cigars, the battle engendered a
gout of poetry. The Manhattan firm of Henry De Marsan, "Publisher of Songs, Ballads, Valentines, Juvenile & Toy-Books, Motto
Verses, Stationery, Playing Cards, A-B-C-Cards &c" issued "Our
Yankee Monitor," a remarkably inept effusion that nonetheless
touches on a truth:

> . . . At Hampton-Roads, the Monitor the Merrimac chased away:
> John Bull says to his parliament: there's danger in delay;
> Let us build Ericson-batteries, all expenses I will pay,
> And do not let America get master of the sea.
>
> France, my cunning neighbor, is beginning to prepare:
> All nations in this struggle will try and have a share;
> But my great boasted navy from Neptune will be hurled
> By Ericson's Iron-batteries, the best yet in the world. . . .
>
> With my money, says the Spaniard, America was discovered;
> My rich and fertile colonies against my will they severed;
> I must build Ericson-batteries, or Cuba will be gone;
> Those enterprising Yankees will call it all their own.

The Russian Bear now looks aghast and knows not what to say;
The largest armies known to fight is in America;
I must have batteries builded, invented by the Swede,
Or I will lose my power, and vast, extensive trade.

The Emperor of Austria, Eastern Continent at large,
Must have some Iron-batteries no matter what's the charge,
To defend their seaboard cities from tyrant devastation;
They know full well defeat to them is sad humiliation. . . .

The ripples of the battle quickly spread across the Atlantic. They reached a France and Britain that had already added the armored ships *La Gloire* and *Warrior* to their fleets, and one British expert remarked, "To the employment of armor she [the *Monitor*] may have given a fresh impulse; but no initiative." This seems too dismissive, for that fresh impulse was powerful. Britain studied the fight at Hampton Roads with fascination, and with an entirely new alarm.

Four months earlier Charles Wilkes, a showy, gifted, glory-hungry US frigate captain, acting without government instructions, had stopped the British mail steamer *Trent* and from it plucked James Mason and John Slidell, Southern commissioners on their way to London to gain recognition for the Confederacy. His action brought Britain to the brink of war. Her Majesty's government called for the release of the envoys and buttressed the demand by sending eleven thousand troops to Canada, while the First Lord of the Admiralty drafted plans for blockading the Atlantic coast north of Virginia. Britain had some worry about the inconvenience of a war, but none whatever about the outcome. The *Morning Chronicle* summed up the national feeling when it derided "that spirit that induces the Americans, with their dwarf fleet and shapeless mass of incoherent squads they call an army, to fancy themselves the equal of France by land and of Great Britain by sea."

Punch magazine published a full-page cartoon showing Britannia, in her helmet, gazing out to sea over the rail of a modern ship. Her shield lies at her feet; her chin rests on her left hand; she is pensive. But not helpless: a naval gun supports her left elbow, and her right hand confidently grasps its firing lanyard. The caption is WAITING FOR AN ANSWER. Clearly, she will get the one she wants.

She did. Although the seizure of the envoys was greatly popular in the United States, Lincoln wanted only "one war at a time." The government backed down, releasing the envoys to a British warship.

Now, after Hampton Roads, that "dwarf fleet" looked very different to the watchers overseas. The *London Times*, saying "nine-tenths of the British Navy have been rendered entirely useless," imagined an engagement between a British squadron and the *Monitor* and the *Merrimack* acting in concert: "What would have been the result? Would our Ariadnes or Orlandos have fared any better than the Cumberland and Congress against an invulnerable enemy? True, they might have availed themselves of their speed and escaped destruction; but if they had chosen, as they, no doubt, would have done, to fight, what would have been the end of the battle?"

The *Illustrated London News* declared "The Naval Revolution" at hand. "Is the Warrior itself a match for the Monitor? It is useless now to talk of speed and magnificence. We don't want our war ships to run away successfully, or to be looked at admiringly, but to fight. How would the Monitor deal with the Warrior? The guns of the first send shot of 170lb.; the guns of the second, shots of 100lb.... Again, the Monitor is practically invulnerable to existing artillery: is the Warrior the same?"

Lord John Russell, the foreign secretary, demanded that Prime Minister Palmerston "stir up the slow and steady Admiralty to some vigour about Iron Ships," because "in six months the United States will be far ahead of us unless the builders in the Navy Department exert themselves. . . . Only think of our position if in case of the Yankees turning upon us they should by means of iron ships . . . renew the triumphs they achieved in 1812–1813 by means of superior size and metal."

The *Illustrated London News* saw Britain "entering a race in which success will no longer be achieved by wealth or material resources, under merely ordinary conditions of skillful development." The dawning epoch demanded "men of skill, science and individual energy"—"men of inventive genius." Here is the beginning of a fundamental shift in an ancient seagoing tradition. Hitherto, shipbuilders merely had to be competent; the fighting captains supplied the genius. Now, the locus of victory was shifting from the quarterdeck to the drafting table.

Three weeks after the battle, Rear Admiral Robert Spencer Robinson, controller of the Royal Navy, alerted the Board of Admiralty to "both the value and the practicability of protecting the batteries and waterlines of screw ships of war" and said that none "should be launched without these protections." The weight of such armor might mean that smaller ships could probably carry only two guns, but—and here he surely was thinking of the *Monitor*—"two guns in a ship that cannot be sunk and where the battery is protected will prove more than a match for twenty in an ordinary wooden ship."

The Board of Admiralty asked, what about our wooden men-of-war nearing completion? Wouldn't it be best to finish them?

No, said Robinson. He was heeded. The Admiralty halted construction on all its wooden warships.

HOWEVER QUICKLY EUROPE FELT THE fight's reverberations, it came as a thunderclap in the warring American states.

The lesson most immediately grasped was that broadside fire from a whole battery of lighter guns was useless against an armored ship. During two days of fighting, the *Minnesota* had fired 78 ten-inch and 169 nine-inch solid shot to no effect. If the *Monitor* hadn't been there with her two guns delivering their 167-pound shot, the frigate would have joined the *Congress* and the *Cumberland*.

Also evident: in this contest between armor and firepower, armor had won. For all the joy North and South, both contestants were still afloat.

John Dahlgren at once saw this, and all its implications. "The *defence* has been gradually making slow way against ordnance," he wrote of the battle. "But the events of this day will definitively shape the future in such matters. . . . Now comes the reign of iron—and cased ships are to take the place of wooden ships."

Gustavus Fox agreed. The man who had so doubted the *Monitor* during his meeting with Lincoln a few days earlier had undergone a conversion as sudden and as complete as Paul's on the road to Damascus. He even declared the destruction of the *Congress* and the *Cumberland* a hidden blessing: "Most fortunately we have met with a disaster—this is the Almighty's teachings always—success never gives a lesson."

What Fox saw as the success of the *Monitor* did teach him one lesson, though, and that was all in Ericsson's favor. After congratulating the ship's officers in their wardroom that Sunday, he had gone ashore at Fortress Monroe and there seen a huge new fifteen-inch gun. *That* would take care of the *Merrimack*, he thought, and wired Dahlgren, "We must have more of these boats with 15-inch guns."

Fox was one of the first to be swept up in what came to be called the "monitor craze." The cantankerous, short-tempered Ericsson had become a beloved national hero. Alban Stimers wrote him, "Thousands have this day blessed you. I have heard whole crews cheer you. Every man feels that you have saved this place to the nation by furnishing us with the means to whip an ironclad frigate that was, until our arrival, having it all her own way with our powerful vessels."

The man who never liked being told what to do didn't bristle at Dahlgren's idea of larger guns. "With all my heart," Ericsson wrote him, "if you can make the guns I will most willingly supply the gear for supporting, working and housing the same. Enforce your plan of employing such heavy ordnance, and in twelve months we can say to England and France, leave the Gulf! We do not want your kings, and monarchical institutions on this continent."

Six days after the battle, Fox went to Franklin Street and met with Ericsson. In the glow of victory, they concocted the Union ironclad program for the rest of the war. An elated Ericsson claimed, "The building of a dozen Monitors is a mere trifle with the enormous engineering capabilities of the United States at this moment."

He would build his dozen, and more. The coasts and rivers of the nation were to swarm with the ships as though the sea itself bred them. The day after Fox and Ericsson met, the inventor received a contract for six more vessels "on the plan of the *Monitor*."

Gideon Welles, who had nervously gambled $275,000 on the *Monitor*, now asked Congress for—and got—$30 million to build her successors. By war's end the Navy had built eighty-four ironclads; sixty-four of them were monitors (the progenitor's name became a generic term almost immediately).

As early as December 23 Ericsson had proposed an improved version of his ship. It would be the first of the *Passaic* class, mounting fifteen-inch guns, with the pilothouse sensibly relocated on top of the turret and port stoppers that could be raised and lowered in seconds without taking a whole crew away from a gun to do it.

Of course the ships were wanted right away, and while Ericsson and Fox were working out the naval future, Welles was grousing, about the *Monitor*, "Instead of giving me credit for my months of labor and care to see that vessel built and ready, I am abused for not having built more."

Nor was there universal agreement on building a fleet of monitors. Benjamin Isherwood, the Navy's engineer in chief, and John Lenthall, head of the Bureau of Ship Construction and Repair, were pushing for a different design. They wanted a larger vessel with a higher freeboard, one that could do more than hold its own in a harbor or on a river. They were looking toward the largest strategic prize—command of the seas.

In a lengthy memorandum to Welles, Lenthall and Isherwood said the United States needed "a navy sufficient for securing a country like ours from foreign aggression," and that meant "a fleet of first-class, invincible ocean ships." They closed with a stirring exhortation: "Wealth, victory, and empire are to those who command the ocean, the tollgate as well as the highway of nations, and if ever assailed by a powerful maritime foe, we shall find to our prosperity, if ready, how much better to fight at the threshold than upon the hearthstone."

Lenthall, who had devoted his working life to designing sailing vessels, and Isherwood, who was up to his ears in the day-to-day minutiae of getting steam engines into whatever ships he had at hand, both saw beyond the farsighted Ericsson to the fleet America would build in the next century.

The two men, getting down to specifics, recommended the turrets that Ericsson's old irritant Cowper Coles had designed. In their present state of development, they rotated on a circle of ball bearings around their base, unlike Ericsson's, which hung on its central spindle.

The proposal annoyed the inventor, who assured Welles that his turret was far superior to Coles's "abortive scheme." By now everything was going Ericsson's way. Fox, who was backing him with all his potent influence, wrote, "I have shouldered this fleet, and I doubt if any one can stand in the way."

The previous July the Navy Department had set up an office in New York City to oversee the private contractors who were building ships along the Atlantic seaboard. In the general tumult of the time, the new entity quickly took on a life independent of the construction bureaus in Washington. When ironclads entered the equation, the office became known as the "monitor bureau." As well it might have: Welles gave New York control over Ericsson's new ships and assigned as general inspector the inventor's friend and ally Stimers.

That galled Lenthall and Isherwood, but they couldn't do anything about it. A Philadelphia shipbuilder named Charles Cramp, who also saw little good coming from the move, said that the two men "had no power to antagonize the Monitor craze successfully" because they had been "entirely set aside, and practically disappeared from the scene as far as new constructions were concerned."

Even so, Stimers resented the very existence of the bureau chiefs, and Ericsson wrote Fox "that unless the malign influence of the Engineer-in-Chief can be wholly removed from the Monitor fleet, to which he is bitterly and openly hostile, the Nation will have much cause for complaint."

Fox tried to stifle them both, although he continued to promote Ericsson, and the program went forward in an increasingly poisonous atmosphere. Cramp complained of a "combination, or 'ring' . . . with head-quarters in New York, to prevent the construction of any type of ironclad-vessel except monitors."

Cramp had a point. Twelve of the first fourteen monitors contracted by the Navy were built in or near Manhattan.

WHILE THE *MONITOR*'S PROGENY TOOK shape in the North, the men aboard the prototype were getting better acquainted with its shortcomings.

Like their counterparts on the *Merrimack*—now undergoing repairs a few miles away in Norfolk—the *Monitor* boys fought their war in reverse. That is, sailors, like soldiers, usually begin their martial career with months of training, and the harsh inculcation of tiresome duties, and empty stretches of boredom, followed by further boredom unpleasantly freighted with the threat of approaching battle. That threat remains distant, though, until after more eternities of cleaning, checking, and again cleaning equipment, and fussing about uniforms, and being made to paint the barracks or chip the metal, they get moved, with a thousand delays, toward the main event.

Not so with these two sets of crews. In the span of a few days, they got, *Here's your ship; you sleep there; all hands to mess; all hands to battle stations; fire.*

They fought first, and the boredom followed. The two sets of antagonists would learn all too well what life was like in an iron home under the Virginia sun, and a good deal else besides.

Keeler was already getting restless when he wrote Anna a week after the battle, "It seems hard that we should be cooped up here so closely but it shews the importance they attach to our service." While the ship was kept in readiness for the *Merrimack*'s reappearance, the surgeon began to get on Keeler's nerves. "The Dr., whose room joins mine, bores me to death by wanting to read me all his correspondence with his lady love."

A few days later the paymaster "had to laugh" when in her most recent letter Anna hopes he "will be allowed to read it in quiet, for . . . in the Dr.'s room, from which I am separated by only a blind door, are a half dozen [shipmates] alternately spouting Shakespeare, criticizing the Opera, Theater, and other places not quite as reputable, while another in a room at my side is exercising his lungs by reading in a loud tone the 'personals' of the 'N.Y. Herald' interspersed with intended witticisms."

The night before, "an empty wine bottle came sailing over the top of the partition into my room about 12 o'clock & its crash echoed all over the ship. . . . Every one looked very innocent at the breakfast table this morning." He concluded grimly, "The youngsters are full of tricks."

He was finding the ship itself trying too. "I'd give a good pair of boots to tread on something besides iron," he wrote Anna late one sleepless night. He longed "to enjoy the delightful sensation of sticking my feet in the mud again. I am tired of everlasting iron. The clank, clank, clank, while I am writing this, of the officer of the deck as he paces back & forth on the iron plates over my head, although suggestive of security is not a good opiate."

Despite this carping, Keeler was enjoying himself. His ship was still a hero, and so was he. When the *Monitor* returned from an eventless "search for the *Merrimack* we passed along close to Newport News. The whole army came out to see us, thousands & thousands lined the shore, covered the vessels of the docks, & filled the rigging. Their cheers resembled one continuous roar." Beneath the roar bands played "all our national airs," while the soldiers yelled, "You're the boys," "You're our Saviours," "You're trumps every one," "Iron sides & iron hearts."

The ship received a deluge of sightseers. "We are hardly up from the breakfast table before they commence and do not cease till dark." Keeler had the job of showing them around, and it kept him so busy that he proposed "to get up a guide book for the *Monitor* & hand a copy to each visitor as he arrives."

These are cheerful complaints. When Vice President Hannibal Hamlin stepped on the deck, "he grasped my hand very cordially saying, 'My dear Sir you do me honor, your country regards you with pride.'" On this same visit, "A Mr. Wall connected with the Navy Department in Washington introduced me to his wife with the request that I would take charge of her for a time—as she was young, handsome & intelligent of course I couldn't refuse. I asked her if she had been in the turret to see the guns. 'Oh, yes,' she said, '& kissed them too. I feel as if I could kiss the deck we stand on.'" A friend of Mrs. Wall's added, "I would like to kiss all who were on board during the fight if I thought they would let me."

Keeler said, "I don't know but that I should have taken advantage of this fit of enthusiasm if I hadn't thought it might by some accident have reached your ears." To this blatant bit of teasing, he appends a perfunctory "How much I wished you could have been with them, your company was all that was wanting to complete my happiness."

CHAPTER 27

Hawthorne Visits the Future

Nathaniel Hawthorne at the time he toured
"the strangest-looking craft I ever saw."

One visitor, down from Boston, saw the bonfire light of the continuous celebration casting some sinister shadows. Nathaniel
Hawthorne found the *Monitor* a weird emissary from a troubling
future, and he was prescient about what it foretold.

The fifty-seven-year-old writer had been ailing in "the long,
dreary January of our Northern year, though March in name."
Spring had shown no sign of arriving, and there was "nothing genial
in New England save the fireside." A friend persuaded Hawthorne
to head south; the weather would be milder, and he could see first-
hand something of the "general heart-quake of the country."

He forsook his land of "frozen ponds" in favor of a New York "whose streets were afloat with liquid mud and slosh." The city had tricked itself out with a "prominent display of military goods at the shop-windows . . . and sometimes a great iron cannon at the edge of the pavement, as if Mars had dropped one of his pocket pistols there, while hurrying to the field."

The populace in Manhattan, and everywhere else, seemed "more quiet than in ordinary times, because so large a proportion of its restless elements had been drawn towards the seat of conflict. But the air was full of vague disturbance."

As Hawthorne had hoped, that air began to soften as he passed through Philadelphia to encounter "a much greater abundance of military people. Between Baltimore and Washington a guard seemed to hold every station along the railroad; and frequently, on the hillsides, we saw a collection of weather-beaten tents. . . . Our stopping-places were thronged with soldiers, some of whom came through the cars, asking for newspapers that contained accounts of the battle between Merimack and Monitor, which had been fought the day before."

On reaching Washington, he toured the Capitol, where he was particularly impressed by "a noble staircase, balustraded with a dark and beautifully variegated marble from Tennessee, the richness of which is quite a sufficient cause for objecting to the secession of that State." He met Lincoln—"a man of keen faculties, and, which is still more to the purpose, of powerful character"—and visited the camps around the city, in one of which he seems to have taken in a baseball game ("Some were cooking the company-rations in pots hung over fires in the open air; some played at ball." What else could that mean?). He was depressed by a landscape "of what had evidently been tracts of hardwood forest, indicated by the stumps of well-grown trees not smoothly felled by regular axe-men, but hacked, haggled, and unevenly amputated, as if by a sword, or other miserable tool, in an unskillful hand. Fifty years will not repair this desolation."

On through Harpers Ferry as a guest of the B&O Railroad, which had just repaired track uprooted by the Rebels. He had little

sympathy for the man who had there done so much to precip-
itate the war: "I shall not pretend to be an admirer of old John
Brown.... Nobody was ever more justly hanged." Then to Fortress
Monroe, the waters around it "thronged with a gallant array of
ships of war and transports, wearing the Union flag,—'Old Glory'
as I hear it called these days."

Among them was the *Minnesota*, at last afloat for good, and
Captain Van Brunt invited Hawthorne aboard. "We . . . were shown
over every part of her, and down into her depths, inspecting her
gallant crew, her powerful armament, her mighty engines, and her
furnaces, where the fires were always kept burning, as well at midnight as at noon, so that it would require only five minutes to put
the vessel under full steam. This vigilance has been felt necessary
ever since the Merrimack made her terrible dash from Norfolk."

The writer was impressed by the scale and intricacy of the frigate. But: "Splendid as she is, however, and provided with the latest improvements in naval armament, the Minnesota belongs to
a class of vessels that will be built no more, nor ever fight another
battle,—being as much a thing of the past as any of the ships in
Queen Elizabeth's time, which grappled with the galleons of the
Spanish Armada."

Thinking thus, he glanced across the water to discover "the
strangest-looking craft I ever saw. . . . It could not be called a vessel at all; it was a machine." The economical form "looked like a
gigantic rat-trap. It was ugly, questionable, suspicious, evidently
mischievous—nay, I will allow myself to call it devilish; for this was
the new war-fiend, destined, along with others of the same breed,
to annihilate whole navies and batter down old supremacies. The
wooden walls of Old England will cease to exist and a whole history of naval renown reaches its period, now that the Monitor
comes smoking into view."

The rat-trap proved more agreeable once Hawthorne entered
it. "Going on board, we were surprised at the extent and convenience of her interior accommodations. There is a spacious wardroom, nine or ten feet in height besides a private cabin for the

commander, the sleeping accommodations on an ample scale; the whole well lighted and ventilated, though beneath the surface of the water. Forward, or aft, (for it is impossible to tell stem from stern,) the crew are relatively quite as well provided for as the officers. It was like finding a palace, with all its conveniences, under the sea. The inaccessibility, the apparent impregnability of this submerged iron fortress are most satisfactory; the officers and crew get down through the little hole in the deck, hermetically seal themselves, and go below; and until they see fit to reappear, there would seem to be no power given to man whereby they can be brought to light. A storm of cannon shot damages them no more than a handful of dried peas."

Yet he suspected this evident invulnerability and saw forward to twentieth-century naval warfare. "In fact, the thing looked altogether too safe, though it may not prove quite an agreeable predicament to be thus boxed up in impenetrable iron, with the possibility, one would imagine, of being sent to the bottom of the sea, and, even there, not drowned, but stifled." Here his prescience borders on the uncanny: "Yet even this will not long be the last and most terrible improvement in the science of war. Already we hear of vessels the armament of which is to act entirely beneath the surface of the water; so that, with no other external symptoms than a great bubbling and foaming, and gush of smoke, and belch of smothered thunder out of the yeasty waves, there shall be a deadly fight below,—and, by-and-by, a sucking whirlpool as one of the ships goes down."

The ironclad haunted Hawthorne, but not as much as the remnants of the first day's battle. "The Monitor was certainly an object of great interest; but on our way to Newport News, whither we next went, we saw a spectacle that affected us with far profounder emotion. It was the sight of the few sticks that are left of the frigate Congress, stranded near the shore,—and still more, the masts of the Cumberland rising midway out of the water, with a tattered rag of a pennant fluttering from one of them. The invisible hull of the latter ship seems to be careened over, so that the three masts stand slantwise; the rigging looks quite unimpaired except that a few ropes dangle loosely from the yards. The flag (which never was struck, thank Heaven!) is entirely hidden under the waters of the bay, but is still doubtless waving in its old place, although it floats to and fro with the swell and reflux of the tide, instead of rustling on the breeze. A remnant of the dead crew still man the sunken ship, and sometimes a drowned body floats to the surface."

Hawthorne thought the *Congress* and the *Cumberland* had gone down in "a noble fight," but, again, a final one, and that the nobility would pass with the wooden ships: "The last gun from the Cumberland, when her deck was half submerged, sounded the requiem of many sinking ships. Then went down all the navies of Europe, and our own, Old Ironsides and all, and Trafalgar and a thousand other fights became only a memory, never to be acted over again; and thus our brave countrymen come last in the long procession of heroic sailors that includes Blake and Nelson, and so many mariners of England, and other mariners as brave as they, whose reknown is our native inheritance. There will be other battles, but no more such tests of seamanship and manhood as the battles of the past; and, moreover, the Millennium is certainly approaching, because human strife is to be transferred from the heart and personality of man into cunning contrivances of machinery, which by-and-by will fight out our wars with only the clank and smash of iron, strewing the field with broken engines, but damaging no one's little finger except by accident."

So Hawthorne's power of prediction finally did run dry; the writer got the future right, and wrong. "All the pomp and splendor of naval warfare are gone by. Henceforth there must come up a race of enginemen and smoke-blackened cannoneers, who will hammer away at their enemy under the direction of a single pair of eyes; and even heroism—so deadly a gripe is Science laying on our noble possibilities—will become a quality of very minor importance when its possessor cannot break through the iron crust of his own armament and give the world a glimpse of it."

MONITOR 172 FT LONG.

ONON

PURITAN   CATSKILL   MONTAUK.   PASSAIC   ROANOKE   WINO

WOODNA

PURITAN 340 FT LONG   W

The *Monitor's* triumph is reflected in this extravagant panorama of her progeny. When the *Harper's* issue in which it ran appeared in September 1862, only a fraction of these ships actually existed. The *Passaic*, first of the *Monitor's* successor class, had been launched just a couple of weeks earlier;

ONG   KAATSKILL   PASSAIC   200 FT LONG   MONTAUK

IRONSIDES   NAUGATUCK   BROOKLYN   MONITOR

ONG   ROANOKE   270 FT LONG

the twin-turreted *Onondaga* was still nearly a year away from completion. The *Roanoke*, with her three turrets, had begun life as a handsome steam frigate, but as the *Harper's* issue went to press, workmen were chopping down her masts and converting her to an ironclad.

One has only to look at another pivotal naval engagement—the carrier battle of Midway—to see that machinery advanced beyond the reach even of Hawthorne's ample and precise imagination would not leach courage, sacrifice, and individual initiative from war's timeless imperatives.

CHAPTER 28

Tattnall's Turn

Two captains of the *Merrimack*: Josiah Tattnall, right,
took over command after Buchanan was wounded.

Gustavus Fox had carried the news of the battle to Washington; Lieutenant Wood was the courier sent to Richmond. Once in the Confederate capital he told the story to Stephen Mallory, President Jefferson Davis, and Secretary of War Judah Benjamin. Wood inadvertently brought a brimstone whiff of battle into the room when he ceremoniously unfurled across the desk the flag of the *Congress*. Brittle with dried blood, it was quickly refolded and removed. Although Wood ended his account by saying, "In the *Monitor*, we had met our equal," an elated Mallory declared that the ship he'd conceived and worried through to completion had "achieved the most remarkable victory which naval annals record."

(He and Welles might have exchanged a smile of sympathy across the chasm of war when Mallory found himself immediately berated in the press for not having supplied more *Merrimack*s.)

As soon as the first reports of Saturday's fight began to come in, he'd envisioned the punishment his ship must be taking and made sure Norfolk had the means at hand to fix it. "Within an hour after the telegraph announced in Richmond on the 8th of March, that the *Virginia* was engaged with the enemy's ships, I gave the order to roll and prepare iron plates to repair her assumed and anticipated damages."

The new plates were on the way from Tredegar in two days, and John Luke Porter was there to see them installed. The *Merrimack* had gone into dry dock as soon as she got back to Norfolk. No shot had breached the casemate, but the ship was thoroughly roughed up. A Norfolk yard worker who deserted to the Union side gave a vivid report of her condition: "One gun broken shot off near the trunnion, and another broken off obliquely, about eighteen inches from the muzzle. Her stern was mashed so that the wood could be strung out like a ball of thread; and they had to squeeze a whole bale of oakum [rope picked apart into its fibers and mixed with tar, a task as unpleasant as it sounds, usually done by prisoners] into it to stop it from leaking—the planking being sprung off and gaping wide. Quite a number of the *Monitor*'s shots had plowed up the roofing so that you could lay a large watermelon in the spot where the shot had struck."

Porter hung 440 ten-inch plates—some three hundred tons' worth—a yard down over the ship's tender sides. While he was supervising the repairs, he became increasingly annoyed by the praise John Brooke was garnering for the success of what Porter saw as *his* ship. This touched off the debate that festered in the press for years and that, like so much surrounding the action, has yet to be settled to everyone's satisfaction.

Bruised pride did not prevent Porter from getting the job done quickly, nor Brooke from having steel-tipped, wrought-iron shot rushed to the vessel for the next round, although the two men's mutual antipathy can be gathered from Brooke's diary entry about their argument over the ship's new ram: "I suggested to the Secretary [Mallory, who seems to have taken Brooke's side] that the iron prow of the *Merrimac* should be square on the cutting edge to insure taking the wood off an enemy's side if struck glancing and not acute angle; Constructor Porter proposed and was making the edge sharp. The Secretary telegraphed to make it as I suggested."

Porter got the *Merrimack* afloat on April 4. A week earlier, a new captain had come aboard. Buchanan would live, but it would be weeks, perhaps months, before he could again command a ship in action. The officers and crew knew whom they wanted to replace him. Lieutenant Minor, wounded the same day Buchanan had been, wrote Brooke, "By no means must any captain or commodore or even flag officer be put over Jones. In old Buck's sickness from his wounds Jones must command the ship."

But even in a new navy—perhaps especially in a new navy—the ancient requirements of seniority had to be honored. On March 21, Mallory gave command of the *Merrimack*, and every other Rebel warship in Virginia waters, to Josiah Tattnall. Flag Officer Tattnall was a sixty-seven-year-old Georgia man—his father had been governor of the state—who had served aboard the frigate *Constitution* during the War of 1812. He was certainly familiar with the theater of operations, having fought right on Craney Island fifty years earlier. He'd done well there. When the British attacked in barges—primordial landing craft—Tattnall had waded out through mudflats with a handful of volunteers to capture the admiral's own barge, which bore the fetching name *Centipede*. He'd taken the first American envoy to Japan, was famous for his skill with a cutlass, stood six feet with an outthrust bunker of a lower lip that had intimidated several generations of subordinates by the time he took over the *Merrimack*.

Even so, Wood wrote the recuperating Buchanan, Catesby Jones "had fitted out the ship and armed her, and had commanded during the second day's fight. However, the department thought otherwise, and selected Commodore Josiah Tatnall." Wood ended the letter with a mix of anger and resignation: "Except [for] Lieu-tenant Jones he was the best man."

Tattnall wasn't all that pleased with his new post. "I have been aware from the first," he wrote Mallory, "that my command is dangerous to my reputation, from the expectations of the pub-lic, founded on the success of Commodore Buchanan, and I have looked to a different field to satisfy them. I shall never find in Hampton Roads the opportunity my gallant friend found."

Mallory also had a different field in mind, but not one Tattnall was considering. He wrote the bed-bound Buchanan, "I submit for your consideration the attack on New York by the *Virginia*. Once in the bay, she could shell and burn the city and the shipping. Such an event would eclipse all the glories of the combats of the sea. . . . Bankers would withdraw their capital from the city. The Brooklyn Navy Yard and its magazines and all the lower part of the city would be destroyed, and such an event, by a single ship, would do more to achieve our immediate independence than would the results of many campaigns."

The destruction of lower Manhattan would surely have had that effect, but Buchanan didn't believe the *Merrimack* could get there. "The *Virginia* is as yet an experiment," he answered Mal-lory, "and is by no means invulnerable as has already been proven." Fortress Monroe had heavier guns than either the *Congress* or the *Cumberland*; if the ironclad managed to run past them, she might founder in the open ocean; and if the sea spared her, how would her deep bottom make its way into New York Harbor? "I consider the *Virginia* the most important protection to the safety of Norfolk, and her services can be made very valuable in this neighborhood."

A busy neighborhood: General McClellan was putting Union troops ashore—389 transports full of sixty thousand of them at first, along with 44 batteries of field artillery and 114 siege guns—to push up the Peninsula and take Richmond. Even though, he wrote, "the appearance of the *Merrimac* at Old Point Comfort, and the encounter with the United States Squadron on the 8th of March, threatened serious derangement of the plan for the Peninsula movement" by closing off the James River, he could still use the York. "The general plans, therefore, remained undisturbed, although"—the ever-cautious commander continued—"less promising in its details than when the James River was in our control."

He was using Fortress Monroe as his jumping-off point, and General Magruder wanted Tattnall to do something about it. This man who as recently as the night before the battle had regarded the *Merrimack* as a waste of time had been as thoroughly won over as Fox. He told Tattnall his ship must "station herself outside Fort Monroe as to intercept all reinforcements of troops and cut off further supplies." Right away too: Tattnall was to have the *Merrimack* "off Sewell's Point in the day and every night off Newport News." Forget the *Monitor*, Magruder said with a soldier's disregard for a seaman's concerns: "We have a country to save and no time for individual duels."

However much Tattnall might have been nettled to be reminded that a war was on, he liked even less hearing about his engines from the man who knew them best. Ashton Ramsay wrote him that they "are not disconnected, and one cannot be worked alone." If the vacuum failed in either, as was likely, both would die. In short: "From my past and present experience, I am of the opinion that they cannot be relied upon."

AS MUCH AS THE *MERRIMACK* worried its owners, it worried the Yankees more, and its only plausible opponent had undergone a confusing shuffle of command.

After Lieutenant Greene made his jaunty understatement to Fox about having merely conducted a little firing practice, the pressure he'd been under since leaving New York made itself felt. He wrote his parents, "I had been up so long, had had so little rest, and been under such a state of excitement, that my nervous system was completely run down. Every bone in my body ached, my limbs and joints were so sore that I could not stand. My nerves and muscles twitched as though electric shocks were continually passing through them. . . . I laid down and tried to sleep, but I might as well have tried to fly."

He felt better the next morning, when "we got under weigh at 8 o'clock and stood through our fleet. Cheer after cheer went up from frigates and small craft for the glorious little *Monitor*. . . . I was Captain then of the vessel that had saved Newport News, Hampden [*sic*] Roads, Fortress Monroe . . . perhaps four Northern ports."

His hour of triumph was fleeting. That afternoon he got a note from Fox congratulating him on the fight, but saying that, given his youth, a new captain had been appointed.

"Of course I was a little taken about," Greene told his parents. "Between you and me I would have kept the command with all its responsibilities and either the Merrimac or the Monitor should have gone down in our new engagement." He added a flick of irony: "But you know all young people are vain, conceited and without judgement."

Greene's successor delivered the order. He was Thomas Selfridge, whose efforts over the past few days must have left him as weary as Greene.

Selfridge had found little to make him smile since the *Cumberland* went into action, but the assumption of his new command did. He was still wearing what the hospitable New York regiment had given him in exchange for the torn, sopping rags he had waded ashore in on the eighth: the regiment's uniform, a flamboyant confection of gilt-embroidered blue jacket and billowing scarlet trousers, adopted from the Zouave battalion of the French Army, which had in turn got it from the Algerians they fought in the 1830s. Selfridge saluted the officer of the deck, and "not wishing to disturb Lieutenant Green, then Executive Officer and acting Captain, from his dinner in the wardroom, I went below and could scarcely contain my amusement at the surprise of the *Monitor*'s officers upon seeing a Zouave back down the narrow hatchway and announce himself as their new commander."

Stimers gave his gaudy captain a four-hour tour of the ship.

Selfridge took in the dented turret, the guns inside it, Ericsson's engines, the intricate toilets. One sight made him feel better about his terrible day on the *Cumberland.* "The marks where the *Merrimac*'s bow had rammed the *Monitor*'s side caused me great satisfaction, since it was clearly evident that, but for the loss of the *Merrimac*'s ram, broken off in the *Cumberland*'s side, the *Monitor* would surely have been destroyed. The *Cumberland*'s epic fight had not been in vain."

Selfridge wanted the pilothouse rebuilt with sloping iron sides, and Stimers immediately set about transforming it from cube to pyramid. That one significant order given, Selfridge too found himself replaced.

After he'd spent a few days guarding the mouth of the Elizabeth against the *Merrimack*'s return, "Mr. Fox again sent for me and stated that, previous to his having ordered me to command the *Monitor*, he had sent a dispatch boat to Commodore Goldsborough . . . directing that Lieutenant Jeffers be sent at once to command the *Monitor.* Mr. Jeffers had just arrived and the Secretary was obviously embarrassed at the situation." Selfridge was a good sport about it, telling Fox "that Lieutenant Jeffers was many years the senior, and that under the circumstances I could have no objection to his superseding me."

CIVIL WAR FACES LOOK OUT across so many intervening changes of dress and hair that we find most of the doors down that long corridor of years shut against us. This isn't the case with William Nicholson Jeffers. One glance at his puffy, petulant features, and you know why nobody aboard the *Monitor* liked him.

Not that he was incompetent.

As a seventeen-year-old in 1841, Jeffers served (with Isherwood's classmate Herman Melville) aboard the aging 1797 frigate *United States* and had gone on to graduate fourth in his class of forty-seven from Buchanan's new Naval Academy in 1846. That year, while still a midshipman, he published a book, *The Armament of Ships of War.*

It presaged a lifelong interest in naval gunnery and brought him an assignment to an experimental ordnance ship where his executive officer was Catesby Jones, and John Dahlgren conducted the ballistic tests. Dahlgren thought highly of Jeffers, which helped lead to his *Monitor* posting.

Along with Jeffers's capabilities came his personality. He has the unique distinction of nearly embroiling the United States in a war with Paraguay when, conducting a survey of the Paraná River, he opened fire on a fort that tried to deny him passage.

He got out of that scrape with little damage to his reputation (the fort had fired too), but his next imbroglio hints at his character and nearly saw him cashiered.

In 1859 Jeffers was ordered to the new steam sloop *Brooklyn* under David Glasgow Farragut. He had been aboard only a few weeks when the man who would become the most famous Civil War sea officer wrote the secretary of the navy, bringing charges against him for "scandalous conduct tending to the destruction of good morale."

The conduct was disappointingly less interesting than it sounds. Taking a walk ashore, Jeffers passed by his captain in the street and failed to salute him. He said that was because Farragut had on an overcoat that concealed his uniform, a ludicrous excuse (the coat didn't cover his face). This is all we know about the contretemps, but Farragut was not an irrational man, and it is hard to imagine that he would have brought charges against his lieutenant had Jeffers said anything even remotely apologetic.

The small storm passed and seems to have done no lasting harm to Jeffers's reputation, as shown by his getting command of what had become the world's most famous warship.

The whole crew liked him at first. Greene, once again the executive officer, said, "Mr. Jeffers is everything desirable, talented, educated and energetic and experienced in battle," while Keeler told Anna (getting yet another name slightly wrong), "Lieut. Jeffards has been in most of the fights along the coast & it is very interesting as we sit at the table to hear him give his experience in the different fights—some of them he sets out in a very amusing light."

The amusement didn't last long. Two weeks later Anna learned that "things don't go as smoothly & pleasantly on board as when we had Capt. Worden. Our new Capt. is a rigid disciplinarian, of quick imperious temper & domineering disposition. . . . So far I have got along smoothly enough with Capt. Jeffers, but I am expecting every day that I may forget to touch my hat, or give him the deck in passing, or grievously offend him in some little point of etiquitte, when I shall get a blast. I keep my seat next to him at the table, but do not find it as pleasant as when Capt. Worden filled his place."

The lower deck felt the same way. George Geer, the New York seaman who had begun writing his wife when his home was still within sight, told her, "I have about $5.00 coming to me for Grog, which, according to the rules of all Government ships, is paid every Quarter, but I hear we will not get it as there is no money in the Ship. What there is, some $200, the captain wants for his own gutts. He is a damnd old Gluttonous Hogg, and I hope the curse of Hell will rest on him. You may think it is strong language, but it is as I feel, as well as all the ships company."

At least Jeffers did not confine his hostility to his crew; he told his officers he wanted a "regular straight out fight with the Merrimack." That would have suited Tattnall, who was vowing revenge on the *Monitor*: "I will take her! I will take her if hell's on the other side of her."

Both captains might be willing to brave hell, but not to defy their governments. During his talk with Lincoln, Worden had said that though his ship could withstand any amount of gunfire, it was vulnerable to boarding. Lincoln took this seriously and wrote Welles, "I have just seen Lieutenant Worden. . . . He is decidedly of the opinion that [the *Monitor*] should not go skylarking up to Norfolk." Welles codified this in an order issued on March 10: "It is directed by the President that the *Monitor* be not too much exposed and that in no event shall any attempt be made to proceed with her unattended to Norfolk."

There was as yet nothing comparable to attend her. "Would to God," said Goldsborough, "we had another ironclad vessel on hand."

Mallory did not put so tight a rein on Tattnall, but his extravagant imaginings of a dash up to Wall Street had cooled, and he became increasingly cautious about hazarding his ironclad.

Keeler was eager to come to grips with it. "If they would only let us go up the river and get the rat in his hole, it would suit us exactly, much better than doing blockading duty in a diving bell." As it was, he wrote later, "I believe the Department is going to build a big glass case to put us in for fear of harm coming to us."

He was right. The *Monitor* and the *Merrimack* had become the two queens on the glittering chessboard of Hampton Roads, radiating lines of terrific power, but moving under strict constraints, both too valuable to risk without being certain of making the coup that wins the game.

On April 10 the *Merrimack* returned to Hampton Roads for the first time since the battle. When the ship and its coterie of gunboats came into view, Van Brunt fired a signal shot from the *Minnesota*, and said Keeler, "There was our old acquaintance with her Satellites dimly seen by aid of our glasses through the fog which covered the water in the vicinity of Craney Island." His ship was prepared: "A stroke of the hatchet loosed us from our moorings & the *Monitor* stood ready for the fight."

The Confederate ironclad "seemed like some huge gladiator just entering the vast watery arena of the amphitheater, while on the opposite side the *Monitor* steamed forth her defiance with her attendant fleet as spectators in the rear—then they stood on the edge of the arena, each hesitating to advance, neither caring to retreat, each desiring the fight to come off on their side of the house that the assistance of their friends might be called in if necessary."

Tattnall, who had imprudently chosen as his battle station an armchair on top of the casemate, devised a plan that had his ship closing with the *Monitor* while men leaped onto her deck from the gunboats to fling bottles of burning turpentine into the blower pipes. (The scheme did not appeal to Virginius Newton of the *Beaufort*: "I would have made my will but that I had no property.")

Captain Jeffers hoped to lure the *Merrimack* under the guns of Monroe or, failing that, tease her out to a spot where a Union vessel could ram and drive her under.

The ships sniffed about each other for hours. Unable to deploy his gunboats as he'd hoped, Tattnall sent them to capture three small merchantmen that had run aground fleeing him. At day's end, these were taken to Norfolk with their American flags hung upside down under Confederate colors. The sight made Keeler's blood "boil with indignation," but as orders dictated, the *Monitor* stood by the *Minnesota*. The ironclads exchanged a couple of pointless long-range shots, and that was that.

So it went for weeks, a frustrating time for both crews: incessant alarms, tentative feints, a mutually humiliating standoff.

The shine began to fade from the *Monitor*. Jeffers probably saw a *New York Herald* article that began, "The public are very justly indignant at the conduct of our navy in Hampton Roads last Friday," which revealed "wretched imbecility."

Tattnall made five sorties into the Roads. On two of them the *Merrimack*'s engines failed. He was "mortified beyond measure by the frequent suggestions, not only from unofficial but from high official sources, of important services to be performed by the *Virginia*, founded on the most exaggerated ideas of her qualities."

General McClellan had the greatest respect for them. The *Merrimack*'s control of the James, said his chief engineer, was "disastrous to our subsequent operations."

Nevertheless, as April dwindled into May, Union troops were pressing up the Virginia Peninsula, the Confederates slowly withdrawing before a force at least twice their size. The Southern hold on Norfolk began to slip.

On May 4, Mallory telegraphed Tattnall, "Please endeavor to protect Norfolk, as well as the James River." Mallory visited the city, saw how things stood, and ordered its evacuation. For the second time in a little over a year men set about preparing to destroy the yard. "What a terrible necessity this is," Wood wrote his wife, with a desolate, angry afterthought: "This is war, stern, terrible war, which our sires have brought upon us."

On May 5 the gunboats *Jamestown* and *Patrick Henry* headed up the James to Richmond, leaving the *Merrimack* alone to defend Norfolk. Tattnall took her out again; Keeler wrote gloatingly to Anna about what proved to be the ship's penultimate foray.

"I had a letter just finished as the cry, the 'Big Thing' (as we have nicknamed the *Merrimac*) is coming, started me from my state room to the deck.

"Sure enough, there she was just emerging from behind Sewall's Point, the black cloud from her bituminous coal hovering over her like the genius of evil omen. She steamed over towards Newport News a piece & then came to a stand." Keeler imagined her "apparently chewing the bitter end [or perhaps "cud"] of reflection & ruminating sorrowfully upon the future.

"She remained there smoking, reflecting, & ruminating till nearly sunset, when she slowly crawled off nearly concealed in a huge, murky cloud of her own emission, black & repulsive as the perjured hearts of her traitorous crew." As he gets caught up in his high tone, Keeler's prose becomes opulent: "The water hisses & boils with indignation as like some huge slimy reptile she slowly emerges from her loathsome lair with the morning light, vainly seeking with glaring eyes some mode of escape through the meshes of the net which she feels is daily closing her in. Behind her she already hears the hounds of the hunter & before are the ever watchful guards whom it is certain death to pass."

Once again, the two ships merely eyed each other, and then the Big Thing returned to its lair.

CHAPTER 29

Lincoln in the Field

Lincoln confers with Major General George McClellan
in September 1862.

On the night of May 6 the revenue cutter *Miami* tied up at Fortress Monroe and President Lincoln came ashore. Unhappy about the slow progress of McClellan's advance, he wanted to get a closer look.

He toured the ironclad first. When he went aboard and was introduced to the officers, he immediately pleased Keeler: "He was very happy he said to find one from Illinois aboard the *Monitor.*"

The paymaster helped show him around: "He examined everything about the vessel with care, manifesting great interest, his remarks evidently shewing that he had carefully studied what he thought to be our weak points & that he was well acquainted with all the mechanical details of our construction."

He was a subdued guest. "Most of our visitors come on board filled with enthusiasm & patriotism ready, like a bottle of soda water, to effervesce the instant the cork is withdrawn, but with Mr. Lincoln it was different. His few remarks as he accompanied us around the vessel were sound, simple & practical, the points of admiration & exclamation he left to his suite."

Keeler was sincere in his stand against liquor. What impressed him most about the presidential visit was that, at its end, "it gives me pleasure to say, & I record it to his credit, that he declined the invitation to whiskey but took a glass of ice water."

Lincoln wasn't there only as a sightseer. Just twice in our history has a sitting president exercised his role as commander in chief in the field. The first to do so was James Madison, in 1814, when the British were advancing on Washington. The other was Lincoln, who took direct operational control in the Chesapeake.

By now Goldsborough had the second armored ship he'd asked God for, the *Galena*, Bushnell's entry in the ironclad sweepstakes. Lincoln told Goldsborough to take it, with two gunboats, up the James River at once. Goldsborough said that three ships "are too few for the work." The President, feeling that he'd already got plenty of this kind of guff from McClellan, overruled the commodore.

John Rodgers, captain of the *Galena*, had command of the squadron. He moved into the James on May 8, during low tide so the *Merrimack* couldn't get at his ships.

In the meantime, the *Monitor*, with several other vessels, began shelling the batteries at Sewells Point. As soon as Tattnall heard the firing, he took the *Merrimack* out. Unable to follow Rodgers into the James, he went to help the batteries and engage the *Monitor.*

One crewman was looking forward to "a lively tussle," but, Lieutenant Eggleston wrote, "At our approach they fled ignominiously and huddled for safety under the guns of Fortress Monroe."

Tattnall wouldn't follow them there, but he steamed about for hours trying to draw the *Monitor* into action. Finally he said to

Catesby Jones, in what Wood remembered as "a tone of deepest disgust," "Mr. Jones, fire a gun to windward, and take the ship back to her buoy." That windward shot was an age-old naval taunt meaning "Come out and fight." Jeffers declined. "It was the most cowardly exhibition I have ever seen," said Wood. "Goldsborough and Jeffers are both cowards."

Keeler thought so too, writing of his captain, "He has always complained that he could not get permission to attack her from the Flag-Officer, but we have reason to think that he had permission to 'pitch into her' if a favorable opportunity offered."

Lincoln had watched the action against the batteries, and the nonaction against the *Merrimack*, and was not pleased. If Norfolk couldn't be taken by sea, he said, it must be done by land. He had himself rowed in close to the enemy shore to make a personal reconnaissance and picked what he believed to be the best place to land the troops, a stretch of beach with the holiday name of Ocean View.

While the soldiers landed, Tattnall was meeting with Army and Navy officials in Norfolk and planning its abandonment. He wanted to attack the whole Union fleet, or to run out to sea and make for Savannah. Even the ever-confident Wood thought the former a bad idea. The transports would flee into shallow water, while the *Monitor* and the other Union ships "would engage us with every advantage, playing around us as rabbits crowd a sloth."

The army representatives liked neither scheme. They said that Tattnall should stay where he was and cover the evacuation of the nine thousand troops holding Norfolk under General Huger, who was going to fall back on the crucial rail juncture at Suffolk, twenty miles away.

The Army won out. Mallory wrote Tattnall, "We look to the *Virginia* alone to prevent the enemy from ascending the James River." The *Merrimack* would remain at Norfolk until Huger was safely away, and then the ship would go up the James. Under normal circumstances, her draft would prevent her passing over the bar into the river, but, Wood wrote, "The pilots said repeatedly, if the ship were lightened to eighteen feet they could take her up the James to . . . where she could have been put in fighting trim again, and have been in a position to assist in the defense of Richmond."

When the Federal troops entered Norfolk, on May 10, they found it abandoned. If they were surprised, Captain Tattnall was enraged. General Huger had assured Tattnall he'd hang on for another week and send word when he planned to move out. He'd done neither.

Tattnall mustered his men, told them the situation, and said that if the ship was to be kept out of Union hands, it must be lightened immediately by five feet to get into the James. "The crew gave three cheers," said Wood, "and went to work with a will, throwing overboard the ballast from the fan-tails, as well as that below—all spare stores, water, indeed everything but our shot. By midnight the ship had been lifted three feet."

At that hopeful point, Tattnall got one more ugly surprise. The pilots told him that to jettison anything else was pointless, as the wind was blowing down the James, piling its surface toward the *Merrimack* like a pushed rug, bringing the bottom so close to the surface that the ship could never enter the river no matter how high she rode.

Tattnall saw this as outright treason on the pilots' part. "Had the ship not been lifted, so as to render her unfit for action, a desperate contest must have ensued with a force against us too great to justify much hope of success, and, as battle is not their occupation, they adopted this deceitful course to avoid it. I cannot imagine another motive."

That is, the pilots had deliberately ensured that the wooden hull rose so far above the surface that, with the *Merrimack*'s heavy upperworks, a single shell could sink her. The ship, Ramsay said, "was no longer an ironclad," and "when morning dawned the Federal fleet must discover our defenceless condition, and defeat and capture were certain."

Tattnall walked through the vessel he'd commanded for less than two months, looked about the harbor, and gave the first of three final orders. The crew should "splice the main brace"—the old naval term for issuing liquor to all hands—and then they were to beach the ship where the men might best get ashore. He steamed up the Elizabeth to just south of Craney Island and ran the *Merrimack* aground there. She couldn't get as close in as he had hoped; the water between the ship and the bank was over any man's head, with only two boats to carry the crew to land. The men embarked, clutching rifles and two days' rations, in a welter of yelling and lantern light that spurted and died on the water below. Behind them, a dozen of the crew carried out Tattnall's final order. Supervised by Wood and Catesby Jones, they laid powder trains and, for the second time in the hard-done ship's career, spread flammable cotton waste about her deck. Jones was the last man off. He put the match to the fuses as he left.

The abandonment began at about 2:00 AM. Tattnall, too ill with strain and betrayal to walk, rode on a cart in the middle of the column that trudged inland toward Huger's new headquarters. As they marched, the men heard behind them the occasional bang of a naval gun. The *Merrimack*'s cannon had been left loaded, and as the burning decks heated the barrels, they one by one fired their shot into the empty morning. In time, the fires reached the eighteen tons of powder in the magazine, and Ramsay wrote, "That last, deep, low, sullen, mournful boom told our people, now far away on the march, that the gallant ship was no more."

The men looked over their shoulders toward the concussion. They had been sailors only for a few months. Now they were soldiers again. But those discouraged orphans were to fight one last battle with the *Monitor.*

"A LURID GLARE IN THE direction of Norfolk continuing the whole of the night," Keeler wrote Anna, "taken in connection with the fact that our soldiers were on their way to that place, led us to the belief that the rebels had applied the torch & then (to use a phrase more expressive than elegant) 'skedaddled.'

"A little after midnight a bright light was seen over Sewall's Point"—that was the burning *Merrimack*—"which continued increasing till about four o'clock in the morning, when a sudden flash & a dull heavy report brought us all on deck to conjecture & Surmise till the morning light should reveal the mysteries of the night."

The light revealed that "the Stars and Stripes were over the Sewall Point batteries. *Merrimac* blown up & Norfolk Navy Yard destroyed by the rebels & the place in full possession of our forces. *Monitor* was the first vessel into Norfolk."

Its crew was disappointed. They had "looked upon the 'Big thing' as our exclusive game. . . . Her career was as short & infamous as her end was sudden & unexpected. We knew her days were numbered, but felt confident that she would die game rather than fall by her own hand."

CHAPTER 30

Not the Way to Richmond

A Confederate gun commands the superb field
of fire afforded by Drewry's Bluff.

Lincoln had no such regrets; to him, the retaking of Norfolk and the *Merrimack*'s disappearance were "among the most important successes of the present war." As he went to tour the re-ruined Norfolk, his ship passed the *Monitor*. He took off his hat and bowed.

Both he and Welles now pressed Goldsborough to move fast, and the Commodore ordered Commander Rodgers to "push on up to Richmond . . . without any unnecessary delay, and shell the place into surrender."

The *Monitor* joining his squadron, Rodgers steamed upriver with *Galena* in the lead, followed by two gunboats, the *Aroostook* and the *Port Royal*, and the *Naugatuck*. This last, a curiosity on loan from the Treasury Department, was an experimental two-gun ironclad built by the Stevens brothers at their own expense during the endless gestation of their Stevens Battery. The task force ran by some lightly held Confederate gun emplacements on the lower river, and at one point, Keeler reported, "We passed about a dozen Negroes at the mouth of a wild ravine who waved their old hats & shook their rags to us & bowed and gesticulated, some even getting down on their knees."

Then they reached Drewry's Bluff.

Today that's just a place name in the northeastern corner of Virginia's Chesterfield County. In 1862, it was Drewry land, the property of Captain Augustus Drewry of the Southside Heavy Artillery. He had been busy setting up a battery there.

Eight miles below Richmond, his bluff was the last defensive position before the city, but it was a fine one: 110-foot-high ground on the south side of a sharp, narrow jink in the James. Drewry's initial emplacement of three guns had just been stiffened with five more borrowed from the James River Squadron. Getting them there had taken nightmarish work, manhandling tons of iron in heavy rain with deep mud sucking underfoot, but by May 14 eight cannon, half of them rifled, had their muzzles pointing down a mile-long shooting gallery of open water.

DURING THE DISPOSSESSED MERRIMACK'S CREW'S slog toward Suffolk, Wood had told them that if any had friends or family back in Norfolk, they were free to go join them. Only two men left.

At Suffolk, while they were waiting for the Norfolk & Petersburg to take them to Richmond, one of them said the women of the town had "prepared for us bountiful tables on both sides of the street, and dispensed gracious and patriotic hospitality to the tired and hungry men, accompanied with words of cheer for their hearts."

From Suffolk, Tattnall sent a five-word telegram to his Navy secretary: "The *Virginia* no longer exists." Mallory saw base incompetence behind his ship's loss: "The destruction of the *Virginia* was premature. May God protect us and cure us of weakness and folly."

So did John Brooke, who blamed Huger and many others for "poor leadership and lack of harmony within the government."

The *Merrimack* crew reached Richmond on the twelfth to find themselves in a city preparing for disaster; the Confederate gold reserves were being crated up for removal. Mallory ordered the men to Drewry's Bluff and put Catesby Jones in charge of the complement, with Wood assisting him. Many arrived demoralized; one, unknowingly echoing the South Carolina artillerists when they'd first seen the floating battery in Charleston Harbor, said he'd been brought to a "slaughter pen."

Jones and Wood didn't agree, nor did Lieutenant Eggleston, who busied himself building barricades in the river. The *Jamestown* ended its above-water military career being sunk to serve as an obstruction.

Eggleston made another contribution to the preparations. During the scramble to abandon the *Merrimack*, he'd noticed the ship's flag lying forgotten on the deck. At the expense of some of his clothes, he packed it and took it with him. Now the *Merrimack*'s colors again flew above her gunners.

RODGERS GOT TO THE BLUFF on May 15. His *Galena* carried thinner armor than the *Monitor*, two-inch-thick iron plates laid horizontally, overlapping one another like the clapboard on a farmhouse. The captain had little faith in this metalwork. "I was convinced as soon as I came on board that she would be riddled with shot, but the public thought differently, and I resolved to give the matter a fair trial."

He took his squadron in under the guns of the bluff shortly before eight that morning. Wood had posted sharpshooters along the banks and their fire began to chime against the *Monitor*'s turret. "Not a man could show himself on the decks," said Keeler, "without a ball whizzing by him. A man on the *Galena* who was sounding was badly wounded & one passed between my legs & another just over Lieut. Greene's head."

Rodgers steamed to within six hundred yards of the bluff and swung the *Galena* broadside to it so her guns would bear. Charles Hasker, a *Merrimack* boatswain who had learned his trade in the Royal Navy, was amazed by the "neatness and precision" with which Rodgers handled his ship in the narrow river; he thought it "one of the most masterly pieces of seamanship of the whole war." Even before Rodgers had carried off this nice maneuver, the Confederate guns had opened up; Captain Drewry fired the first one. Two shots struck the *Galena*'s port bow—and penetrated it. "The batteries soon got the range," wrote Keeler, "& their shot began to tell fearfully on the *Galena*, against whom they seemed to concentrate their fire. Her iron sides were pierced through & through by the heavy shot, apparently offering no more resistance than an egg shell, verifying the Commodore's [Rodgers] opinion that 'she was beneath naval criticism.'"

Seeing the flagship in trouble, Jeffers took the *Monitor* in to cover her. He couldn't help. His guns elevated only enough to put tangles of hillside scrub in their sights. The *Merrimack*'s gunners remembered what their best efforts had done to that ship and simply ignored her. She was hit three times during the battle; the *Galena*, forty-three.

As Jeffers backed away to get the tilt he needed to play his fire on the crest of the bluff, Keeler saw the *Galena* "being roughly used as shot & shell went crashing through her sides, still she held out & the thunder of her guns pealed out from the sulphurous cloud that enveloped her sending their iron messengers with remarkable accuracy. We could see large clouds of dirt & sand fly as shell after shell from our vessels exploded in the rebel works."

A member of the Southside Artillery wrote, "Shells from the *Galena* passed just over the crest of our parapets and exploded in our rear, scattering their fragments in every direction, together with the sounds of the shells from the others, which flew wide of the mark, mingled with the roar of our guns, was the most startling, terrifying and diabolical sound which I had ever heard or ever expected to hear again."

One of the gunners on the bluff thought the squadron "would finally overcome us," but after three hours the engagement was clearly going their way. Rodgers said the "batteries on the Rebel side were beautifully served, and put shot through our sides with great precision."

When the *Monitor* had retreated to where her guns could bear, her crew worked hard. "No one on board was hurt," said Keeler, "but all suffered terribly for the want of fresh air. It was one of those warm, muggy days with a very rare atmosphere which, shut up closely as we were, made ventilation very difficult. At times we were filled with powder smoke threatening suffocation to us all. Some of the hardiest looking men dropped fainting at the guns."

Despite the effort, the ship was too far away to do much against the smoking heights. The *Naugatuck* had to withdraw because her 100-pound rifle burst when firing its tenth round, and Captain George Morris of the *Port Royal*—who had survived the destruction of the *Cumberland*—was wounded by a sharpshooter.

At about eleven thirty, Keeler said, Rodgers "hailed us & said that he should have to leave as he had expended all his ammunition, having fired 360 rounds."

The battered flotilla withdrew. As the *Monitor* turned to head downstream, John Wood shouted to the pilothouse, "Tell Captain Jeffers that is not the way to Richmond!"

STEPHEN MALLORY HAD BEEN ON the bluff—along with Robert E. Lee and Jefferson Davis—and witnessed the battle; it helped reconcile him to the loss of the *Merrimack*. He had been having a lonely time. On the day he ordered the evacuation of Norfolk, he'd written his wife, Angela, who had recently left with the children for Florida, "Everything is as quiet about the house as the grave. The table is so empty that I cannot endure to remain more than two minutes at it, and the bed is so large and desolate that I sit up reading all night. We all must endure much suffering, my dear wife, ere we win our independence." Now, immensely cheered, he wished only for another Union try at the Drewry's Bluff defenses: "I am afraid that the enemy will not make a second attempt to pass them" and "I have got the river so strongly protected now that I earnestly desire the whole Yankee fleet to attempt its passage."

The fleet did not; Richmond would stand for three more years. A snappy little jingle commemorated the victory:

> The *Monitor* was astonished,
> And the *Galena* admonished,
> And their efforts to ascend the stream
> Were mocked at.
> While the dreaded *Naugatuck*,
> With the hardest kind of luck,
> Was very nearly knocked
> Into a cocked-hat.

Fox said Lincoln "was very disappointed at the gunboats not being in Richmond," and Goldsborough quickly insisted that "without the Army the Navy can make no real headway towards Richmond. This is as clear as the sun at noonday to my mind."

Keeler, heading downriver, put the best face he could on the day: "We do not regard the matter in the light of a defeat as we accomplished our purpose, which was to make a reconnoissance, ascertain the nature & extent of the obstructions & the strength of the batteries. We found them of such a nature that it was impossible to force them." Geer's summary is shorter and truer: "We have been fighting all day and have come off 2ⁿᵈ best." Rodgers assessed the *Galena*'s achievement with a jab of dark humor: at least "we demonstrated that she is not shot-proof."

Keeler saw just how unshotproof she was and sent a surprisingly frank account that Anna must have found disquieting: "I went on board the *Galena* at the termination of the action & . . . she looked like a slaughter house. . . . Here was a body with the head, one arm & part of the breast torn off by a bursting shell—another with the top of the head taken off and the brains still steaming on the deck, partly across him lay one with both legs taken off at the hips & at a little distance was another completely disemboweled. The sides & ceiling overhead, the ropes & guns were spattered with blood & brains & lumps of flesh while the decks were covered with large pools of half coagulated blood & strewn with portions of shells, arms, legs, hands, pieces of flesh & iron, splinters of wood & broken weapons were mixed in one confused, horrible mass.

"Twenty five wounded were groaning in agony" alongside thirteen dead.

Jeffers sent Goldsborough an account of the *Monitor*'s performance that Ericsson hated. The best Jeffers could say for the ship was that nobody had got killed aboard her. "I have hitherto refrained from making any official report relative to this vessel," but "notwithstanding the recent battle in Hampton Roads . . . I am of the opinion that protecting the guns and gunners does not, except in special cases, compensate for the greatly diminished quantity of artillery, slow speed, and inferior accuracy of fire." The temperature rose to 140 degrees in the turret; the captain could not direct the guns from the pilothouse; "the ports have not sufficient elevation to allow the guns to be pointed at a battery on an eminence"; the muzzle blast would kill everyone in the wheelhouse if the cannon fired closer than 30 degrees on either side of it and would crack the boilers if trained within 50 of the stern, thereby narrowing the theoretical 360-degree field of fire to 200.

Goldsborough passed on the report to the Navy Department, but the monitor enthusiasm had gathered such momentum that the program went forward with no real change.

CHAPTER 31

Doldrums

The universally disliked William Jeffers.

N̲ow the dolors of summer patrol duty along the James settled on the *Monitor.* Even with the Big Thing gone incessant call-to-quarters alarms came, but none of them amounted to much. One cry of "Boarders!" brought the crew out on deck with swords and rifles to confront a slave who had fled the Shirley Plantation despite the master's having said that the Yankees would take him out to sea and drown him. Instead, Jeffers enlisted Siah Hulet Carter as "first-class boy," and he served aboard the *Monitor* for the rest of her career.

The weather grew warm, then warmer. "Yesterday was a hot uncomfortable day," Keeler wrote, "& we lay broiling on or in our iron box or Cage, as it has now become." When sharpshooters didn't threaten from the banks, the men went swimming, revealing a panoply of tattoos. "I wish you could see the body's of the sailors," wrote Geer. "They are regular Picture Books. . . . One has a Snake coiled around his leg, some have splendid done pieces of Coats of Arms or states, American Flags, and most . . . have the Crusifiction of Christ on some part of their Body."

Then as now the Navy ran on coffee. The *Monitor* men drew the water steaming from the boilers, but the heat diminished the brew's palliative qualities, and it often contained visitors. A sailor on another Union ship wrote, "One thing I never got used to, and that was finding cockroaches in my coffee, although after picking a few out of my tin cup I could manage to worry the liquid down." A more constant annoyance arrived with the cloud of insects that seethed about the ship all summer long. "You may imagine me writing this," said Keeler, "with a towel in one hand brushing off mosquitoes & wiping off perspiration, my brains in a sort of mix with the buzzing of mosquitoes, the hum of flies, the trickling of sweat."

Twice a day, before breakfast and supper, the boatswain blew his call for grog, and the men would line up to draw their four-once ration. Keeler was one of the few who, on September 5, thanked Senator James W. Grimes of Iowa for the "great good" of passing the law that "the liquor ration will be abolished after the 1st of next month & no liquor will be allowed on board our men of war except for medicinal purposes."

Its disappearance only fueled another popular diversion. Geer said, "Gambling still keeps going, though some of the worst ones have lost all he had and everybody is glad. One boy who had only 50c when he commenced now has $40."

A surefire generator of ill feeling, the cards and dice ignited quarrels. Something of the mood of the season comes across in Geer's observation that "the English and Irish portions of the crew are out with each other and have several times come very near having a general fight, and have had several small fights I wish they would have a big fight and eat each other up, so we can get clear of them and get some desant men here—if there is any in the navy, which I begin to doubt."

The sultry, torpid days magnified Keeler's dislike of his captain and expanded it to include his commodore. He wrote Anna, "Your question of 'what is the *Monitor* doing' is more easily asked than answered, though it is very evident that she is doing nothing."

That was Goldsborough's fault: "The fact is, & it is the opinion of all the officers, that the Commodore is not the man for the position he occupies—real merit never placed him there. He is coarse, rough, vulgar & profane in his speech, fawning and obsequious to his superiors—supercilious, tyrannical, & brutal to his inferiors.

"He hasn't the first qualification of an officer or a gentleman & I don't know of any other who respects him in the least. He is monstrous in size, a huge mass of inert animal matter & is known throughout his whole fleet by the very significant appellation of '*Old Guts.*'"

Geer told his wife that on a normal summer day, with nothing out of the ordinary happening, the mercury in the engine room stood at 127 degrees, and 155 in the galley. The cooks escaped that infernal heat when a fire in the stove's wooden backing brought them topside to do their work, to nobody's satisfaction. "Potatoes taste like I don't know what," said Geer, "—anything that no taste at all—and the Beef is all parts of the Cow cooked together until it is next to a Jelly and will drop to pieces."

While McClellan was losing battles on the Peninsula, Keeler complained about never getting reliable news. "We hear so much that is absurd & improbably mixed with items plausible that we are at a loss now to separate it & tell what to believe & what to reject & wish we could get the *papers to learn the news.*" He didn't trust the papers he did see. "I find they are trying to make this retreat out as 'a piece of strategy'—'a masterly movement'—'a change of front by which we get possession of Richmond in a few days' & c. This may sound well to those at a distance, but it don't go down here."

A small mercy came when, on August 15, Keeler happily told Anna, "Captain Jeffers has been detached from the *Monitor* &

Capt. Stevens of the [gunboat] *Maratazna* takes his place. —I don't know Captain S. but we can't be any worse for the exchange." Four days later, the paymaster had met the new captain and said good-bye to the old. "Yesterday our 'most noble Captain' bade us adieu & left for the east. . . . I can assure you we parted from him without many regrets. He is a person of a good deal of scientific attainment, but brutal, selfish & ambitious. Commander Stevens, who takes his place, has the appearance of a quiet modest man, so far I like him, but I find that first impressions are not always to be trusted." Besides: "He has the reputation of taking a glass too much occasionally, the curse of the navy."

Commander Stevens was Thomas H. Stevens, son of a naval hero of 1812, destined to see more action than most Union captains, and to finish the war universally admired. He didn't stay on the *Monitor* for long, but Keeler—and the crew—liked him, and the paymaster's mild forebodings went unfulfilled.

Better still for morale, the *Monitor* quit the James River at the end of August. McClellan had fallen back from Richmond, and the ironclad got to leave what Keeler called "the heated furnace like air of the James" for "the breeze of old ocean" in Hampton Roads. She anchored off Newport News on the thirtieth, and everything improved, most notably the food.

Civil War sailors always ate better than their soldier counterparts. Unlike the Army, the Navy had specially posted cooks and went to great lengths to supply its ships with fresh meat and ice in warm weather.

In the fall, Keeler could boast to his wife about an astonishing diet that would have met the demands of the next generation's notorious trencherman Diamond Jim Brady. "Our breakfast is usually fried oysters, beefsteak, fish balls, mutton chops with an abundance of vegetables, *sweet* and common potatoes & c. For lunch we usually have oysters or cold tongues, lobster (in cans), cold boiled ham, sardines, crackers, cheese, etc., etc.

"Dinner is *the* meal. Soups, steam'd oysters, boiled Salmon, Roast beef, Mutton or Turkey, or boiled ham, & so on through a whole hotel bill of fare with all the sauces, condiments & fancy pickels."

By then they were in the Washington Navy Yard. Long overdue for a refit, the *Monitor* had been released from Hampton Roads by the advent of the *New Ironsides*, the third and most conventional vessel commissioned by the Ironclad Board.

During the dog days of August, the *Monitor* had grown so luxuriant a beard of marine crud on her hull that she had to be towed to the capital by a tugboat. Despite this ignoble arrival, Washingtonians greeted her as warmly as had the citizens of Newport News after the battle. Marine guards had to be posted to control the crowds, and Keeler got another chance to bait Anna about women clustering around him: "Our decks were covered & our ward room filled with ladies & on going into my state room I found a party of the 'dear delightful creatures' making their toilet before my glass, using my combs & brushes. We couldn't go to any part of the vessel without coming in contact with petticoats. There appeared to be a general turn out of the sex in the city, there were women with children & women without children, & women—hem—expecting, an extensive display of lower extremities was made going up & down our steep ladders."

After the receptions were done, the crew got leave, and the ship got a thorough overhaul. Workers widened the berth deck by ripping out the storerooms that lined it and installed an improved ventilation system Ericsson had designed, one of his few acknowledgments that the *Monitor* fell short of perfection.

"The ragged shot marks in our sides," Keeler said, "have been covered with iron patches & the places marked 'Merrimac,' 'Merrimac's Prow' [the dent that so pleased Selfridge], 'Minnesota' [from what is now known by the oxymoron *friendly fire*], 'Fort Darling' [Drewry's Bluff]. New awnings have been furnished us, ventilation for our deck lights & many other little conveniences which would have added greatly to our comfort could we have had them then."

He liked the "new nice black walnut steps" connecting the

berth deck and the wardroom, the spotless oilcloth on his floor, the steam radiators, all the improvements that had made his home "as bright & cheerful as could be desired." What he liked most, though, was the memorial to a battle not yet a year in the past:

Our guns have been engraved in large letters, on one of them

MONITOR & MERRIMAC
WORDEN

on the other

MONITOR & MERRIMAC
ERICSSON

The men came back from leave in late November, but not all of them. Some deserted; one, Coal Heaver William Durst, wrote he was "sick from some trouble to my heart and stomach, contracted from bad air in the *Monitor*"; Seaman Hans Anderson, out for a little fun in New York City, entered a "rum hole," got a glass of drugged beer, and awoke to find himself a deckhand on a merchant ship bound for London.

George Geer didn't take to their replacements: "These men are damdest lazyest set of Hoggs I ever saw, and out of 13 there is but two saylors. The rest of them never were on salt water."

But one of history's more durable lessons is that landsmen can be made into good seamen quite quickly, and the *Monitor* began working that transformation on November 8, when she returned refurbished to Hampton Roads under the command of John Pyne Bankhead.

A forty-one-year-old South Carolina bachelor who had gained the respect of his superiors in the blockading squadron, Bankhead had requested duty "in an iron ship" and got it on September 10.

So many Navy officers of this era have close and elaborate family ties that it is a little surprising to find Bankhead with scarcely any. Throughout the 1850s he'd given the Navy Department one or another Manhattan hotel as his address. His parents both died in 1856, and his staying with the North severed the tenuous ties with whatever Southern relatives he had left.

Our closest observer of *Monitor* life doesn't have much to say about him, but the two men clearly got on well. "Everything goes along quiet & smoothly on board," Keeler wrote, "—very different from what it was under" Jeffers.

By December the ship was enjoying a quiet time back off Newport News, still refreshing itself. Geer and another seaman painted the turret, while Keeler wrote Anna, "I have spent the day in my little snuggery reading & writing by the aid of the few rays of light which straggled down from a bright unclouded sun through the little circular opening over my head, closed by the thick plate of glass & covered by some six (or eight) inches of water. I went to sleep last night to the swish, swash, of the waves as they rolled over my head & the same monotonous sound still continues & will be my lullaby tonight."

On Christmas Eve, Second Assistant Engineer Campbell brought into the wardroom a mince pie and a pitcher of cider, and even though it must have been hard cider, Keeler assisted in hanging "our blankets over the sky lights & other openings making the officer of the watch believe the report made to him by the Master at Arms of 'lights out sir.'"

The paymaster seems to have let his temperance convictions slip a little. Seduced by the mince pie and "some real nice crullers," he "had a fine time till 12 o'clock."

Christmas Day brought more bounty. "A number of our officers living in New York, Brooklyn, Phila., Baltimore & other places not too far off have had boxes of 'good things' sent them to keep Christmas with."

As these gifts were being set out along the wardroom table, Captain Bankhead said to Keeler, whose Illinois family was beyond the reach of 1862 Christmas Day delivery, "Well, Purser, I think you & me will have to depend on the rest for our good things—I have neither Mother, wife or sister to send me such things but I hope some of my New York friends will send me some good wine & cigars."

The ship's complement hadn't been starving, but the Christmas spread was extravagant even by their recent standards. Keeler again treats Anna to a comprehensive menu ("five different kinds of nuts," "Strawberries, Raspberries, plums, cherries," "Meats enough to start a Chatham Street eating house") and then, imaginations fired by "Cider, Blackberry & Currant wine," the wardroom planned the victories their miraculous craft would gain in the year ahead. "The rebels on the Rappahannock were annihilated, Richmond taken, Charleston blotted out . . . the secesh [secessionists] thrashed all over the country—we 'iron clads' reigning over the conquered provinces which were divided among us—Johnny Bull taken across our knees & most thoroughly and convincingly thrashed with our 15 inch guns—ditto the French if they were found at all saucy—in fact we arrived at the conclusion that the Star Spangled Banner next to us 'iron clads' is about the 'biggest thing' to be found just now outside of Barnum's Museum."

Some of that would happen, but the *Monitor* wouldn't be there to see it.

CHAPTER 32

Hatteras

"The *Monitor* is no more."

On that merry Christmas Day she got orders to proceed to Beaufort, North Carolina, in company with two new *Passaic*-class monitors. Welles wanted to attack Wilmington, but it lay beyond Cape Hatteras, whose seas had daunted sailors forever.

Remembering the voyage down from New York, Samuel Greene wrote, "I do not consider this steamer a seagoing vessel. She has not the steam power to go against a headwind or sea."

The crew felt the same way. The new hands had heard about the fraught voyage south from the old, and all worried.

Those were the orders, though, and Geer set about readying the hatches for the journey "with Red lead putty, and [for] the Port Holes I made Rubber Gaskets and in fact had everything about the ship in the way of an opening water tight." Captain Bankhead unwittingly made his ship less watertight by having the turret caulked with oakum. Ericsson would have done all in his power to prevent this, but Ericsson wasn't there.

Rough weather blew through the Roads on the twenty-seventh and twenty-eighth, and Keeler was glad to see it. The "*Monitor* shall hold on here till the storm is over & take advantage of the calm that follows for our trip down the coast."

By the twenty-ninth the December Atlantic was wearing her courtesan's smile. The *Monitor* ran two towlines to the USS *Rhode Island*, the sturdy side-wheeler that would take her south. They set out at two thirty in the afternoon. Keeler believed he saw his weather prediction justified: "A smooth sea & clear skies seemed to promise a successful termination of our trip & an opportunity of once more testing our metal against rebel works & making the 'Little *Monitor*' once again a household name."

The next morning brought storm clouds. "We began to experience a swell from the southward," Bankhead wrote, "with a slight increase of wind from the southwest, the sea breaking over the pilothouse forward and striking the base of the tower. . . . Found that the packing of oakum under and around the base of the tower had loosened somewhat as the vessel pitched and rolled. Speed at this time was about five knots, ascertaining from the engineer of the watch that the bilge pumps kept her perfectly free, occasionally sucking. Felt no apprehension at this time."

The apprehension came as the day waned. The *Monitor* passed the Hatteras light at around one and strained toward the cape. Once they'd rounded it, Geer said, "It would clear up."

Instead, a full gale boomed down on the ships. Now Bankhead "found the vessel towed badly, yawing very much. . . . Ordered engineers to put on the Worthington Pump and the bilge injection and get the centrifugal pump ready and report to me immediately if he perceived any increase in water."

The Worthington pump couldn't keep ahead of it; neither could the centrifugal one. The latter ejected three thousand gallons a minute, but with the oakum washing away, by nine o'clock the water was sloshing about the knees of the men in the engine room.

"But our brave little craft," said Keeler, "struggled long & well. Now her bow would rise on a huge billow & before she could sink into the intervening hollow, the succeeding wave would strike her under her heavy armor with a report like thunder & a violence that threatened to tear apart her thin sheet iron bottom & the heavy armour which it supported.

"Then she would slide down a watery mountain into the hollow beyond & plunging her bow into the black rolling billow would go down, down, down, under the surging wave till naught could be seen but the top of the 'cheese box' isolated in a sea of hissing, seething foam."

At ten o'clock the shipped water drowned the boiler fires. The engines slowed and stopped and, with them, the pumps.

Bankhead had told the *Rhode Island*'s captain that if the *Monitor* got in trouble, he would hang a red lantern in the turret. The lantern was lit, but the *Rhode Island* couldn't see it through the boisterous gloom. Nor did the ship heed the flares the ironclad sent up.

Its crew huddled together topside. Keeler wrote, "Words cannot depict the agony of the moments as our little company gathered at the top of the turret, stood with a mass of sinking iron beneath them, gazing through the dim light, over the raging waters . . . for some evidence of succor from the only source we could look to for relief. Seconds lengthened into hours & minutes into years."

At last the clouds parted enough for the moon to cast its cold gleam on the two ships, and the *Rhode Island* backed toward her charge, hove to a quarter mile away—a collision in those seas would have sunk both vessels—and began to lower her boats.

Diligent Keeler remembered his paymaster's records and left the turret to go "down into the Ward room, where I found the water nearly to my waist & swashing from side to side with the roll of the ship, & groped my way . . . into my State room. It was a darkness that could be felt. The hot, stifling, murky atmosphere pervaded every corner."

He scrabbled together a bundle of papers, realized he couldn't save both them and himself, then thought of the cash in his care. He "took out my safe keys with the intention of saving the Government 'green backs.' The safe was entirely submerged; in the thick darkness, below the water & from the peculiar form of the lock I was unable to insert the key. I desisted from the attempt & started to return."

He nearly didn't make it. "My feelings at this time it is impossible to describe, when I reflected that I was nearly at the farthest extremity of the vessel from its only outlet . . . & the vessel itself momentarily expected to give the final plunge . . . the waves dashing violently across the deck over my head; my retreat to be made through the narrow crooked passage leading to my room; through the Ward room where the chairs & tables were surging violently from side to side, threatening severe bruises if not broken limbs; then up a ladder to the berth deck; across that & up another ladder into the turret; around the guns & over gun tackle, shot, sponges & rammers which had broken loose from their fastenings, & up the last ladder to the top of the turret."

By the time he escaped, the *Rhode Island*'s boats "were pitching & tossing about . . . or crashing against our sides, mere playthings of the billows." As the officers bawled through speaking trumpets, sailors climbed down to the deck and made for the boats beneath the spitting blue glare of the distress rockets.

Some were swept away forever; Keeler was washed overboard and then deposited back on the gyrating deck. Captain Bankhead too lost his footing and the sea sucked him in; Lieutenant Greene pulled him to safety aboard a boat.

Some of the men would not leave the turret. The boats were too small, the seas too high; they wanted to keep the illusory safety of iron beneath their feet. Bankhead ordered, then begged, them to join him. They refused.

Aboard the *Rhode Island* the shivering survivors got blankets, dry clothes, and, of course, coffee. On this, the worst New Year's

Eve they'd ever known, most went to the rail to watch the *Monitor*'s lantern, winking in and out of visibility between the cresting waves. For a half hour or so the garnet ember glowed across the water. Then it was gone.

"What the fire of the enemy failed to do, the elements have accomplished," said Keeler. "The *Monitor* is no more."

CHAPTER 33

Landfall

The USS *Brooklyn* brings John Ericsson home to Sweden.

On January 3, 1863, Gideon Welles wrote in his diary, "A word by telegraph that the *Monitor* has foundered and over twenty of her crew including some officers are lost [actually, sixteen, four of them officers]. The fate of this vessel affects me in other respects. She is the primary representative of a class identified with my administration of the Navy. Her novel construction and qualities I adopted and she was built amidst obloquy and ridicule."

Her sinking made Welles take stock, and doing so gave him a good deal of satisfaction. "Such a change in the character of a fighting vessel few naval men, or any Secretary under their influence would have taken the responsibility of adopting. But the Board which I appointed seconded my views, and were willing to recommend the experiment if I would incur the risk and responsibility. Her success with the Merrimac directly after she went into

357

commission relieved me of odium and men who were preparing to ridicule were left to admire."

He shared the credit. "Understanding that Ericsson the inventor was sensitive in consequence of supposed slight and neglect by the Navy Department or government some years ago, I made it a point to speak to Admiral Smith Chairman of the Board, and specially request that E. should be treated tenderly, and opportunity given him for a full and deliberate hearing. I found Adl Smith well disposed. . . . Adl Smith beyond any other person is deserving of credit, if credit be due any one connected with the Navy Department for this vessel. Had she been a failure, he, more than any one but the Secretary, would have been blamed, and was fully aware that he would have to share with me the odium and responsibility. Let him therefore have the credit that is justly his."

There was credit enough to go around.

The *Monitor* and the *Merrimack* were done with their war. The men who had built the ships, and those who had survived the battle between them, went their various ways. "I very much doubt," Geer wrote his wife, "their ever seeing us again if we once get out the Navy Yard Gate."

Some of them did, though. The *Monitor* crew had been loyal to one another to the last. Captain Bankhead reported that Quartermaster Richard Anjier had wrestled the wheel until "the vessel was sinking, and when told by me to get into the boat replied, 'No, sir, not until you go.'"

Quartermaster Peter Williams, who, according to John Driscoll, "saw more of her [the *Merrimack*] than anyone else" during the battle, got the Medal of Honor.

Hans Anderson escaped from the British ship that had shanghaied him and returned to serve, with several other *Monitor* veterans, on the *Passaic*-class *Catskill*.

John Worden received from New York State a gold sword fashioned by Charles Lewis Tiffany and commanded monitors until he was called to Washington to help design new ones. He regained the sight in his right eye, but never really recovered from his wounds.

In 1895, two years before his death, he wrote, "My head was all knocked to pieces at Hampton Roads. For three months, I lay unconscious and when I woke to life again, I was a mental wreck. Since then I have never known the time when I wasn't suffering both physical and mental pain."

After Buchanan's injuries healed, he too went back aboard an ironclad, the CSS *Tennessee*. When Farragut bulled his way into Mobile Bay in the summer of 1864, the Confederacy's only full admiral fought with all his angry determination until the larger Union fleet overwhelmed his.

Among the ships he engaged that day was the much-modified but never satisfactory *Galena*. Lieutenant Wood, who had seen that luckless vessel off from Drewry's Bluff with his helpful tip to Jeffers about where he could find Richmond, got command of the *Tallahassee* and made her one of the South's most feared commerce raiders.

Catesby Jones gained the rank of captain, but was posted away from the water to end the war running an Alabama cannon foundry.

A week after the *Monitor* went down, William Keeler staunchly told Anna, "I still hope to visit Charleston in an iron clad." His ironclad days were over, though. Captain Bankhead got command of the side-wheel steamer USS *Florida* and took his paymaster with him. Keeler found himself on less glamorous blockade duty. He was cheered by the presence of his *Monitor* friend Samuel Greene, until Greene tried to slough off a lot of paperwork on him. This so got the paymaster's back up that he wanted to take the issue right through to the Navy Department. Greene retreated, and the squabble didn't rupture their friendship. With the war long over and Keeler returned to Anna and his children, the two regularly exchanged letters until 1884.

Their correspondence ceased on the saddest possible note. Twenty years after Appomattox, the *Century* magazine began commissioning veterans of both sides and every rank to write about their experiences. The accretion of articles culminated in the wonderful—and still wonderfully readable—four-volume *Battles and*

Leaders of the Civil War. Asked to tell about his role in the fight with the *Merrimack*, Greene composed a vigorous, fluent account, sent it off to the editors, and put a bullet in his brain.

Gideon Welles kept his cabinet post throughout the war; so did his counterpart Stephen Mallory, who was still urging ironclads into existence when Lee surrendered.

John Ericsson stayed famous for the rest of his life. Proud of the *Monitor* when she was still the object of what Welles called "obloquy," his admiration did not wane after she became renowned. In 1867 he declared, "It was the cannon in the rotary turret that tore the fetters from millions of slaves." A grotesquely inflated claim, but to paraphrase his most important supporter, President Lincoln, there's something in it.

Much of what the inventor had helped shepherd from theory to reality during his lifetime went on display in the 1876 Philadelphia Centennial Exhibition, a lavish showcase for all the strides American mechanical power had made in the century since the colonies declared their independence.

Ericsson met his son there for the first time.

The Swedish government sent Hjalmar to the fair as one of its commissioners. He had inherited his father's abilities, and Sweden wanted his assessment of the American railroad system. John Ericsson had, characteristically, got into an imbroglio with the Centennial's organizers and made himself so obnoxious that they declined to display any of his inventions.

He visited the fair anyway and got together with Hjalmar; they corresponded frequently thereafter, and some sort of fondness seems to have grown between them.

Ericsson survived his son by two years. He died at eighty-five, on the anniversary of the Hampton Roads battle, in 1889. He'd always thought funerals a waste and wanted what he saw as a proper engineer's farewell: "The best thing they can do with my body is to throw it into a retort, convert it into matter and let it mingle with the atmosphere."

He lies beneath the Swedish atmosphere. There was a movement to get him buried beside Robert Fulton in Trinity Church in Manhattan, but Sweden demanded its famous son back.

On August 23, 1890, his remains were in Battery Park, not far from where he had waited with his luggage while the *Princeton* steamed disdainfully past. He lay in a caisson, the *Monitor*'s torn old flag spread across it, Marines standing beside, and John Worden, a rear admiral now, leading the cortege to the Hudson, where the USS *Baltimore* was waiting beside the Statue of Liberty.

Ericsson's departure was untidy. A carefully choreographed show of warships was to steam in line, but so many people who remembered the *Monitor* crowded the harbor that their boats threw the procession into disorder.

Once the coffin was aboard, the *Baltimore* stood out to sea. A two-year-old protected cruiser, the flagship of the North Atlantic Squadron, she was three times the length of the *Monitor*, five times her weight, and carried five times as many heavy guns. But the turrets on her decks, the metal hull that supported them, the twin screws that drove her—all these her only passenger had made indispensable to the naval world for decades, perhaps centuries, to come.

One of the first to benefit from Ericsson's inaugural turret was John Driscoll, still lively as a tick while World War I was muttering on the horizon, showing tourists where it had all happened so long ago, pointing out to the Roads and saying, "That's where we . . ." and "That's where she . . ." Thomas Selfridge died, full of years and honors, more than five years after that war ended, in 1924.

The monitors outlasted everyone who had been there at their birth. Of the sixty-four the North built during the war, only six failed to survive it. Thirty were still in commission when the twentieth century began. The longest-lived was the *Milwaukee*-class *Chickasaw*. Having fought in Mobile Bay, she was sold out of the service in 1874 to the New Orleans Pacific Railway, becoming a coal barge and then a ferry carrying strings of boxcars before she finally sank in the Mississippi in the 1950s.

The last American warships to be called monitors patrolled the rivers of Vietnam.

ALL THIS TIME THEIR PROGENITOR lay 240 feet down on the Hatteras seabed.

In 1973 underwater searchers, armed with the most advanced equipment, located it. Nearly thirty years later they retrieved the thirty-ton engines, and on August 5, 2002, divers under the direction of Barbara Scholley—the fourth woman ever to command a US naval vessel—brought up the turret, the wounds from the *Merrimack* still clearly visible under the impasto of sea spackle. Today it is at rest, along with the cannon it contained, in the superb Mariners' Museum in Newport News, on display in ninety thousand gallons of treatment solution that is slowly, gently laving away the decades of marine encrustation.

During the trip back to shore, the recovery vessel's crew discovered skeletal remains in the turret. That is not how Commander Scholley reported the find. Navy traditions are long, and strong. She said, "It appears we might actually be bringing home more of our shipmates."

GEORGE ORWELL, PERHAPS NOT THE first person you'd expect to have such a thought, said that the sight of artillery always makes "one's heart leap."

Today the *Monitor*'s two Dahlgrens in their long, long revivifying bath may or may not hearten the viewer, but they are there for us to see, a symbol of the triumphs and disasters we face as we strain, as we always must, eagerly or reluctantly, toward the future. While the pretty Virginia seasons turn above them, the electrolytes, busy winter and summer, by microscopic degrees are bringing the incised words WORDEN and ERICSSON closer to the daylight.

A Note on Sources, and Acknowledgments

In 1916 the eighty-year-old John Driscoll, once a fireman on the *Monitor*, points out across Hampton Roads to where he spent the most eventful day of his life.

The *Monitor* and the *Merrimack* have interested me for nearly as long as I can remember. At summer camp in the mid-1950s I produced a series of pencilings that imagined the meeting between the ironclads, a rewarding subject for a nine-year-old because although the two ships look very different, both are satisfyingly easy to draw. And the drama of their encounter, which took place, as Gustavus Fox observed, just when the novelist would have deployed it, is easily grasped even by a child.

Unlike, say, my early fascination with dinosaurs, this one stayed with me. I spent four decades working for *American Heritage*, and those two epochal days in Hampton Roads percolated through the magazine's pages the whole time I was there. I would find myself embroiled in closely argued controversies about which ship had been the victor, or—and this came up often—what properly to call the Confederate contender. I had the good fortune to write about the battle as my micro-contribution to the Burns brothers' great Civil War documentary, and to be able to commission my friend Harold Holzer—whose knowledge of the war is about on the same level William Tecumseh Sherman's was—to give us an article about the heroic, near-miraculous recovery of the *Monitor*'s world-changing turret.

So I knew that I wasn't alone in my enthusiasm, but I learned just how legion were my fellow enthusiasts only when my terrific editor, Colin Harrison of Scribner (can you think of anyone else who is as good an editor as he is a novelist? I can't), gave me the go-ahead on this project.

One often comes across statistics about Civil War books: something like one a day published since 1861. A surprising amount of them are about those inaugural ironclads. I found not only the sheer number intimidating, but also how *good* so many of them are. All those who are drawn to the confluence of history, technology, and human courage in Hampton Roads will find months of rewarding reading to engage them. Touching only on relatively recent contributions to the field, I'd mention John Quarstein's studies of both ships, which not only tell their careers but also give the individual biographies of their crews; Jim Nelson's lively *Reign of Iron*; Harold Holzer and Tim Mulligan's *The Battle of Hampton Roads*, a series of essays examining the most recent scholarship about the battle; and Carl D. Park's *Ironclad Down*, an absorbing history of the *Merrimack* grown out of a ship modeler's frustration at trying to winnow from conflicting accounts what the never-photographed vessel actually looked like. In *Clad in Iron*, Howard Fuller gives an impressively thorough account of the battle's impact overseas; Donald Canney brings immense knowledge to his books both on the wooden ships of the warring navies and on the ironclads that made them obsolete; *Lincoln and His Admirals*, by Craig L. Symonds, is the model of how such a collective biography should be written; and in *War on the Waters*, James M. McPherson has given us a fine account of the whole conflict at sea.

The list goes on and on—and back and back, to books born as early as 1862, and certainly to the monumental and always fascinating *Battles and Leaders of the Civil War*, published in 1887 when most of the veterans were still alive and had plenty to say.

My gratitude keeps expanding: to the historian Edward L. Ayres, who told me the "iron-plated/contem-plated" joke, and to Claudia Jew, who directs photographic services at the Mariners' Museum in Newport News and who energetically saw that I got the pictures I needed just as soon as I wanted them, and to Anna Gibson Holloway, who is maritime historian at the Park History Program there. Dr. Holloway saved me from a serious gaffe. A couple of years ago, eBay's sloppy, infinite, glorious souk turned up a photograph that I was excited to lay hands on. Although a press picture issued in the 1960s, it copied a century-old photo that, the caption said, showed crewmen repairing the *Monitor.* As far as I'd known, the only photos of the ship—and we are damned lucky to have any—were taken in the James River the July after the battle with the *Merrimack*. But here was the *Monitor* being reconditioned in the Washington Navy Yard that fall!

Fortunately I was prudent enough to send a copy to Dr. Holloway, who agreed that the photograph was extraordinary, but, alas, not of the *Monitor*; rather, it showed the *Passaic*-class *Lehigh* a year or so later.

Beyond this particular debt, I must thank Dr. Holloway for the extraordinary job she and her colleagues do with their museum. Along with all the other maritime history the Mariners' unfurls, it makes the Hampton Roads action immediate even before one gets to the *Monitor*'s turret and its Dahlgrens. The very first artifact you encounter is thrilling: a *Merrimack* gun with its muzzle shot away in the first day's fighting, its trunnions bearing the scars of the futile efforts to hammer them off as the Union abandoned the Gosport Navy Yard. This museum is worth a special detour if you find yourself within five hundred miles of it.

American Heritage was one of the first voices to assert that a photograph or a painting can be as revelatory and significant a historical document as any title deed or diary or muster roll, so I'd had a fair amount of experience with visual sources. But not until Scribner started publishing my books did I have to supply the illustrations myself.

The pleasure of doing so has far outweighed the trouble and cost. Despite the will-o'-the-wisp of my *Monitor* repair photograph, eBay has been invaluable, as any number of sources there offer public-domain images easily and inexpensively.

I would be both ungrateful and remiss were I not to mention my superb agent, Emma Sweeney, and my friend Ellen Feldman, who bravely read the book when it was a cumbersome bundle of typescript and whose sharp novelist's eye has spared me many infelicities.

Henry Ford, about whom I wrote my previous book, said that an automobile was never finished until it was ready to be put in the hands of its owner, and the only person who could see to that was the dealer. He'd receive the car nicely painted and nearly complete, but had to make the all-important small adjustments that got it ready for the road. For the writer, that dealer is the copy editor, and I have been most fortunate in having my manuscript fine-tuned by the masterly Steve Boldt. He filed many burrs off my prose, discovered and defused internal contradictions, and saved me from such embarrassments as declaring January 31 to be New Year's Eve and misspelling Captain Tattnall's name every time it appeared. Let me put this in the starkest terms: unless you're Vladimir Nabokov or Max Beerbohm, without a copy editor much of your book will read like a ransom note.

Perhaps more eccentrically, I also want to thank Volare Restaurant. A kindly providence planted my home a block away from this establishment, and during my *Heritage* days I took to coming there to work, free of interruptions, at lunchtime. The habit became so ingrained that I have written this book in the last booth on the right in a long, low-ceilinged dining room that has been generating happy customers for well over a century now. The present propri-etors, Sal and Falco, will make you feel as welcome as I am at 147 West Fourth Street. Even if you're not planning to write a book there, I'd urge a visit. It's a "real old Greenwich Village Italian," but leagues better than that makes it sound. And because, as John Masefield put it, life's a very narrow street, I there met construc-tor John Luke Porter's great-great-granddaughter and her husband, who make a point of stopping in whenever they're up from Virginia. Thanks to them you can see, at the Mariners' Museum, the drafting instruments Porter used when he was making a new kind of war-ship out of the *Merrimack*.

My most immediate gratitude, though, goes to my wife, Carol, who has supported me in all I have tried to do since she came to *American Heritage* as its publisher thirty years ago. She's now the publisher of *Harper's BAZAAR*, and without her formidable competence to buoy me I would have had to write the above in a branch of the New York Public Library rather than in my favorite restaurant.

Bibliography

Adams, Scaritt. "The Miracle That Saved the Union." *American Heritage*, December 1975.

Allen, Frederick E. "The *Monitor* Rises." *American Heritage of Invention & Technology*, Winter 2003.

Allen, Oliver E. "The *Monitor* Is Mine!" *American Heritage of Invention & Technology*, Winter 1996.

Anderson, Bern. *By Sea and by River: The Naval History of the Civil War.* Knopf, 1962.

Ayers, Edward L. *What Caused the Civil War?* Norton, 2005.

Barnes James. "The Birth of the Ironclads" and "The Most Famous American Naval Battle." In *The Photographic History of the Civil War, Volume Six, The Navies*, edited by Francis Trevelyan Miller. Review of Reviews, 1911.

Barthell, Edward E., Jr. *The Mystery of the* Merrimack. Dana Printing, 1959.

Bathe, Greville. *Ship of Destiny: A Record of the U.S. Steam Frigate* Merrimac, *1855–1862 with an Appendix on the Development of the U.S. Naval Cannon from 1812–1865.* St. Augustine, 1951.

Baxter, James Phinney, III. *The Introduction of the Ironclad Warship.* Harvard University Press, 1933.

Beach, Edward L. *The United States Navy: 200 Years.* Holt, 1986.

Bennett, Frank M. *The* Monitor *and the Navy Under Steam.* Houghton Mifflin, 1900.

———. "The United States Ironclad 'Monitor.'" *Cassier's Magazine*, April 1898.

Bradford, James C., ed. *Captains of the Old Steam Navy: Makers of the American Naval Tradition, 1840–1880.* Naval Institute Press, 1986.

Broadwater, John D. *USS* Monitor: *A Historic Ship Completes Its Final Voyage.* Texas A&M University Press, 2012.

Brockmann, Robert F. *Commodore Robert F. Stockton, 1795–1866: Protean Man for a Protean Nation.* Cambria Press, 2009.

Brodie, Bernard. *Sea Power in the Machine Age.* Princeton University Press, 1943.

Brooke, George M., Jr., ed. *Ironclads and Big Guns of the Confederacy: The Journals and Letters of John M. Brooke.* University of South Carolina Press, 2002.

———. *John M. Brooke: Naval Scientist and Educator.* University Press of Virginia, 1980.

Bruce, Robert V. *Lincoln and the Tools of War.* Bobbs-Merrill, 1956.

Bruzek, Joseph C. *The IX" Dahlgren Broadside Gun.* United States Naval Academy Museum, n.d.

Burton, Anthony. *The Rainhill Story: The Great Locomotive Trial.* W & J Mackay, 1980.

Campbell, R. Thomas, and Alan B. Flanders. *Confederate Phoenix: The CSS Virginia.* Burd Street Press, 2001.

Canney, Donald L. *The Confederate Steam Navy, 1861–1865.* Schiffer, 2015.

———. *Lincoln's Navy: The Ships, Men and Organization, 1861–1865.* Naval Institute Press, 1998.

———. *The Old Steam Navy: Frigates, Sloops, and Gunboats, 1815–1885.* Naval Institute Press, 1990.

———. *The Old Steam Navy: The Ironclads, 1812–1885.* Naval Institute Press, 1993.

Cannon, Le Grand Bouton. *Recollections of the Iron Clads,* Monitor *and* Merrimack, *and Incidents of the Fights.* Burlington, 1875.

Chittenden, L. E. *Recollections of President Lincoln and His Administration.* Harper, 1891.

Church, William Conant. *The Life of John Ericsson.* Scribner, 1906.

Clancy, Paul. *Ironclad: The Epic Battle, Calamitous Loss, and Historic Recovery of the USS* Monitor. McGraw-Hill, 2006.

Cooley, James. "The Relief of Fort Pickens." *American Heritage,* February 1974.

Daly, R. W. *How the* Merrimac *Won: The Strategic Story of the C.S.S.* Virginia. Crowell, 1957.

Davis, William C. *Duel between the First Ironclads.* Stackpole, 1975.

deKay, James Tertius. Monitor: *The Story of the Legendary Civil War Ironclad and the Man Whose Invention Changed the Course of History.* Ballantine, 1997.

Deogracias, Alan J., II. *Battle of Hampton Roads: A Revolution in Military Affairs.* U.S. Army Command and General Staff College, 2003.

Dew, Charles B. *Ironmaker to the Confederacy: Joseph R. Anderson and the Tredegar Iron Works.* Library of Virginia, 1999.

Donald, David, ed. *Why the North Won the Civil War.* Macmillan, 1960.

Doubleday, Abner. *Reminiscences of Forts Sumter and Moultrie in 1860–61.* Nautical and Aviation Publishing Company of America, 2005.

Douglass, Frederick. *A Narrative of the Life of Frederick Douglass, an American Slave, Written by Himself.* New American Library, 2005.

Durkin, Joseph T. *Confederate Navy Chief: Stephen R. Mallory*. University of North Carolina Press, 1954.

Emerson, Jason. *Lincoln the Inventor*. Southern Illinois University Press, 2009.

Fehrenbacher, Don E., and Virginia Fehrenbacher. *Recollected Words of Abraham Lincoln*. Stanford University Press, 1996.

Field, Ron. *Confederate Ironclad vs. Union Ironclad: Hampton Roads, 1862*. Osprey, 2008.

Flake, Elijah W. *Battle Between the* Merrimac *and the* Monitor *by Elijah W. Flake, One of the Survivors of the* Merrimac. Privately printed, 1914.

Fuld, George, and Melvin Fuld. *Civil War Patriotic Tokens*. Whitman, 1960.

Fuller, Howard J. *Clad in Iron: The American Civil War and the Challenge of British Naval Power*. Naval Institute Press, 2010.

Gardiner, Robert, ed. *Steam, Steel & Shellfire: The Steam Warship, 1815–1905*. Conway Maritime Press, 1992.

Gibbon, Richard. *Stephenson's Rocket and the Rainhill Trials*. Shire, 2010.

Goodheart, Adam. *1861: The Civil War Awakening*. Knopf, 2011.

Grace, Trudy A., and Mark Farlow. *West Point Foundry*. Arcadia, 2014.

Greene, Jack, and Alessandro Massignani. *Ironclads at War: The Origin and Development of the Armored Warship, 1854–1891*. Combined Publishing, 1998.

Greene, Samuel Dana. "I Fired the First Gun and Thus Commenced the Great Battle." *American Heritage*, June 1957.

Hattaway, Herman, and Archer Jones. *How the North Won: A Military History of the Civil War*. University of Illinois Press, 1991.

Hawthorne, Nathaniel. "Chiefly about War Matters." *Atlantic*, July 1863.

Hearn, Chester G. *Admiral David Dixon Porter*. Naval Institute Press, 1996.

Holzer, Harold, ed. *Lincoln's White House Secretary: The Adventurous Life of William O. Stoddard*. Southern Illinois University, 2007.

Holzer, Harold, and Tim Mulligan, eds. *The Battle of Hampton Roads: New Perspectives on the USS* Monitor *and CSS* Virginia. Fordham University Press, 2006.

Hoogenboom, Ari. *Gustavus Vasa Fox of the Union Navy*. Johns Hopkins, 2008.

Hunter, Alvah F. *A Year on a Monitor and the Destruction of Fort Sumter*. University of South Carolina Press, 1987.

Jack, E. A. *Memoirs of E. A. Jack, Steam Engineer, CSS* Virginia. Brandylane, 1998.

Johnson, Robert Underwood, and Clarence Buell, eds. *Battles and Leaders of the Civil War, Volume I*. Century, 1887.

Joint Committee on the Conduct of the War. *Heavy Ordnance*. 1864.

Jones, Catesby ap R. "Services of the *Virginia (Merrimac)*." *Southern Historical Society Papers*, January 1883.

Jones, John B. *A Rebel War Clerk's Diary*. Sagamore Press, 1958.

Keeler, William F. *Aboard the USS* Florida: *1863–65; The Letters of Paymaster William Frederick Keeler, U.S. Navy to His Wife, Anna.* Edited by Robert W. Daly. Naval Institute Press, 1968.

———. *Aboard the USS* Monitor: *1862; The Letters of Acting Paymaster William Frederick Keeler, U.S. Navy, to His Wife, Anna.* Edited by Robert W. Daly. Naval Institute Press, 1964.

Konstam, Angus. *Confederate Ironclad, 1861–65.* Osprey, 2001.

———. *Hampton Roads, 1862: Clash of the Ironclads.* Osprey, 2002.

———. *Union Monitor, 1861–65.* Osprey, 2008.

———. *Union River Ironclad, 1861–65.* Osprey, 2002.

Lamm, Michael. "The Big Engine That Couldn't." *American Heritage of Invention & Technology*, Winter 1993.

Langley, Harold D. *Social Reform in the United States Navy, 1798–1862.* University of Illinois Press, 1967.

Lewis, Michael. *England's Sea Officers: The Story of the Naval Profession.* Henderson and Spalding, 1948.

Luraghi, Raimondo. *A History of the Confederate Navy.* Chatham, 1996.

Macartney, Clarence Edward. *Mr. Lincoln's Admirals.* Funk & Wagnalls, 1956.

Mahin, Dean B. *One War at a Time: The International Dimensions of the Civil War.* Brassey's, 1999.

Marvel, William. *The* Monitor *Chronicles: One Sailor's Account; Today's Campaign to Recover the Civil War Wreck.* Simon & Schuster, 2000.

McCordock, Robert Stanley. *The Yankee Cheesebox.* Dorrance, 1938.

McDonald, Joseph. "How I Saw the *Monitor-Merrimac* Fight." *New England Journal*, July 1907.

McGowan, Christopher. *The Rainhill Trials: The Greatest Contest of Industrial Britain and the Birth of Commercial Rail.* Little, Brown, 2004.

McPherson, James M. *War on the Waters: The Union & Confederate Navies, 1861–1865.* University of North Carolina Press, 2012.

———. *The War That Forged a Nation: Why the Civil War Still Matters.* Oxford, 2015.

Meade, Rebecca Paulding. *Life of Harrison Paulding, Rear-Admiral, U.S.N.* Baker & Taylor, 1910.

Melton, Maurice. *The Confederate Ironclads.* Yoseloff, 1968.

Merli, Frank J. *Great Britain and the Confederate Navy, 1861–1865.* Indiana University Press, 2004.

Miller, Edward M. *U.S.S.* Monitor: *The Ship That Launched a Modern Navy.* Leeward Publications, 1978.

Mindell, David A. *Iron Coffin: War, Technology, and Experience Aboard the USS* Monitor. Johns Hopkins, 2012.

Morison, Elting. *Men, Machines, and Modern Times.* MIT Press, 1966.

Muiscant, Ivan. *Divided Waters: The Naval History of the Civil War.* Harper-Collins, 1995.

———. "The Fires of Norfolk." *American Heritage*, March 1990.

Muller, Stephen H., and Jennifer A. Taylor. *Troy, New York, and the Building of the USS* Monitor. Hudson Mohawk Industrial Gateway, 2009.

National Trust for Historic Preservation. *The* Monitor, *Its Meaning and Future: Papers from a National Conference.* Preservation Press, 1978.

Nelson, James L. *Reign of Iron: The Story of the First Battling Ironclads, the* Monitor *and the* Merrimack. Morrow, 2004.

Newton, Virginius. *The Confederate States Ram* Merrimac *or* Virginia: *The History of Her Plan and Construction, and Her Engagements with the United States Fleet, March 8 and 9, 1862.* Heritage Press, 1907.

Niven, John. *Gideon Welles: Lincoln's Secretary of the Navy.* Oxford, 1973.

Official Records of the Union and Confederate Navies in the War of the Rebellion, Series I, Volume 7: North Atlantic Blockading Squadron, from March 8 to September 4, 1862. Government Printing Office, 1896.

Park, Carl D. *Ironclad Down: USS* Merrimack–CSS Virginia *from Construction to Destruction.* Naval Institute Press, 2007.

Parker, William Harwar. *Recollections of a Naval Officer, 1841–1865.* Scribner, 1883.

Pearson, Lee M. "The *Princeton* and the Peacemaker: A Study in Nineteenth-Century Naval Research and Development Procedures." *Technology and Culture*, Spring 1966.

Peck, Taylor. *Roundshot to Rockets: A History of the Washington Navy Yard and U.S. Naval Gun Factory.* Naval Institute Press, 1949.

Porter, David Dixon. *Incidents and Anecdotes of the Civil War.* Appleton, 1885.

Quarstein, John V. *The CSS* Virginia: *Sink before Surrender.* History Press, 2012.

———. *A History of Ironclads: The Power of Iron over Wood.* History Press, 2006.

———. *The* Monitor *Boys: The Crew of the Union's First Ironclad.* History Press, 2011.

Ringle, Dennis J. *Life in Mr. Lincoln's Navy.* Naval Institute Press, 1998.

Roberts, William H. *Civil War Ironclads: The U.S. Navy and Industrial Mobilization.* Johns Hopkins, 2002.

Sandler, Stanley. *The Emergence of the Modern Capital Ship.* Associated University Presses, 1979.

Schenkman, David. *Tokens & Medals Commemorating the Battle Between the* Monitor *and* Merrimac. Numismatic Association, 1979.

Schneller, Robert J., Jr. "The Battle of Hampton Roads, Origins of Ordnance Testing Against Armor, and U.S. Navy Ordnance Development During the American Civil War." *International Journal of Naval History*, December 2003/April 2004.

——. *A Quest for Glory: A Biography of Rear Admiral John A. Dahlgren.* Naval Institute Press, 1996.

Sears, Stephen W. *To the Gates of Richmond: The Peninsula Campaign.* Ticknor & Fields, 1992.

Selfridge, Thomas Oliver, Jr. *Memoirs of Thomas O. Selfridge, Jr., Rear Admiral, U.S.N.* Putnam, 1924.

Sheridan, Robert E. *Iron from the Deep: The Discovery and Recovery of the USS Monitor.* Naval Institute Press, 2004.

Shippen, Edward. *Thirty Years at Sea: The Story of a Sailor's Life.* Lippincott, 1879.

Silverstone, Paul H. *Warships of the Civil War Navies.* Naval Institute Press, 1989.

Simson, Jay W. *Naval Strategies of the Civil War: Confederate Innovations and Federal Opportunism.* Cumberland House, 2001.

Sloan, Edward William, III. *Benjamin Franklin Isherwood, Naval Engineer: The Years as Engineer in Chief, 1861–1869.* Naval Institute Press, 1965.

Smith, David R. *The* Monitor *and the* Merrimac: *A Bibliography.* University of California Library, 1968.

Smith, Gene A. *Iron and Heavy Guns: Duel between the* Monitor *and* Merrimac. Ryan Place, 1996.

Spears, John R. *The History of Our Navy: From Its Origin to the End of the War with Spain, 1775–1898.* Scribner, 1899.

Still, William N., Jr. *Confederate Shipbuilding.* University of Georgia Press, 1969.

——. *Iron Afloat: The Story of the Confederate Ironclads.* Vanderbilt University Press, 1981.

——. *Ironclad Captains: The Commanding Officers of the USS* Monitor. United States Department of Commerce, 1988.

——. Monitor *Builders: A Historical Study of the Principal Firms and Individuals Involved in the Construction of USS* Monitor. National Park Service, 1988.

Stoddard, William O. *Inside the White House in War Times: Memoirs and Reports of Lincoln's Secretary.* University of Nebraska, 2000.

Swanberg, W. A. *First Blood: The Story of Fort Sumter.* Scribner, 1957.

Symonds, Craig L. *Confederate Admiral: The Life and Wars of Franklin Buchanan.* Naval Institute Press, 1999.

——. *Decision at Sea: Five Naval Battles That Shaped American History.* Oxford, 2005.

——. *Lincoln and His Admirals.* Oxford, 2008.

Tazewell, William L. *Norfolk's Waters: An Illustrated Maritime History of Hampton Roads.* Windsor Publications, 1982.

Thulesius, Olav. *The Man Who Made the* Monitor: *A Biography of John Ericsson, Naval Engineer.* McFarland, 2007.

Trexler, Harrison A. *The Confederate Ironclad "Virginia" ("Merrimac").* University of Chicago Press, 1938.

Tucker, Spencer. *Arming the Fleet: U.S. Navy Ordnance in the Muzzle-Loading Era.* Naval Institute Press, 1989.

Underwood, Rodman L. *Stephen Russell Mallory: A Biography of the Confederate Navy Secretary and United States Senator.* McFarland, 2005.

Walters, Kerry. *Explosion on the Potomac: The 1844 Calamity Aboard the USS Princeton.* History Press, 2013.

Webster, Donald B., Jr. "The Beauty and Chivalry of the United States Assembled . . ." *American Heritage,* December 1965.

Welles, Gideon. *The Civil War Diary of Gideon Welles, Lincoln's Secretary of the Navy: The Original Manuscript Edition.* Edited by William E. Gienapp and Erica L. Gienapp. University of Illinois Press, 2014.

Wells, William S., ed. *The Original United States Warship* Monitor: *Copies of Correspondence Between the Late Cornelius S. Bushnell, of New Haven, Conn., Captain John Ericsson, and Hon. Gideon Welles . . .* Cornelius S. Bushnell National Memorial Association, 1899.

West, Richard S., Jr. *Gideon Welles: Lincoln's Navy Department.* Bobbs-Merrill, 1943.

———. *Mr. Lincoln's Navy.* Longmans, Green, 1957.

White, E. V. *The First Iron-Clad Naval Engagement in the World: History of Facts of the Great Naval Battle between the* Merrimac-Virginia, *C.S.N., and the* Ericsson Monitor, *U.S.N., Hampton Roads, March 8 and 9, 1862.* Privately printed, 1906.

White, Ruth L. *Yankee from Sweden: The Dream and the Reality in the Days of John Ericsson.* Holt, 1960.

White, William Chapman, and Ruth White. *Tin Can on a Shingle: The Full Story of the* Monitor *and the* Merrimac. Dutton, 1958.

Worden, John L., Samuel Dana Greene, and H. Ashton Ramsay. *The* Monitor *and the* Merrimac: *Both Sides of the Story.* Harper, 1912.

Wrigley, Herbert Wilson. *Ironclads in Action: A Sketch of Naval Warfare from 1855 to 1895, with Some Account of the Development of the Battleship in England.* Little, Brown, 1896.

Zeller, Bob. *The Blue and Gray in Black and White: A History of Civil War Photography.* Praeger, 2005.

Index

About the Author

Richard Snow is the author of eight books, among them two historical novels, a volume of poetry, and an account of America in the Battle of the Atlantic during World War II. His most recent work is *I Invented the Modern Age: The Rise of Henry Ford*. He spent nearly four decades at *American Heritage* magazine, serving as editor in chief for seventeen years, and has been a consultant on historical motion pictures, among them *Glory*. He was awarded a John Simon Guggenheim Memorial Foundation Fellowship in 2012.